DATE DUE

| | |
|---|---|
| | |
| | |
| | |
| | |
| | |
| | |
| | |
| | |
| | |
| | |
| | |
| | |
| | |
| | |
| | |

BRODART                              Cat. No. 23-221

# THE ESCHER CYCLE:
## CREATING
## SELF-REINFORCING
## BUSINESS ADVANTAGE

*Finn Jackson*

THOMSON™

Australia · Canada · Mexico · Singapore · Spain · United Kingdom · United States

**The Escher Cycle: Creating Self-Reinforcing Business Advantage**
Finn Jackson

COPYRIGHT © 2004 by Finn Jackson.

TEXERE, an imprint of Thomson Business and Professional Publishing, a part of the Thomson Corporation. Thomson, the Star logo, TEXERE, and Thomson Business and Professional Publishing are trademarks used herein under license.

ISBN: 1-58799-194-2
Printed and bound in the United States by Edwards Brothers
1  2  3  4  5  6  7  8  9  07  06  05  04

For more information, contact Thomson Learning, 5191 Natorp Boulevard, Mason, OH  45040. You can also visit our website at www.thomson.com/learning/texere.

Composed by: SettingPace LLC
A CIP catalogue record for this book is available from the Library of Congress.
2004017212

This book is printed on acid-free paper.

*For*
## *Talli Binshtock*
*who pointed me in the right direction*


*and also for*
*Neville Symington, Leila Shelton, Paul Bascombe, Marc Cools,*
*Martin Fry, Suzanne White, David Musson, Jeremy Kourdi,*
*Lucy Armitage, Ian Waddington, Phil Pinto, Kate Cooper,*
*John Dickson, Chris Brown & Gayle Souter-Brown,*
*Sheila Harrison, Clare Jackson, David Wilson, Loretta Nauth,*
*and everyone else at Thomson-Texere*


*who all helped*
*(knowingly and unknowingly)*
*to make this book what it is,*


*with love, and thanks,*
*and apologies for the long wait.*

# Contents

# Prologue

*The point is not to understand the world, the point is to change it.*

—KARL MARX

I WANT TO USE this prologue to step back from the detail of the book you are about to read and to say something instead about where it came from and where it is going to take us.

This book grew out of the tension between two conflicting views of what it takes to make a business successful.

The first view, which I learned as a consultant and later at business school, says that success in business comes from having the right strategy. The second view, which I learned while working in a firm known as "The Marine Corps of Implementation," says that success comes only from action.

Both these views are useful, but neither has the complete picture. A successful business is a combination of good strategy *and* good implementation. Both ways of looking at the world are important. But one is a top-down view and the other is bottom-up, and the problem is that they do not meet in the middle.

For nine years I created sustainable strategic change in an action-oriented corporation. I worked at all levels, in almost all functional areas of the business, and in more than a dozen countries worldwide. What I found, over and over again, was that whenever the time came to convert a good high-level plan into practical reality, or connect a practical low-level process into the higher-level aims of the business, there was always a disconnect, a mismatch. It always became necessary to flip from one way of thinking about the business to the other.

In effect, we use one language to talk about strategy, and another to talk about tactics.

This means that the actions the business takes can never quite live up to the ambitions of its strategy. And the strategy it chooses can never quite be based on the full reality of how the business actually works. So changing or leading a business becomes like watching a movie that starts out in one language, and then switches to another one halfway through.

That may not seem like a problem if we can hire people who understand and speak both languages. But what it means is that the two elements that are critical to business success—strategy and action—never quite line up correctly, because something is always lost in translation. And so business performance is never quite what it could be.

What we want and what we need is a new way of thinking about the world, which explains how to be practical *and* strategic, visionary *and* pragmatic—*all at the same time.* That is what this book provides.

Of course, new ways of thinking can sometimes seem to be difficult if they clash with what we know already. But they often turn out to be even simpler than what we knew before.

And new ways of thinking also give us the opportunity to create new results. Imagining that the world might not be flat gave Christopher Columbus the possibility of discovering America. Imagining that people might want to listen to music on a tape player that didn't record gave Sony the possibility of developing the Walkman.

In the case of this book, we shall learn to see strategy and action not as separate, but as the same thing. And this will enable us to achieve dramatic new results both in terms of how we operate our businesses and in how we understand them.

As readers learn the minimum activities a business needs to do to be successful, they will understand that competitive advantage comes from being better than rivals at one or more of these activities. Ultimately they will see how to link them together in a way that creates ever-increasing levels of performance at each activity. In other words, they will learn how to create self-reinforcing business advantage.

That will create new results. And because the plans that they came from were created using the same language and concepts as the implementation, the feedback between plans and results, strategy and action will be accelerated —so our *understanding* of what it takes to create results will be accelerated also.

The point of this book, as Marx told us, is not just to understand the world. The point is to *apply* that understanding to improve the results that we create. By linking the two elements together, strategy *and* action, we gain the opportunity to improve them both, and so become practical *and* strategic, visionary *and* pragmatic.

FINN JACKSON

GUILDFORD, ENGLAND

SPRING 2004

# CHAPTER 1

# *Introduction*

*The whole of science is nothing more than a refinement of everyday thinking.*

—ALBERT EINSTEIN

BUSINESSES TODAY face two major challenges. The first is how to find some form of competitive advantage that will last in the face of almost constant innovations by rivals. The second is simply how to get done each day all the things that need to get done.

This book addresses both issues.

At first sight the two problems seem unconnected. After all, the first is strategic, and the second is highly practical. But in fact they are closely linked. If the firm has strategic advantage today, then the pressure on day-to-day activities will be less. If it finds a new way to create advantage for tomorrow, then the pressure on workload will have to increase while it puts the new ways of working into practice.

Strategy and action are two sides of the same coin.

Strategy by itself adds no value. Only actions create value. But actions that are not aligned to a good strategic direction can just as easily destroy value as well as create it. How can we tell which actions are which?

This book starts out by looking at the second of the two challenges, and asks: "What is the *least* a business needs to do to be successful?"

It finds that there are *just three things*. These are described in the next section. But knowing what they are, and *focusing* on them, helps the business to reduce its workload. This addresses the second of the two challenges, getting things done.

The other challenge has to do with creating competitive advantage, and this comes when a business carries out an activity better than its rivals.

So, starting from the *least* a business needs to do, the book shows how strategic advantage builds in layers as the business develops greater levels of ability and skill at each activity. The greatest advantage of all comes when the business learns to link its activities together in a way that generates higher levels of performance at them *all*. This creates a self-reinforcing loop of improving ability—a self-reinforcing loop of strategic advantage—that addresses the first of the two challenges by creating strategic advantage that not only lasts but actually *grows* the more of it a business has.

*FOUR LAYERS OF STRATEGIC ADVANTAGE* What *are* the minimum activities a business needs to do to be successful? (You might like to pause for a moment and write these down for yourself.)

The first thing we can say is that it has to *satisfy a customer need*. No matter what industry a business is in, no matter who its customers are or what products or services it provides, if a business does not satisfy a customer need then nobody will buy from it, and the business will go out of business—fast.

---

**PRODUCTS AND SERVICES**

Throughout this book, boxes will be used to expand on points outside the main flow of the text. This one discusses products and services.

In his famous book *Competitive Strategy* (1980) Michael Porter wrote that "to avoid needless repetition, the term 'product' rather than 'product or service' will be used to refer to the output of an industry, even though the principles of structural analysis developed here apply equally to product and service businesses."

A little over 20 years later I face the same problem: how to avoid endless repetition of "product or service." But I am going to choose the opposite solution, for two reasons.

The first is that services now account for more than 50 percent of the global economy. (In more developed countries the percentage is even higher.) And the second is to remind us that even when customers buy a physical *product,* it is not the features of the product they are paying for, but the ability of those features to satisfy or service their underlying needs. If a completely different product provides a better *service* against their needs (a typewriter instead of chalk and slate, or a word processor instead of a typewriter) then the customers will buy that instead.

It is not the *product* that customers want but the service/solution to their needs. And in a competitive world, this focus on the customers' needs, rather than the physical features of the product, is an important difference to remember.

So, to avoid needless repetition, the term "service" rather than "product or service" will be used to refer to the output of a business, even though the principles developed here apply equally to "product" and "service" businesses.

*Satisfying customer needs* is a start, but it is not enough. The business also has to *use resources* in some way in order to achieve that goal. Different businesses have different resources, and different ways of using them. That is what makes them look different. But this is still not enough to define what it takes to create a successful business. To be successful the business also needs to make money—otherwise it will lose money and fade away to nothing.

So, the very least a business needs to do to be successful is to *make money* by *using its resources* to *satisfy customer needs.*

These activities form the first, *operational,* layer of strategic advantage. The first way in which a business can gain competitive advantage is by being better than its rivals at simply *carrying out* these core activities. Chapters 2–4 look at them in detail, and show what it takes to achieve each one.

A business that has become good at carrying out these core activities can improve its performance by balancing them against each other. Portfolio management, for example, can increase the amount of money that the business makes, by balancing the range of customer services that it provides against the costs of the resources that are used.

These balancing, or coordinating, activities are discussed in Chapters 5 and 6. They optimize the performance of the business over time by linking the individual activities of the first layer together. Capability, skill, and expertise at these activities form the *second layer* of business advantage: *Leadership*.

Combining these two layers together, we understand that a business is a system that *makes money* by *using resources* to *satisfy customer needs, today* and *in the future.* We can draw this as a picture:

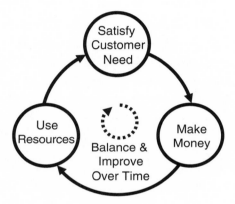

Like any system, the performance of the business depends on how well it fits with its environment. For a business that environment is what we call the *economy.*

So, in Chapter 7, the book draws a map of what happens when tens or thousands of these simple businesses come together to form an industry or economy. It finds that different activities are important in different parts of the economy. In some areas it is important to focus on satisfying customer needs. In others it is important to focus on making money. And so on. *This explains where strategy comes from.* A good strategy simply means finding a way to carry out the core activities of the business so that they match better with the particular part of the economy where it is operating.

Getting good at focusing on the right activity in this way forms the *third layer* of advantage: *Strategy.*

But there is a fourth and final layer of advantage to be gained.

Because different activities are important in different parts of the economy, some businesses are better than others at carrying out each one. Their expertise then spreads and flows to other businesses for whom performance at that activity is important, but not critical enough to develop the leading edge themselves. It flows through managers who are hired from one firm to another, through books and articles that are written about successful companies, through consultants who develop ideas for one client and then reapply them to another, and so on.

This flow of innovation and improvement runs through the economy in a never-ending cycle. Over time it creates the evolution we call *progress.*

By understanding this flow, a business can copy it. That accelerates its own evolution, and brings higher levels of performance at all the activities that matter.

Competitive advantage, strategic advantage, or business advantage then come when a business is able to carry out an activity better than its rivals.

So knowing what those least activities are, and building a self-reinforcing cycle of improving capability at each one, creates a self-reinforcing cycle of competitive advantage.

Skill at doing this is what brings the *fourth layer* of advantage: *The Escher Cycle.*

**WHO WILL FIND THIS BOOK USEFUL, AND WHY**  This book is for anyone interested in finding practical ways to generate strategic results.

Chief executives and the people who support them—corporate planners and consultants—will clearly be interested in building self-reinforcing advantage. They will also find the frameworks presented useful for analysis of competitive strategic positioning and for mergers and acquisitions. The activity-led nature of the book means that any strategic conclusions reached are easily converted into actions.

At the other extreme, managers with individual functional responsibilities will find the book a helpful reminder of *what* it is they need to achieve. Understanding the deliverables they need to produce (and how those contribute to the business as a whole) will not only increase their efficiency and effectiveness, but will also prepare them for more senior roles.

Divisional managers and the managers of other operating units—the people charged with implementing strategy—will find the book useful for both these reasons. The integrated view of their business that this book presents will help them not only to *identify* their goals, but also to align all the different parts and levels of their organization towards *achieving* those goals.

This integrated viewpoint will also benefit MBA students. For them it represents "joined-up business": a skeleton structure on which all the individual subjects that form the rest of their studies can be fitted together.

And "joined-up business" also helps entrepreneurs. Their priority is to convert an idea or opportunity into a successful business. This book gives a simple introduction to all the different building blocks they will need and shows how to put them together.

Finally, for management theorists, this book provides a new, simpler, integrated view of the firm. It explains all the different phenomena of the business world, from the micro-scale to the macro-scale, using a model that is built around just *three* basic activities: making money, using resources, and satisfying customer needs.

This book will be useful for anyone who wants to think about strategy in a practical way, or to carry out operational execution and implementation in a strategic way.

It is an activity-driven approach to understanding and implementing the actions that create strategic business advantage.

*HOW TO USE THIS BOOK*   The chapters in this book have been written to build logically, step by step, from the least activity a business needs to do to be successful to the activities that bring the greatest advantage.

Each chapter is written as a stand-alone section. Each one explains the essence of what it takes to carry out that particular part of the business, and then asks what it would take to bring another layer of advantage. That leads to the next chapter.

There are three main ways in which to read this book.

The first is to read the book from start to finish. This will build an understanding, layer by layer, of what a business is and what a business does. This approach is probably most useful for people with relatively little knowledge of business.

The second approach is to start anywhere. Choose the chapter you already know most about, or the problem you most want to solve, and start there. Understand the tools presented in the chapter and apply them to your business. Then move forward or backward as needed.

The third approach is to do what you should never do with a thriller: read the conclusions first. The earlier half of that chapter gives a detailed summary of the whole book. Reading it will give a better understanding not only of each part, but also how they fit together. You will then be better placed to decide whether to start at the beginning or in the middle.

But as Chapter 6 explains, the best understanding of the whole comes from a detailed understanding of the parts, and the best understanding of the parts comes from a detailed understanding of the whole. So there is no one best way to read this book.

Enjoy!

## SUMMARY

This book argues that competitive advantage comes when a business carries out an activity better than its rivals.

What are those activities? The book says that the least a business needs to do to be successful is to *make money* by *using resources* to *satisfy customer needs.*

And therefore:

- *Doing* these activities well forms the first layer of strategic advantage: Operations.
- *Balancing* them against each other and maintaining that balance over time forms the second layer: Leadership.
- *Fine-tuning* the activities to match the particular part of the economy where the business is operating forms the third layer: Strategy.

- And *connecting* the activities together, within the business and with customers and suppliers, forms the fourth and final self-reinforcing layer of business advantage: The Escher Cycle.

The book shows what it takes to be successful at each layer, and how each one leads to the next.

By understanding these we will not only learn how to build a more successful business, but will also find a checklist for creating competitive advantage. Understanding how to turn that into *self-reinforcing* advantage will show us the business of the future.

LAYER 1

# THE OPERATIONAL PERSPECTIVE: RUNNING THE SYSTEM

# CHAPTER 2

# Satisfying Customer Needs

*"We are all different!"*

*"I'm not."*

—MONTY PYTHON'S *LIFE OF BRIAN*

DIFFERENT PEOPLE WANT DIFFERENT THINGS, and the foundation stone of any business is the set of customer needs that it aims to satisfy.

If it serves a lot of people with strong needs then there is potential to build a large and thriving business.

The weaker the needs, or the more short-lived they are, the weaker and more short-lived any business will be that tries to fulfill them.

This chapter looks closely at what it takes for a business to satisfy customer needs.

It finds that to do this a business needs to achieve three outcomes:

i)   understand the customers' needs,

ii)  choose which needs to satisfy, and

iii) bring customers and service together

The better a business is at achieving any or all of these things, the stronger its advantage will be. The final part of the chapter looks at how a business can improve the activities in this area over time, and turn *satisfying customer needs* into a source of long-term strategic advantage.

## UNDERSTANDING CUSTOMERS' NEEDS

*ALL ORGANIZATIONS HAVE CUSTOMERS* The starting point for any discussion about customers has to be that customers are always *people*. This is obvious for consumer businesses, but it also applies in cases where the customer is a government or another business. Here, even though an organization is paying for the service, the decision about which service to buy is still made by a *person*. What is different in each case is who or what will benefit from the service being bought.

When people buy services to satisfy their *own* needs or the needs of people close to them (friends and family) we call this a "consumer" business. When people buy services as part of their role within an organization, it is the *organization's* needs that are being met, and we call this "business to business" or "business to government." And when people pay for a service that will benefit someone or something other than themselves or their organization, then we call this "philanthropy" or "giving to a charity."

So whatever and whoever will benefit from the service, three things are true. The first is that the decision about which service to buy is made by an individual.

The second is that their decision is based on a combination of the value it brings to them and the value it brings to whoever will receive the service. This is why cat food companies advertise to cat owners instead of to cats—they tell them their cats will love them, "Oh, and by the way, the cat food tastes good, too." This is why tax-deductibility encourages charitable donations. And this is also why the IBM campaign "Nobody ever got fired for buying IBM" was so successful.

And the third thing that is true is that whatever the *legal* form we have invented for the organizations that will fulfill these needs—whether we call them businesses or charities or not-for-profit organizations—they all need to satisfy our definition of a "business" to be successful. They all need to make more money than they spend, by using their resources to satisfy their customers' needs, today and in the future. And when two organizations are working to satisfy a similar set of needs (no matter who benefits from the service), the one that does these things better will be more successful over time.

Charities and not-for-profit organizations can therefore also benefit from this book. They already understand that the customer is the person who decides which service to buy, not necessarily the person who receives the service or the person who pays for it.

*ALL CUSTOMERS ARE PEOPLE*   So, customers are people, and they look to different organizations to help them fulfill their needs in their roles as husbands, fathers, mothers, daughters, bosses, subordinates, and philanthropists.

If businesses want customers to choose *their service* as the best way to help solve their needs, they need to understand what those needs are. And since in this book we want to understand what is common between all businesses, we need to understand the needs of all six billion people on the planet, in all their different roles. For this we need to understand human psychology.

Abraham Maslow was a psychologist who found that all people's needs could be classified into five distinct groups. What he also found was that these groups were arranged in layers, or levels—a hierarchy of importance —such that people would only try to satisfy high-level needs once their needs had been satisfied at the lower (more urgent) levels.

The first level he identified were the physiological needs: for air, food, water, and warmth. Once these had been taken care of then the needs for safety and security became important. The third level covered needs to do with love and belonging, while the fourth level needs were to do with self-esteem and respect for and from others. The fifth and final level he called "self-actualization": the need to realize one's personal potential and find fulfillment.

Now, these are very broad-brush categories, and readers who want to learn more about human psychology can look elsewhere. But what this tells us is that the Californian who buys organic food, the Swede who drives a Volvo, the Texan who buys a gun, and the Kalahari bushman who cuts down

MASLOW, ABRAHAM H.; FRAGER, ROBERT D.; FADIMAN, JAMES, MOTIVATION AND PERSONALITY, 3rd Edition, © 1997. Reprinted by permission of Pearson Education, Inc., Upper Saddle River, NJ

a thorn tree to build his stockade, are all doing so partly in order to fulfill the same basic need: the need to protect their family.

The five Maslow levels are shared by all the people in the world. What is different are the *ways* in which they try to fulfill those needs. And *that* varies between different cultures, in different parts of the world, and at different times in history.[1]

This obviously affects the services that people buy, and businesses can apply and use this understanding in three main ways.

*USING MASLOW TO IDENTIFY NEEDS*  The first way is to remember that the only reason customers ever buy a service is to help satisfy at least one of their needs. Understanding *what* the needs are that are being satisfied is therefore the first step to the business being able to control its own destiny. *Encyclopedia Britannica,* for example, thought that they were in the business of selling large books containing lots of information, so they did not see personal computers as a threat. But the need they actually satisfied was just one possible answer to the question, "What can we buy for around $1,000 that will help our children's education?" And when the makers of personal

---

[1]For evidence that human nature is not so very different from what it was 500 or even 2,000 years ago, see the plays of Shakespeare and the poems of Catullus.

computers came up with a better answer to that question, *Encyclopedia Britannica*'s business suffered.

Defining the service that the business offers in the *customers'* terms—defining the exact needs that are being satisfied—rather than in terms of the features it provides or what it takes to deliver the service, is the first step to a business being able to control its own destiny and build some form of sustainable advantage.

---

**"I'D LIKE TO BUY THE WORLD A COKE—OR FANTA, OR SPRITE, OR TEA, OR WATER. . ."**

The Coca-Cola Corporation has long been thought of as having a single aim—to get the world to drink Coke. Indeed, Roberto Goizueta, chairman and chief executive until 1997, famously said that he would never be satisfied until the "C" on the cold tap stood for Coke.

But in its 2000 annual report the corporation showed a different approach. It talked about how different customers had different needs from the service called "beverages," and that as a result the corporation had decided to "reshape" its business, dividing it into "four basic interacting segments."

Those segments matched four different sets of underlying needs that Coca-Cola saw in its customers. It called those groups of needs or segments: "refreshment," "rejuvenation," "health and nutrition," and "replenishment."

For customers who wanted "refreshment," "Coca-Cola, Fanta, Sprite, and a host of other carbonated soft drinks [would] continue to provide customers with special moments of refreshment."

Customers who wanted "rejuvenation" would be able to choose from a range of ready-to-drink teas and coffees, "whether . . . for a lift during the day or enjoyment after the workday ends."

Customers who wanted "great-tasting beverages that also provide nutrients for healthy growth and keep them looking and feeling their best" could buy juices and milk. This was a key segment because, as Coca-Cola noted, "health and nutrition beverages represent roughly 40 percent of all ready-to-drink commercial beverages consumed around the world."

Finally, the company said, "even as lifestyles change all over the world, there is one beverage that remains the essential element for all people—water." So, here the company would offer a "portfolio of replenishment beverages to meet different local tastes for water and to provide sports drinks that quench the thirst of people with active lifestyles."

The decision to reshape the business in this way reflects a deeper truth: that different people have different needs, and that ultimately the way for businesses to be more successful is to change their own services to match people's needs, rather than try to change people's needs to match their services.

What Coca-Cola (and marketing people in general) call a "segment" is just a shorthand word for a closely related set of needs.

The different segments that Coca-Cola identified are mostly concerned with meeting needs on the first, physiological, level. Coca-Cola's four segments are subdivisions within that category.

The full five levels of the Maslow hierarchy account for all the different services that are offered by all the businesses in the world—not just the beverage industry. What matters is to use the Maslow hierarchy as a starting point, and then to use whatever classifications are important and meaningful for the particular group of customers.

But this example also shows us that a service can meet customer needs on more than one level of the Maslow hierarchy. And that is what we shall look at next.

---

The second of the three main ways in which the Maslow hierarchy can help a business is by understanding that services often satisfy a need on *more than one level.*

We can see this in the Coca-Cola example in the box, where water, juices, and milk provide a mix of basic physiological needs, while Coca-Cola, Fanta, and Sprite also offer (especially for children) the chance to fulfill needs on the third and fourth levels: the chance to be "cool," to feel part of a group.

Another example of this lies with automobiles. As cars have evolved from the Model-T Ford to the Volkswagen Beetle and the Lamborghini Diablo, so the needs that form part of the decision process of buying a new car have grown from simply "getting from A to B" to include safety (Maslow level 2), country of manufacture (Maslow level 3), exhaust emissions (level 4), as well as brand name, color, and styling (level 5).

These features and others all matter differently to different people, and so each person buys the particular model that seems best to match against their particular set of priorities and needs. The more needs the service is able to meet, the more valuable it becomes, the more it becomes superior to the competitor's service, and the more the customer is willing to pay.

(This is especially true the more a service provides value at the higher Maslow levels. Then there is a stronger *emotional* connection for the customer, which translates into higher customer loyalty to the service, and strategic advantage for the business. This explains why soap powder manufacturers spend so much money on advertising: to transform a basic chemical product into something that enables the buyer to *care*, for their family and/or the environment.)

The third important thing that understanding the Maslow model reminds a business is that people only begin to focus on higher levels once their lower-level needs are being satisfied. This means that new needs are continuously emerging. And as customer needs change, the business needs to focus on correctly identifying the *current leading edge* of those changes— the new features that would have most impact on customer needs that are *just emerging.*

An over-sophisticated service, one that is ahead of its time, can be just as unattractive to customers as one that is out of date. This is part of the reason that the Betamax video format lost out to VHS. When they were launched together, the whole idea of being able to watch movies at home was completely new to consumers, so they were unsure about what mix of features they wanted. Betamax offered a better quality picture, while VHS had a wider range of movies and a lower price. Now, if Betamax had taken off, then its price would have come down, too (see the Experience Curve in Chapter 3) and the range of movies would have increased. And we know that people *do* want better picture quality than VHS, because since then they have chosen to pay for watching DVDs. But *at the time,* simply being able to play movies at home was novelty enough, and so most people bought VHS rather than Betamax.

At the time they saw better picture quality as an expensive "nice to have," and many of the other features they are now happy to pay for on DVD systems would have been over-engineered irrelevancies when video first appeared. It was not so much that people did not *want* the better quality picture, but that they did not want it *yet*.

Timing is important. The business needs to match the features of its service to the needs that are *newly* emerging because higher-level needs only become important once lower-level needs have been satisfied. (See "Surfing the Wave of Emerging Needs" box.)

These reminders to look at the *boundary* between satisfied and unsatisfied needs, as well as looking for needs on higher levels, also help businesses to find ways to make their services more valuable to customers. For example, it used to be that the only way to add value to brands of instant coffee was to emphasize the kind of beans that had been used, the roasting method, or the country where it was grown—after all, surely the only way to make better coffee was to make it taste better, right? Not according to the makers of "fair trade" coffee, whose customers also want the people who produced it to be paid a "fair" price for doing so. The customer may not benefit directly from this second part—or rather the benefit they get may be different from the coffee they are buying—but it is a service that they are most definitely willing to pay for. And in the same way, people who buy organic and free-range produce are paying as much for the animals and soil to be treated in a certain way as they are for the nutritional and health benefits that these foods bring them and their families.

In summary, then, Maslow's insights into human nature are useful to businesses because they tell us how to focus on the needs that are being satisfied rather than on the service being provided; they remind us that needs exist on more than one level (higher levels generating more emotion, more loyalty); and they tell us that once one set of needs has been satisfied, new sets of needs will emerge.

How to find out what these different needs are is the task of market research. In summary, this involves a combination of asking customers what they *might* buy, measuring what they actually *do* buy, and watching closely how they use what they *have* bought—understanding the benefits that match their needs, and how they might be increased. How best to do these things will vary for the different services of each business, and is a level of detail that is beyond the scope of this book.

The "Surfing the Wave of Emerging Needs" box shows a simple way to use the market research information, once it has been obtained, to help the business improve the service it offers. But of course, the fact that customers want or need something does not necessarily mean that businesses will provide it. The fact that legislation exists on car and aircraft safety and emissions and noise levels, for example, shows that market demand is not always enough. Businesses do not produce what the market wants: they produce what the market wants *and* what the businesses can make money from. This is part of what we shall look at in the next section: choosing which needs to service.

---

**SURFING THE WAVE OF EMERGING NEEDS**

No customer ever buys a service in order to satisfy just one need—services always bring benefits that help to satisfy a number of different needs.

What those needs are, and how important they are, varies between customers. But they can always be classified into three basic groups.

First, there is a set of features that the service absolutely "must have." Next, there are features that the customer "also wants." And finally there is a set of needs and features that are less important, and which the customer might think of as "nice to have."

The "must have" items represent the core of the service, if you will, so we can draw these different priorities of need as a target diagram, shown on the next page.

Once a business has identified the needs or features that matter to its customers, placing them in these different categories will improve the depth and quality of its understanding.

It tells the business what matters most to customers, and what matters least.

Combined with a good competitor analysis, it tells the business whether its strengths actually matter to customers or not. And that then helps the business to decide whether and how to compete with other businesses (see the next section): to compete directly against them, to focus on a subset of the needs, or to join forces with other

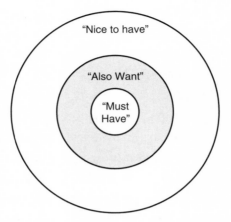

businesses to offer a combined service that uses the strengths of each as the best total solution to the customer needs.

Thinking this way helps the business to switch away from thinking in terms of features that it knows and has grown comfortable with, to focusing on the needs that actually matter to customers today.

Over time, features migrate between the different zones (usually from "nice to have" to "must have"), so this picture can also help the business to identify where changes or improvements in the service would generate the most value (for customers).

The "must have" zone looks attractive, because this is what matters most to customers. But needs here are usually already met by the existing service—and by the services of competitors. Improving them will probably bring more cost to the business than it brings value to customers.

The outer ring is probably also not the best area for improvement. It is probably easy to develop new features, but if the needs they satisfy are not yet important to customers, then they are only "bells and whistles" and there is no drive to buy them.

The key area to focus on is the "also want" zone. This is the area that drives how customers choose between businesses that all provide the "must have" features.

To be successful, a business needs to focus on this middle ring. It needs to spot when "also wants" are becoming "must haves." And it needs to spot where new features and needs have entered the "also want" ring. To be successful over time, the business needs to surf the wave of emerging needs that forms the leading edge between needs that are currently well satisfied for customers and those that are not.

It is in developing features that satisfy needs in this "also want" band that the battle for tomorrow's market share is fought.

Choosing which markets to enter and which battles to fight is the subject of the second section of this chapter, after we have looked at how to measure and quantify the needs we have identified.

*MEASURING THE NEEDS—THE SPIDER CHART* Of course, *identifying* needs is not enough—the business also needs to *measure* them. Only then can it hope to know which needs are more important to which customers, be able to prioritize, and measure how good a job it and its competitors are doing at satisfying each one.

Different services satisfy different needs. But when it comes down to it there are just three things that any customer cares about when choosing between services. One is value, one is cost, and one is timing.[2]

The "value" part is what we normally think of a service as providing. This, as we have seen, is a combination of the benefit that comes to the buyer and the benefit that comes to the person or organization that receives the service. Whenever we buy a birthday gift or present, our choice always includes an element of what will make us feel good about ourselves, as well as what we think the birthday boy or girl will like.

The second part of the needs that customers have has to do with cost. This can be cost in terms of money, cost in terms of time, or cost in terms of any other resources that will be needed to buy and then to use the service. In personal terms, a buying decision might be influenced by whether I can buy the service during my lunch break or from the comfort of my own desk, or whether I have to drive 100 miles to visit the nearest showroom. Are there hidden costs, such as the lifetime supply of batteries? For businesses, does one service offer a lower total cost of ownership? Or is another supplier easier to do business with, and won't tie up the organization in chasing unmet promises?

---

[2]We shall see the flipsides of these three items in the next chapter as effectiveness, efficiency, and adaptability, the *measures* of the processes that produce the service.

The third set of needs that customers have is to do with timing. These needs have to do with either availability of the service (being able to obtain it or begin it before a certain date), its reliability, or its durability (whether it will break, how long it will last, how quickly it will become out of date, whether it can easily be upgraded, and so on).

All these different factors come together under these three headings to define the total "value" that a customer might get from a particular service, and which they use to decide which competitor's service to buy.

A simple, visual way to show all these different needs together is to use a spider chart.

Based on a standard chart used by coffee tasters, it can easily be adapted to measure and compare the features of any service—or even a course of action, as we shall see with the Balanced Scorecard in Chapter 5.

As a simple example, suppose I want to buy an apple.

Things that are important to me about an apple are its size, color, taste, freshness, and price. These are the "value" and "cost" needs I have. Let's suppose that I am also on my lunch break, so I only have 15 minutes to buy it. That is my "time" need.

These are six simple and straightforward attributes, and I have drawn them out in the chart below. It has six axes, one for each of the six items that are important to me. The shaded area shows the upper and lower limits that I am willing to accept for each characteristic, and the dark line represents my ideal apple:

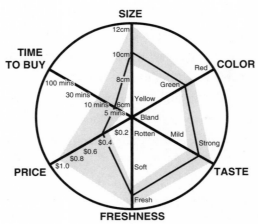

In other words, this picture shows that I want an apple that is between 9 and 12 cm in diameter (around 3 to 5 inches across). It must be green or red-green, but not red or yellow. I like my apples to have a strong taste, and will not compromise on freshness. I am willing to pay up to a dollar for the right apple, but believe that a price lower than 30 cents probably means low quality. And I have between 5 and 15 minutes to buy it.

These are *my* preferences, and the preferences of another customer would show a different profile, a different shape.

Other customers might also care about other properties that they want their apples to have *or not to have*: the country of origin, regular or irregular shape, whether it contains maggot holes, or whether it is organic, genetically modified, or coated with wax. Whatever is important, for any service, whether quantitative or qualitative, the axes on the chart can easily be adapted to measure and plot it.

But now think about the alternative apples that I can choose among. I know that the apples in the canteen are close by, but they have only the red and yellow apples I don't like. (This is shown as the dotted line in the picture below.) The supermarket has the apples I like best, but it is too far away for me to be able to get there and back in the time available. (This is the dashed line.) So, I buy an apple from the convenience store on the corner—it is not my ideal apple, and it is expensive, but it is a good enough match to all my different requirements, and is shown as the solid line below:

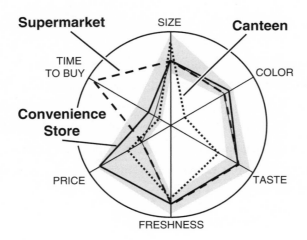

This chart shows the key features of my buying decision, and by using it a business can examine how good a job it does at providing for the different needs that its customers have, and how well that compares with the services offered by competitors.

Apple growers could use this chart to think about which stores will be best at getting their apples to the end customers. Retailers can use it to understand what customers want, and where they provide more or less value than the competing outlets—which also helps them set the best price.

This particular example contains more information than would normally be shown at once. Usually it is enough to plot just *two* spider profiles, and when color is used this spider chart then gives a good overall picture, as well as highlighting the specific strengths and weaknesses of each alternative. It gives an instant overview that is quantitative *and* qualitative.

Whether or not your business actually *draws* this chart, it is important to be able to *imagine* it, because this is effectively what happens inside customers' heads every time they buy a service (or decide not to).

They have a set of needs (the axes in the diagram), which might be well defined or vague. They have a set of performance requirements against those needs, which again might be quite specific or very vague. And the way that they then make their buying decision is by comparing the spider profile that they *think* they want (precise or vague) with the spider profile that they *think* each service has (precise or vague).

Even when their key driver for buying something is "gut feel," *that* is the measure they are using, and *that* is what they test each service for to see if it provides.

So every buying decision involves a comparison between the spider profile that customers *think* they want, and the spider profile that they *think* each service has.

Different people have different needs and different spider profiles. So a particular service will sell better or worse, depending on how many people's spider charts it matches. (Or rather, depending on how many people *think* it matches their needs.)

Choosing which set of needs to satisfy is the subject of the second part of this chapter. Getting people to understand how well *this* particular service will meet their spider chart of needs is the subject of the third part of the chapter.

——— **MAKING IT REAL** ———

- Who are the customers for *your* service?
- What are the needs your service satisfies?
- Which Maslow levels do these match against?
- What is the relative importance of each need to the customers?
- Which needs are becoming more important; which make the difference to the customer purchase decision?

## CHOOSING WHICH NEEDS TO SATISFY

*STRATEGIC POSITIONING—IDENTIFYING ALTERNATIVE CUSTOMERS AND NEEDS* Human beings have too many needs for one service to be able to satisfy them all. So each business has to focus on satisfying a relatively small set of those needs.

When businesses try to satisfy the same set of needs, we call them competitors in a marketplace. When the businesses provide similar services in similar ways, we say that they are in the same industry.

But even within a particular industry, even with a service as simple and straightforward as an apple, we know that different customers want different things: they all have different spider profiles.

So, any business has to choose not only what industry or marketplace it wants to be in, but also (within that area) how generalist or how specialist it wants to be. It has to choose a combination of which customers it wants to service, and how wide a range of their needs it wants to satisfy.

This is called strategic positioning.

It is critical to the business because it determines what the total demand for the firm's services will be. It determines, first of all, how many customers will be interested in those services, and how strong their interest will be. And it determines how many other businesses will be competing to sell services that might satisfy those same needs.

In other words, the combination of customers and needs that the firm's services aim to satisfy defines which other firms the business will be competing against. These two items *together* establish what the total demand for the firm's services will be.

An example will help to make this clearer.

Think about the convenience store we talked about earlier. It knows it is in the business of being a food retailer, and it has to strategically position itself against the other stores in the neighborhood. Like them, and like any business in any industry, it has to decide which customers it wants to service, and how wide a range of their needs it wants to satisfy.

Essentially it has to decide whether to target few or many customers, and few or many needs, which gives it four basic alternatives to choose among:

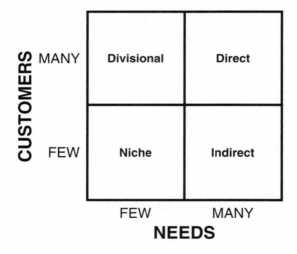

Trying to satisfy as many customers as possible seems like the best strategy, but different people want different things, so it may make sense to focus on a smaller number of people who want (nearly) the same thing. Getting this balance right is what positioning the business is all about: knowing who your customers are and what they want.

If we think about the different ways in which modern businesses have so far found to satisfy the food needs of customers, then the top right-hand corner is clearly occupied by supermarkets. These sell a huge variety of foods (and non-foods) to a huge variety of people. Each customer probably buys the same set of groceries each week, and no single customer probably ever buys more than 1 percent of the total range of items on sale. The strategic positioning of the supermarket is to cater to pretty much all the food needs of the vast majority of customers.

The convenience store could choose to compete directly with them—the so-called "direct" strategy. To do so successfully it would need to become better than the supermarkets at satisfying the *same* full set of needs for the same wide set of customers. Doing that successfully is not only difficult but would also turn the convenience store into a supermarket.

So, an alternative approach would be the so-called "indirect" strategy. This aims to satisfy roughly the same set of needs, but changes the priority of customers' different buying criteria. In this example, supermarkets generally offer low price with acceptable quality. An indirect strategy could swap these priorities to become high quality with acceptable price. This is what delicatessens provide. Like supermarkets, they sell a wide range of foods, including breads and canned goods, meats, cookies, fruit, wine, and specialty items. But unlike supermarkets, they emphasize that the most important thing about food is its quality or taste or links to a specific country, *not* its price. Customers who agree with this approach buy from the deli. Customers who disagree shop elsewhere.

Like supermarkets, delicatessens meet a wide range of food needs. But unlike them, they focus on one small set of customers. This places delicatessens in the bottom right-hand corner of the diagram on page 26. Over time a business like this may change its services but remain focused on serving the needs of a particular customer group.

(The staff canteen also follows this indirect strategy. For its customers, the key benefit is not price or quality, but *convenience.* Again, we see the mix of the three fundamental values—cost, benefit, and time—which have different importance for different people.)

The third alternative is the "divisional" strategy. This approach divides up the total needs of a customer or customers, and focuses on being the best at servicing a small set of them. In food retailing, butchers, bakers, liquor stores, and others all fall into this category. They all satisfy a narrower range of needs than the supermarket, but offer more services within that range. This means that they can appeal more *precisely* to *individual spider profiles* within that smaller set of needs. These businesses all sell a narrower range of foodstuffs, but still to a broad customer base, so they occupy the top left-hand corner of the diagram on page 26. Change over time in this corner is based on innovations in the services delivered and the processes used to deliver them, no matter who the customers for the services are.

The final approach is called the "niche" strategy. This offers a specialist range of services to a specialist set of customers. In the food industry, a specialty tea or coffee shop might once have fulfilled this role. But delicatessens can easily sell these items as part of their overall range—and economies of scale (which we shall look at in Chapter 3) make it easy for supermarkets to offer more standard teas and coffees as part of their overall range. So the niche strategy can make money because of its focus and the lack of competition. But it tends to be rather narrow—a limited range of services to a limited number of customers—which makes it difficult to adapt over time. In the case of specialty tea and coffee shops, they either expanded to become cafés or concentrated on becoming wholesalers to other retailers.

But where does this leave the convenience store? It does not offer as wide a range of services as the supermarket. It does not specialize in the way that either the bakery or the delicatessen does. And it certainly does not fulfill a niche role. So, it sits in the middle. It borrows a piece from each of its competitors, offering a mix of different services (and needs) to a mix of different customers. (See diagram on next page.)

This teaches an important lesson. It shows that whatever names we might come up with to describe different possible strategies, they are only *descriptions,* not solutions.

Just because we identify a box and call it a strategy does not mean that a business that follows that strategy will be successful. And just because a

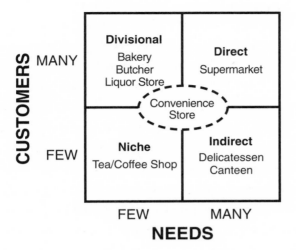

business does something that does not fit into any of the identified strategies does not mean that it will fail.

The strategies are just names, inventions. The reality is the individual customers and their individual needs. All that matters, as the first step to building a successful business, is that the business finds a set of customer needs that it can satisfy better than other businesses. And the root to understanding *that* lies in understanding the different spider profiles.

Each of the businesses shown in the diagram above has the potential to be successful if there are people who have needs that it can satisfy. What limits the *size* of that success, and the size that the business will achieve, is how many customers have that need, and whether other businesses have a better match to their spider profile.

In the USA and the UK, well over 50 percent of customers currently find that their needs are best satisfied by the solution offered by supermarkets. In other countries, where people want different things, the market potential offered by the supermarket approach is smaller.

In other industries, other markets, the structure will be different, and the balance of the numbers of people that want the same or different things will be different. So, what constitutes the "best" strategy will be different. YKK has been extremely successful in following a divisional strategy within the total clothing fasteners industry: it provides more than half the world's zips/zippers, for almost any application, but it focuses on a very narrow range of needs. My local country store finds success by selling a huge range of items, including clothing, hardware, and animal foodstuffs and medicines. The common thread is the farmers and other people who live out of town and need these different things. Private banks offer small or wide ranges of services to a small group of customers. And many small companies, especially consultancies, can find extremely lucrative niches, sometimes providing a single service to a single customer. Just because they are small does not mean that they cannot be successful.[3]

Ultimately, defining the strategy that a business follows as one category or another makes sense only in relation to the other businesses that are in its marketplace. YKK's strategy may be divisional within clothing fasteners, but it is a direct coverage of just about all the market for zips/zippers, which itself is just a very small (and successful) niche within the worldwide garment industry as a whole.

Every market, or set of needs, has other markets within it, and is also part of larger marketplaces. What we think of as a market is just a subset of the total set of human needs. (See box: "The Business Defines the Market, Not the Other Way Around.") We shall return to this in Chapters 7 and 8, as we look at strategy and how to build self-reinforcing business advantage.

Strategic positioning helps a business to think about itself in comparison to other businesses, and in comparison to other spider profiles of needs that it might satisfy.

Being able to choose between these different alternatives requires a way to rank and prioritize them. That is what we shall look at next.

---

**THE BUSINESS DEFINES THE MARKET, NOT THE OTHER WAY AROUND**

We tend to think of businesses as operating within a certain marketplace. But in fact it is the limits of *business* that define the edge of the *marketplace,* not the other way around.

---

[3]Managing the portfolio mix of customers and/or services that a business offers is something that we shall look at in Chapter 5. Expanding it is covered in Chapters 7 and 8.

When Jack Welch was CEO of General Electric, he had a simple rule of strategy: "If you don't have competitive advantage, don't compete."

The direct result of applying this approach was that all of General Electric's business units then achieved the number 1 or number 2 market share positions in their markets. Business units that could not achieve this position were either sold or closed down.

The financial impact of this approach was that the corporation made a lot of money, and stock prices and shareholder value increased dramatically.

Broadly speaking, money made equals value given minus cost incurred. (See Chapter 4 for more on this.)

By focusing on becoming market leaders, Jack Welch and General Electric found an approach that matched their attitude to risk, which meant that every business unit now combined high customer value with low cost incurred: high customer value came from the high market share; low cost incurred came from the Experience Curve (see Chapter 3).

But as well as making a lot of money for GE investors, and good copy for business writers and stock market analysts, this also shows us something *fundamental* and important about the way that businesses, markets, and competitive advantage interact.

For Jack Welch and General Electric, the rule of thumb that measured whether a business had enough competitive advantage to compete was becoming market leader 1 or 2. But what was the market for each business? If we turn the thinking around, we realize that a market is something that has a market leader. If there is no market leader, there can be no market.

So what Jack Welch and General Electric are telling us, and *showing us through their results,* is that *what defines the market is the sustainable competitive advantage of the market leader.*

All the other businesses in the market then follow a direct, indirect, divisional, or niche strategy, *in relation to that leader.*

But, for the leader, competitive advantage is not relative to any other business—it is built around a set of customer needs that it has found a way to satisfy better than its rivals. And as long as those needs survive, and as long as it still has the best way of satisfying them, then the market leader will survive also.

If the needs fade then the market fades, and the leader fades or shrinks with it.

And if another business finds a better way to satisfy the needs, then the market becomes redefined around what that *new* leader can do: if its way of doing things is useful for satisfying other needs, as well, then the markets begin to converge, as telecommunications and computing have done.

It is the individual customers and their needs that are fundamental and real, and any high-level market analysis is an approximation.

Together, the needs of the six billion humans on the planet form a continuous "sea." Within that field, the edges of individual markets are defined by the limits of what the technologies of particular market leaders allow them to do. When those capabilities change, the markets change also.

As we develop legislation and new technologies/capabilities (such as the global transport and telecommunications infrastructures) that enable individual businesses to satisfy a greater share of the needs of more customers, so we automatically create a world in which companies inevitably grow larger. A larger (legally defined) market requires a larger market leader, and a larger market leader defines a larger market.

The implication for any individual business is that success is never defined relative to what some other business is doing. The foundation stone of any business is the set of customer needs that it aims to satisfy, and success comes when a business finds a set of needs that it can satisfy better than its rivals.

The best competitive approach for a business is therefore not to compete at all, but to find a set of customer needs that only it can satisfy. The best competitive approach is to become the market leader in its own market.

Doing this implies that every successful business needs ideally to find its own particular niche, in the way that General Electric's business units have done. This requires being able to combine high value to customers with low costs of delivery. Chapter 8 will show us how to do this, in a way that is not only sustainable but also self-reinforcing.

The limits of the capabilities of the *business* define the edge of the *marketplace,* not the other way around.

*RANKING THE ALTERNATIVES* Understanding needs and spider profiles tells the business what different groups of customers might want. And strategic positioning shows what competitors are doing.

The best way forward for the business will involve a balance between these different factors.

As a simple example of how to approach this, I am going to work through the convenience store's decision about which types of fruit to stock. But the process, the approach, could equally well be applied to the decision about whether or not to stock fresh fruit as a category, in comparison to canned or frozen fruit, vegetables, bread, ready meals, and so on. And it could also be applied to the decision that a conglomerate or investment fund might make about whether to include a convenience store in *its* business portfolio; in comparison with supermarkets, delicatessens, bakeries, restaurants, hotels, golf courses, and so on.

These cases seem very different, but each one is just a different level within the total set of human needs. Each one involves a customer with a set of needs, and so in each case there is a spider profile, and so in each case the methodology applies.

In each case, what the business has to do is to assess its options against three questions.

The first is to define how much value each alternative would bring to the potential customers. Ideally the answer would be defined in specific dollar terms. But that is not always possible, and so a ranking scale of 1–10, or even "high, medium, low," can be used, at least as a first step.

It usually makes sense to break this question down into smaller parts. In the case of the convenience store we might say that the potential value to customers is a combination of the number of people that like each type of fruit and how much they like it. For other services, items such as customer urgency to buy, ability to pay, market size, and so on might be appropriate.

For the convenience store example, the table on the next page uses a simple scale of 1 (low), 2 (medium), and 3 (high). It shows that a small number of people (1) like grapes, and they *really* like them (3). On the other hand, lots of people (3) quite like (2) apples. This is then repeated for the other fruit. The two numbers are then combined to create an overall rating for the value to customers of each alternative.

The second step is to find what value each alternative offers for the *business*. Again, it is necessary to break this question down into separate indicators, such as the likely volume of the business (how many units would be sold), the profitability of each sale, what the long-term growth potential is, and so on. The marketing potential (or brand image) to be gained from going into different business areas might also be important.

In the convenience store example, the table shows the likely sales volume (number of sales) and profitability (mark-up) for each type of fruit. Again, the numbers are combined to create a single overall measure of the value to the business.

Finally, each alternative needs to be assessed for the ability of the business to implement and sustain it—what we might call "competitive resilience." This is a combination of the business's ability to put the new service into place and the ability of competitors to do a similar or better job. Timing is often important in this section (e.g., time to implement, financial payback, or how long it would take a competitor to respond), and if it applies to the first two questions (customer and business value), then they too can be split out into short-term and long-term assessments.

Again the specific questions that are appropriate depend on the individual business and its specific situation. In the convenience store example (and to save space) I have simply shown a single overall figure.

| | VALUE TO CUSTOMER | | | VALUE TO BUSINESS | | | USING RE-SOURCES | OVER-ALL TOTAL |
|---|---|---|---|---|---|---|---|---|
| | NUMBER | STRENGTH | SUB-TOTAL | VOLUME | PROFIT | SUB-TOTAL | | |
| Oranges | 1 | 2 | 1.5 | 1 | 2 | 1.5 | 1.5 | 3.4 |
| Apples | 3 | 2 | 2.5 | 3 | 2 | 2.5 | 2 | 12.5 |
| Pears | 2 | 2 | 2 | 1 | 3 | 2 | 2 | 8.0 |
| Peaches | 2 | 3 | 2.5 | 1 | 3 | 2 | 2.5 | 12.5 |
| Grapes | 1 | 3 | 2 | 1 | 3 | 2 | 3 | 12.0 |
| Bananas | 1.5 | 2 | 1.75 | 1 | 2 | 1.5 | 1.5 | 3.9 |
| Etc... | | | | | | | | |

In order for the alternatives to be successful they need to add value to the customer, *and* make money for the business, *and* represent an easily achievable way of using resources. So the overall attractiveness of each type of fruit is obtained by multiplying the individual ratings together.

The result, in this example, is that apples and peaches (with scores of 12.5) both appear to offer the best opportunities for the convenience store to build a successful business, closely followed by grapes (12.0).

We can put the same information into picture form:

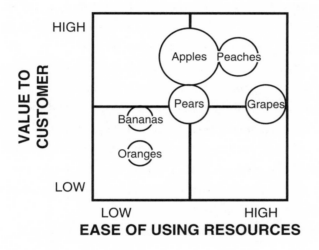

In this diagram the size of each circle shows the potential value to the business. The left axis shows the value to the customer. And the bottom axis shows how comparatively easy it would be for the business to deliver each service.

Which option the business chooses then determines the mix of *market* risk and reward that it is likely to have—that will become (as we shall see in Chapter 4) the *financial* risk and reward that its shares will have in the stock market.

If this business chooses to sell grapes, then it is choosing to enter a market where the value to the customer is medium, and so is the reward to the business. But the ease of getting into the business is very high—and so, in other words, the risk is low.

If the business chooses to sell apples, then the value to customers and the value to the business are both higher, and (in this example) the business is more difficult to implement. In this case risk is higher and so is reward.

Different businesses, and different people within those businesses, will tend to prefer different mixtures of risk and reward. Some prefer low risk, low reward. Others prefer high risk and high reward.

What most people would probably like is low risk and high reward. In our diagram this would appear as a large circle in the top right corner: very valuable to customers and to the business, and very easy to deliver. But life does not usually work that way—or if it does, then other businesses will soon appear to compete in that same marketplace. Which alternative seems most attractive will vary from business to business, and the ones that are chosen then determine the inherent *market* risk and reward of the business: the strength of demand from the customers, and the potential value that the business can extract for itself. Combined with the *operational* risk (and costs) of delivering the service (as we shall see in Chapter 3) these then become the *financial* risk and return that the business represents, and we shall look further at this in Chapter 4.

For now, though, in this particular example, we can again see that apples, peaches, and grapes are the front-runners, with pears not close behind. The numbers are the same as they were in the table, but the picture is clearer this time, because we can see the different *reasons* that each one is a priority, the different nuances of risk and reward.

Now this was a highly simplified example, and the results for a real convenience store might have looked different. But whether the table was filled out based on the opinions of a single store manager, a group of managers, or by spending (say) 1 percent of turnover on some detailed market research, would not alter the process. All it would change would be the accuracy and confidence in the findings, as well as the time and cost it took to generate them. (Remember this in Chapter 7.)

What approach the business chooses to fill out the table will depend on its attitude to risk. But a successful business is always a combination of value to the customer, value to the business, and sustainable use of resources, and so the approach always clearly shows the advantages and disadvantages of each alternative, and so enables a more informed decision to be made.

The approach also usually throws up at least one surprise: it usually finds at least one top-ranking alternative that was not considered before. When that happens the next step is always to think back through the scores that have been given, and *test* whether they are correct. More often than not the overall result still stands.

The reason for this is that most people tend to look at only one part of the problem—the part that they are most expert in. But choosing which needs to satisfy is about choosing which needs offer the best chance to combine them *all* and build a competitive, sustainable business.

So, the best option for the business is the one that offers the best opportunity to build the first layer of strategic advantage: to make money by using resources to satisfy customer needs.

By looking at the whole picture, unexpected opportunities are found, and the weaknesses in pet projects are also revealed. That is the strength of this approach: it combines both qualitative and quantitative measures from all sides, allowing trade-offs to be made and hidden opportunities to be revealed.

Chapters 2, 3, and 4 help readers to expand their understanding of the right questions to ask under each heading. The remaining chapters show how to balance the three together, and ultimately Chapter 8 shows how to combine them all to create a self-sustaining "niche" market.

Now that the business has understood its customers' needs and chosen a set that it is well-placed to satisfy, the next and final step is to get those needs satisfied—to bring together the customers and the service that the business has developed. That is the subject of the next section.

——— **MAKING IT REAL** ———

- What are the alternative services your business is thinking of choosing between?
- Rank the value to the customer of each one on a scale of 1–10.
  (Identify at least three sub-measures for this.)

- Rank the value to the business of each one on a scale of 1–10. (Identify at least three sub-measures for this.)

- Rank the ease with which each alternative can be achieved and maintained, on a scale of 1–10.

- Find the overall attractiveness of each option by multiplying the three scores together.

- Are the results what you expected? If not, why not?

## BRINGING CUSTOMERS AND SERVICE TOGETHER

*THE CUSTOMER CHAIN* Having picked a combination of customers and needs to satisfy, every business now faces the same situation: six billion people on the planet, some of whom *might* find the service useful, most of whom will *not* find it useful, and *none* of whom yet knows *anything* about the service or the value it could bring to them.

The aim is to bring customers and service together, and the first step is to get at least some potential customers to become aware of the service, to know that it exists.

This is what teaser campaigns do—they tell potential customers that the service is there, but say nothing (at first) about what it might do for them. That is the second step: to build understanding.

As people get more information about the service (from advertisements, from friends, or wherever) an image builds inside their minds about what the service might do for them. They then compare that image against their own spider profiles of needs (for cost, value, and timing) and eventually decide whether they like the service and are willing to try it, or dislike the service, since it has nothing to offer them.

These are the next two groupings, and how many people move into each one—"Like" or "Dislike"—and how many simply remain "Aware" of the service, depends on three things, all of which can be *partly* influenced by the business.

The first is how many people have needs profiles that the service matches. Although the *needs* are fundamental, the profiles of *acceptable* levels of performance depend on a mix of cultural and economic factors, and can be influenced by what we broadly call advertising. The second factor is how many people with matching profiles the business has communicated with. In other words, it depends on how well targeted its activities have been. This is why businesses pay for mailing lists, for example, and it is also why spam and junk mail are so annoying—because they are not targeted to the needs of the people who receive them. The third factor that influences how many people decide they "Like" the service is how accurately and effectively the value it might bring to them has been communicated. (For more on this see "Secrets of Communication—The Six Cs.")

Since the business *can* influence all three of these factors, it might seem like a good idea to push as hard as possible to persuade *everybody* to move from "Knowing" the service to "Liking" it. But let's see what happens next.

When people try the service, they get the most direct information they will ever have about whether or not it meets their needs. "The proof of the pudding is in the eating," as the saying goes, and from this point there are three things that can happen.

The first is that customers decide that they do not like the service after all—it is not what they expected or they were misled into thinking the service was something other than it is—and so they now "Know and Dislike" the service.

Surveys repeatedly tell us that a very dissatisfied customer can tell ten other people about their bad experience. So, the result of pushing too hard to persuade just *one* more customer to try the service could therefore be that the business has *eleven* more customers who actively "Dislike" it. This won't happen every time, but the point is that the business needs to be careful about what messages it gives to which customers. Pushing too hard can backfire.

The second possibility is that having tried the service, customers then find that they do like it. They continue to buy it from time to time, but they also buy from competitors: they become and remain what I call "Fickle" customers.

The third possibility is that they like the service so much—they find it matches so well with their spider profile of needs—that they become

"Loyal" customers, buying the service frequently and never buying from competitors.

Together, these five attitudes (Unaware, Know, Like, Use, and Trust[4]) form a "customer chain" that describes five different sets of customer behavior towards the service.

Managing this chain is what the third part of satisfying customer needs is all about:

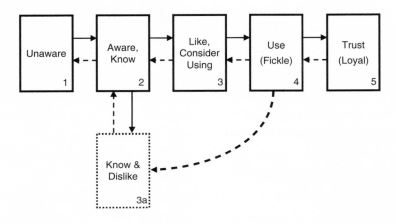

## The Customer Chain

New customers and customer needs are being born (and dying) all the time, so if the business does nothing, then customers as a whole will tend to drift back towards the unaware state.

Stopping this from happening, and reversing the flow, requires the business to spend money and effort to move customers between the different links along the chain. Each step is different, and so each change in customer

---

[4]The five boxes shown are illustrative only. The key is to choose whatever categories match *actual observed customer behaviors.* Classical marketing, for example, talks about AIDA (for awareness, interest, desire, action). This makes no distinction between loyal and fickle customers. Other businesses will want to differentiate between "loyal" and "very loyal," or between "dislikes" and "actively campaigns against us." Politicians have a similar chain, with people perhaps classified as "contact," "friend," "supporter," or "ally."

thinking involves a different message, delivered in a different way, using a different set of resources.

This is what most of marketing is all about: the four Ps, direct selling, spin selling, junk mail, viral marketing, point-of-sale materials, advertising, PR, promotions, buy-one-get-one-free. . . . All are aimed at moving customers between the links in this chain, or at keeping them in the category that they are already in. (The rest of marketing is either about understanding customer needs or choosing which needs to satisfy.)

Delivering what we think of as the service is *just one part* (one very important part) of this overall customer chain.

Once we realize this, we understand that the customer needs which the business is being asked to satisfy are often much greater than the ones being met by the core service alone. For example, I not only need my apple to taste good, I also need to be able to buy it during my lunch hour.

In fact, this broader set of needs often includes some elements that *cannot* be met by the core service alone. The aim of cosmetics, for example, is to make the wearer *feel* beautiful—but since she cannot see her own make-up once it has been put on, strong advertising helps the customer to conjure up the mental images (or self-images) that are what is *really* being paid for. Here, superb advertising combined with average make-up is probably a better business proposition than average advertising and superb make-up.

Whatever the business, customer satisfaction is always something that happens (or fails to happen) *in the mind of the customer.* So success at satisfying customer needs is about success at managing customer perceptions at *all* stages along the customer chain, not just in delivering the core service.

Sometimes what it takes to manage that perception is a message or piece of information, such as advertising. At other times, perceptions change as the result of something physical, such as cleanliness or on-time delivery. (More examples are given in the table on page 43.)

Realizing that it is the *full* customer chain that matters helps us to think back to the first part of this chapter and understand better what the *full* needs of the customer are. It then becomes the job of the business to align its full resources (as will be discussed in Chapter 3) to optimize the way it manages the *full customer chain,* not just the delivery of the core service.

It also reinforces the decision taken in this book to talk about services rather than products—because even a pure product business has a customer chain, which contains the other, *service*-related, needs that its customers have.

So, for obvious reasons, I call this whole approach customer chain marketing.

It is vitally important, because it also drives the financial success of the business. The business has to spend money in moving customers between every link of the chain, but the only customers who bring any money *into* the business are the loyal and fickle ones. So how much money the business actually makes is driven by the balance between how many customers there are in these two groups (and the revenues they bring), and how much money the business has to spend to get them there and keep them there.

Just as delivering a successful service requires the business to get the right profile of cost, value, and timing needs, so successfully managing the customer chain also requires the business to get the right mix of these three things into every link along the chain.

*How* to do this varies between businesses, as well as between links in the chain. Some examples are given in the table opposite.

Television advertising, for example, is a common way to inform people that a service exists, as is word of mouth and hanging a shingle outside the store. Advertising can also be used to keep customers loyal, by reminding them what a great service they have bought. But what makes for good advertising in all these cases is very different.

To be successful at every stage, the business needs to get away from general terms such as advertising or PR, and focus instead on identifying the *specific* changes in thinking that would induce customers to switch between the different groups; what *specific* messages would achieve those changes; and what *specific* resources would be best placed to deliver those messages. (See also the "Secrets of Good Communication—The Six Cs" box on page 51.)

Being successful at this means the business has to get close to its customers—both in terms of understanding them, and in terms of being able

| | UNAWARE → AWARE | AWARE → LIKE | LIKE → BUY | BUY → LOYAL | REMAIN LOYAL |
|---|---|---|---|---|---|
| **Supermarket** | • TV advertising<br>• Store location | • TV advertising<br>• Exterior façade<br>• Word of mouth | • TV advertising<br>• Exterior façade<br>• Word of mouth | • Quality/price<br>• Store layout<br>• Range of goods | • "Loyalty" cards<br>• Special offers<br>• … |
| **Airline** | • TV advertising<br>• Internet research | • TV advertising<br>• Word of mouth<br>• Pricing | • Flight schedule<br>• Pricing | • In-flight experience<br>• Timeliness | • Frequent traveller discounts<br>• Cabin crew |
| **Car** | • TV advertising<br>• Passed in street<br>• Magazines | • TV advertising<br>• Word of mouth<br>• Test drive | • Discounts<br>• Sales staff<br>• Word of mouth | • Ownership experience | • Servicing<br>• TV advertising<br>• Owner clubs |
| **Novel/Author** | • Press advertising<br>• Bookstore stack | • Critic's review<br>• Back cover blurb | • Flick through<br>• Amazon reviews | • "Good read" | • "Test of time" |
| **Industrial Gases** | • Word of mouth<br>• Trade press | • Word of mouth | • Word of mouth<br>• Negotiated terms | • Reliability | • Reliability |
| **Vacation** | • Advertising<br>• Word of mouth | • Press advertising<br>• Brochure | • Price, availability<br>• Travel agent staff | • Vacation experience | • Repeat vacation experience |
| **Plumber, Electrician, Music Teacher** | • Word of mouth<br>• Yellow pages | • Word of mouth<br>• Yellow pages | • Visit<br>• Price quote | • Quality of service<br>• Friendliness | • Continued quality of service |
| **Insurance by Telephone** | • TV advertising<br>• Internet research | • TV advertising<br>• Word of mouth | • Ease of getting price quote | • Hassle-free renewal<br>• Price | • Experience of making a claim |
| **Sports Shoes** | • TV advertising<br>• Fashion | • Celebrity endorsement | • Fashion<br>• Price | • Fashion<br>• User experience | • Fashion<br>• User experience |

Examples of *some* of the factors that *can* influence people to switch between customer groups in different businesses.

to communicate clearly with them. In fact, the word "communication" is enough, since it has to be two-way in order to be effective.

It is beyond the scope of this book to define the specific activities that work best for any one business (though Chapter 3 will look in more detail at *how* to go about using resources).

But knowing where to focus to improve the chain is key to improving business performance, and so a general example of that is what we shall look at in the next section.

---

**LOYAL AND FICKLE CUSTOMERS: THE CONSUMER ADOPTION PROFILE**

As we know, Maslow's hierarchy tells us that different people have different needs, and so the *number* of the six billion people on the planet who have a very strong match to any particular service will be relatively small, with many more of them having a low or very low match. This is drawn as the "Suitability" curve below.

At the same time, the strength of match between a customer and a service depends on how closely the two spider profiles match. If the match is very strong then the customer will need little persuading to buy the service—a loyal customer. If the match is weaker, then the customer will need more convincing—a fickle customer. Mathematically, loyal customers have a high probability of buying the service, and fickle customers have a low probability (so the business has to work harder to convince them to buy). This is drawn as the "Probability" curve below.

Putting these two things together gives us the bell-shaped curve that we see in real life, describing how many people like a service "a lot," "some," or "a little," and which classical marketing calls the Consumer Adoption Profile.

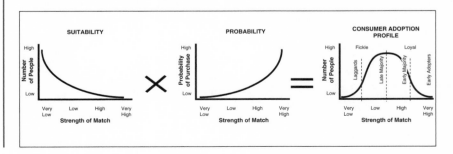

---

When a new service is launched, a small number of customers will buy it almost immediately. These are called the "Innovators" and "Early Adopters," and they need very little convincing to buy the service. The reason is that their spider profiles match closely with the service.

As time passes, more people begin to buy the service, and these are called the "Early Majority." The reason is that the service has become better known and maybe the price has come down. These are customers with a high match to the service, who take a little bit more convincing to move along the customer chain from "Aware" to "Use."

Next comes what classical marketing calls the "Late Majority," and then the "Laggards." Again, these are people for whom the match is slightly weaker. They probably form what I call the fickle customer group, and the business has to work harder to convince them to buy the service.

The total bell-shaped curve that results is called the Consumer Adoption Profile. Its shape is different for different services, and sometimes it is not bell-shaped. But whatever the actual shape of the curve, where it comes from is always the two fundamental things we have looked at: the Maslow hierarchy of needs, and the spider profile.

It is one of the foundations of marketing, but in summary all it says is that some people need a lot of persuasion to buy the service, while others need very little.

*CUSTOMER CHAIN MARKETING—AN EXAMPLE* This is not a book about marketing, but it is worth spending time on a detailed example of the Customer Chain, because this will give a better feel for how the business's different resources interact with different parts of the chain, and how the business needs to focus not so much on *controlling* the customer's movement between different perceptions of the service, but on *facilitating* it.

Different businesses all have different customers and different customer chains. For example, the time it takes customers to move from "Unaware" to making their first purchase can vary from several minutes to weeks, months, or even years, depending on the business.

But whatever the business, and whatever its service, doing a better job at managing the Customer Chain always comes down to two basic things: picking the right part of the chain to improve, and finding the best ways to do so.

As an example let's take a look at a traditional British fish and chip shop (or fish bar) that has noticed a reduction in sales since a Chinese take away (carry out) was opened just around the corner.

The fish bar hires a firm of marketing consultants, who stand in the street with clipboards and ask 100 passers-by about each business.

The results are summarized into two Customer Chain diagrams:

**Fish and Chip Shop:**

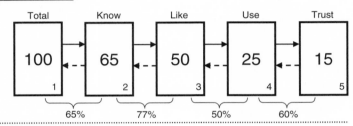

**Chinese Take-Away:**

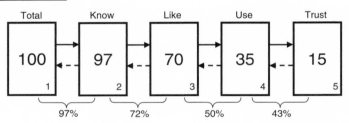

These figures show us that 65 percent of the people questioned know that the fish and chip shop is there. (When the other 35 percent explained why they had not noticed it before, they said that it is down a side street or alleyway that they never visit, or that the shop front just blends into the background.) Of the people who do know about it, most like the fish bar—they know or have heard that it serves good food—but only half of them again (25 percent of the total) have used it in the past month (defined as the measure of customers who "currently use" the business). Of those people a high proportion (60 percent, nearly two-thirds) are defined as loyal customers.

By comparison, nearly everybody (97 percent) has noticed the Chinese restaurant. This is partly because the owners recently leafleted all the homes in the area, and partly because of the bright colors and neon lights which have been used on the exterior. Again, a high proportion of the people who know about the business say they like it, although only 35 of the 100 people have actually tried the food. So, the high number of people liking the new business probably has more to do with the 10 percent discount offered during the first two weeks, or the donations given to the local school, than it has to do with the actual food being good.

Although more people have used the new restaurant in the past month (35 percent compared with 25 percent for the fish and chip shop) the proportion of them who have become loyal customers is lower: 43 percent compared with 60 percent for the fish bar. The net result is that both businesses now have about the same number of loyal customers (15 percent of those questioned), with the Chinese restaurant having an additional 20 people in every 100 who are fickle customers, and the fish and chip shop an additional 10.

That describes the situation. What should the fish and chip shop do?

Well, that depends on what results it wants to achieve, and what attitude it wants to adopt relative to the Chinese restaurant (see the section above on strategic positioning). If the fish bar wants to compete *directly* with its rival, then copying everything that rival does is a simple way to create exactly the same results—and reduce the money made by each business, since each would be serving exactly the same (limited) set of customers.

Alternatively, the fish bar owner might believe that there are some people in the neighborhood who like fish and chips, some who like Chinese, and some people who like both. In that case, the fish and chip shop could expect to suffer a drop in sales to start with as customers try out the new premises *instead of* fish and chips, followed by a possible rise in sales as more people get into the habit of buying restaurant food (of every kind).

So, let's assume that the owner decides that (s)he wants to continue to run a fish and chip shop—serving a slightly different set of customers from the Chinese restaurant, providing a better service against a different set of needs—and wants to find ways to ensure that the future turns out better than the past.

The ultimate goal is to increase the number of loyal customers (and possibly fickle ones as well). So long as the business has loyal customers, it will survive.

The obvious way to do that, for any business, is to improve the service, and in this specific case, that might mean buying more expensive fish or hiring a better chef, reducing prices or offering home delivery. But comparing the figures with the Chinese restaurant Customer Chain shows that the business is actually *already very good* at creating loyal customers—60 percent of its paying customers are classified as loyal, compared with 43 percent for its rival. *So improving the service is unlikely to bring much benefit.*

What *would* benefit the business is to find a way or ways to get more people simply to know that it is there—and the Chinese restaurant has shown that it is possible to get that number up to 97 percent!

To achieve this same result, the fish and chip shop could simply copy everything the Chinese restaurant did. But the fish bar serves a different set of customers, with different needs. And so covering the outside of the building with bright neon lights (for example) *might* not fit with what the loyal customers want or expect from their fish bar. Repainting the shop front or moving premises to a busier location are probably better alternatives.[5]

The Chinese restaurant, in its turn, might also learn something from the fish bar, which is much better at converting its fickle customers into loyal ones. The reason might be that people who like fish and chips are intrinsically more conservative (loyal), compared to people who like Chinese food, who are intrinsically more adventurous (fickle). Or it might be because the fish shop has friendlier staff, better décor, chairs to sit on, newspapers to read while customers are waiting, and so on. It might even be because it has better food.

---

[5]To choose which alternative(s) to implement, the business needs to predict the effect that each will have on the number of people in each group along the Customer Chain. Converting that to a sales forecast and combining it with the expected costs (see Chapter 4) enables the business to estimate the short-term impact on the value of the business. Chapter 5 shows how to take a wider range of measures into account. And Chapter 6 looks at testing how well each alternative might fit within the longer-term plans for the business.

Whatever the reason, by probing into greater detail and understanding the reasons, the Chinese restaurant could also learn new ways to influence people to move along *its* chain, and so could improve *its* business.

This is what market research or marketing research should be about—not simply understanding how to make the *service* better, but how to improve the entire Customer Chain.

Whatever the solution, understanding the Customer Chain helps a business be more focused and precise about *where* it needs to improve performance, and *how.*

Comparison with other businesses almost always helps, and it might seem to make sense to compare figures for two identical businesses (in this case two fish shops), rather than two slightly different ones as we have done here.

Comparing two very similar businesses can be a quick and easy way for the weaker business to catch up. But knowing what to do does not make it possible. And copying will rarely help the stronger business.

If two businesses do exactly the same things in the same way they will get exactly the same results. They will end up serving exactly the same set of customers with the same service, which is bad news for both businesses, because they will both have only fickle customers—fickle customers that each business then has to pander to, because if they do not, then those customers will simply switch to the rival business.

To be successful, to be the best at serving the customer needs in *its* marketplace, any business has to create its *own* ideas, find its own ways of understanding, choosing, and satisfying its customers' needs. It cannot simply copy everything a rival business does.

To do that, like the fish and chip shop, it has to look at other businesses that are *different* from itself. And it then has to *borrow, adapt,* and *combine* ideas from different areas to create its own individual total way of doing things. The ultimate way of doing *that* successfully is what we shall look at when we come to creating self-reinforcing advantage in Chapter 8.

So far we have seen that success in satisfying customer needs does not come simply from having a good service—it comes from having a good *total* Customer Chain.

The messages, methods, and resources that are used need to match not only with each particular part of the chain, but also with the customers that the business has chosen to satisfy. (For more details on this see the "Secrets of Good Communication" box below.) Simply deciding to improve the service or spend more money on advertising is like throwing darts while wearing a blindfold—they can sometimes hit the mark, but more by luck than judgment.

The chosen set of customers and needs are embodied in the people who become the loyal customers. These are the ones whose needs most closely match with what the service has to offer. And it is these people who form the common thread between all the different links along the chain.

When marketing people talk about coherence of the total marketing message, they are talking about aligning every link along the chain. And the way they best achieve this is by matching the loyal customers' *own* processes for moving along the chain—processes that are intrinsically coherent because they are dealing with moving the *same person,* the same loyal customer, between the different mental states or perceptions and opinions about the service.[6] This is why free samples and free trials work—they let customers make up their own mind about the service. It is also the idea behind customer lifetime management.

Doing a better job than competitors at efficiently managing the Customer Chain means understanding customers' individual journeys from unaware to loyal, and helping them to make that journey. It means not only free samples but also the toll-free numbers and reply-paid coupons that make it quick and easy to move forward. It means creating the possibility of as many different routes or chains as there are distinctive groups of customers.

Managing this successfully has three parts. First, the business has to understand how its customers currently move between the different parts of

---

[6]For businesses where most customers are fickle, coherence becomes much less important. This is because the business has not been able to identify a piece of value that would make most customers loyal.

the chain and find ways to make that as easy as possible: facilitate what is already happening. Second, the business needs to experiment with new ways of enabling the process (such as the Internet). And third, it needs to manage its whole portfolio of these different channels to market, keeping the profitable ones and pruning back the ones that don't work. (This is described in detail in the first part of Chapter 5.)

Satisfying the different customer needs along *all* the links of the chain, in all stages of awareness, and in all stages of the customer's lifetime means much more than simply delivering the service. To achieve it successfully the business needs to use many different resources from different parts of its organization. But although the *organization* may have many parts, the *business* (and the customer) is a single whole—so if it is to be successful, those different parts need to pull together in the same direction, aligned around the common thread of the loyal customers' needs.

This idea of seeing the business as a single coherent whole is a theme throughout the book. This issue of organizational alignment is addressed specifically in Chapter 5.

But what we are going to look at next, in the final section of this chapter, is how to *optimize* the total Customer Chain.

---

### SECRETS OF GOOD COMMUNICATION—THE SIX Cs

If customer satisfaction is something that happens in customers' minds, then we can think of the things that convince them to switch between categories along the customer chain as messages.

Sometimes these messages are literally messages, such as advertising, leaflets, or store signs. And sometimes they are subtler messages, such as whether there are chairs to sit on while you wait, or how clean a room is, or the way that customers are treated.

No matter how a message is delivered, its effectiveness is determined by the six Cs.

The first C is for *Customer Chain*. The message needs to fit with the place on the chain where the customer already is, and the change that the business wants to bring about. A message which is perfectly suited to moving a customer from "Knows" to "Likes" will probably be of very little use in getting a fickle customer to become loyal, and vice-versa. This is why it is so important to understand and focus on the right part of the customer chain first.

The second C is for *Content:* does the content come across as value to the customer, rather than as a feature? We have already discussed this in relation to the actual service. The same applies to advertisements and the rest of the Customer Chain.

The third C is for *Culture:* does the message explain the value in a way that makes sense to customers, a way that fits with their culture, language, and style? (Teenagers speak a different language than people over 50.)

The fourth C is for *Channel.* Marshall McLuhan told us that "The medium is the massage"—it "massages" the way the hearer hears the message. So, first the medium or channel needs to be a source of information that the customer normally pays attention to, not one that they blank out or ignore. And second, the channel needs to fit with the message being delivered: newspaper advertisements are a good way to convey factual messages; television is a good medium or channel to convey emotions.

The fifth C is for *Context.* When and how the message is received needs to fit in with the context of what the customer is doing and thinking at the time. Showing trailers at the beginning of a movie or a video is a good idea, but only if they are roughly similar to the main film. Vending machines make sense in the context of station platforms, where people spend time standing around waiting—but not in stairways or corridors where they are hurrying from one place to another.

And the sixth C is for *Consistency* or *Coherence.* Is there coherence between all the different elements of the message? For example, I might normally watch television and I might like Tiger Woods, the golfer—but I probably wouldn't pay much attention if he appeared in a television commercial for tennis rackets, however much I wanted one.

Consistency between the different elements that impact the different links along the Customer Chain is important not because of any benefit to the *business,* but because it is the same customer and the same set of customer needs that the business is trying to appeal to along the whole length of the Customer Chain.

In summary, the most successful messages will be the ones that (by accident or design) match with who and what customers normally listen to or pay attention to and when and in what situation they listen to them, and articulate the message in a way and in terms that are relevant to customers. (These six items reappear in a different form in Chapter 3, as the "six honest serving-men" in the "Defining a Process" box.)

> In other words, the most efficient communications are those that go with the flow of the Customer Chain—not *drift* with the flow, but *go* in the direction that the flow is already flowing—to encourage customers along their *own* natural processes of change and tip or nudge something that was about to happen anyway.

———— **MAKING IT REAL** ————

- What are the key groups or stages along the Customer Chain for your business?

- Of 100 (or 1,000) customers in your target market, how many would fit into each category for your business?

- What are the key processes, resources, or activities that you rely on to move customers between each of the categories?

- Of 100 (or 1,000) customers in your target market, how many would fit into each category for your two competitors?

- What methods do *they* use to manage *their* customer chains?

- What are the key areas where you need to improve your performance? How could you do that?

- What are the key areas where you have advantage? How will you maintain that advantage?

## BUILDING COMPETITIVE ADVANTAGE: OPTIMIZING THE CUSTOMER CHAIN

*SETTING A PRICE* So, we have understood the customer needs, chosen a set to satisfy, and learned that managing the Customer Chain is what being good at delivering on *satisfying customer needs* is all about.

It involves not only providing or delivering the service, but also carrying out the activities we call sales, selling, advertising, promotions, networking, public relations, customer support, and so on.

Every one of these subjects is worth a dozen books, and new methods are being invented all the time. So defining what approach would work best in every single situation is clearly beyond the scope of this book. But we *can* say something about what it takes to manage the Customer Chain *as a whole*. Being able to do this better than competitors is clearly something that will give a business an advantage.

In other words, together with the other activities in satisfying customer needs, optimizing the Customer Chain is something that can be used to create a long-term source of business advantage.

We know that to be successful the business needs to make money. So as a starting point, let's focus on the only two customer groups that bring money into the business: loyal and fickle customers.

Of these two groups, the loyal customers have the best match to the spider-profile of features offered by the service. For them the service has the greatest value, and they will be willing to pay the most for it.

Of course, not all loyal customers are the same. A few will be prepared to pay a very high price. More will be willing to pay less. But as a group, the loyal customers form the first focus for the business—the people who will be most grateful to the business for its service.

Fickle customers will also buy the service. But for them the value is lower, so they are willing to pay less.

Putting these two groups together gives us the bell-shaped curve shown above in the Consumer Adoption Profile. This represents the total potential *maximum* value that the business could extract from the marketplace. But the business cannot (usually) charge a different price to each customer. What usually happens is that the business sets a single price for the service, and people then buy the service *if the value to them is greater than the price.*

If the business sets the price too high then very few people will want to buy. If it sets the price too low, then more people will buy, but most will pay far less than they would have been willing to.

In order to help us think about this, we need to redraw the information in the bell-curve in a different way.

The bell curve shows the number of people who are willing to pay each specific price. We need to see the number of people willing to pay that same price, *or higher.*

Redrawing the same information in this different way gives us another well-known chart of economics: the Demand Curve.

The picture now shows the number of people (along the bottom axis) who are willing to pay *at least* the price shown on the left-hand axis.

### THE FULL DEMAND CURVE

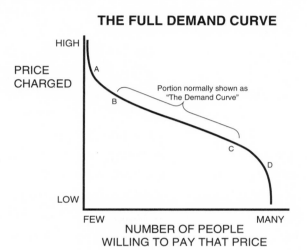

Economists usually focus on just the central part of the curve, the part that is almost straight. But the two ends are very important for businesses also.

What the curve first shows us is that for any service there are a *small* number of people who would be willing to pay a very high price for it—perhaps the service is *exactly* what they are looking for, or maybe they simply have money to burn. This is the area marked on the curve as "A," and it is very important for businesses launching new services to think about who these customers are, and how to contact them.

Then, in the central section, from "B" to "C," is the line usually drawn by economists. This is where businesses most usually operate, and here (broadly speaking), the lower the price, the more people will be willing to pay it.

But at the right-hand end, the part marked as "D," there is a certain point, a certain price, beyond which reducing the price will have almost no effect on the numbers of people who buy it. Beyond this point, people are saying: "I don't care how cheap it is, I don't want it!"

The total sales or revenue that the business earns will be equal to the number of people who buy the service multiplied by the price they pay. So, setting the price is a key driver of how well the business manages its Customer Chain.

If the business sets the price at "C," for example, then it immediately has a large number of customers. But it loses out on the money it could have earned from the customers at "A" and "B" who would have been prepared to pay more.

If the business starts by charging price "A" and then slowly reduces it to "B" and "C," it gains the maximum value from its customers, but it is under threat to a competitor who comes straight in at price "C."

Choosing the right price to set is a complex area that depends on many things. But in general, if there are few competitors, or if competitors would find it difficult to launch a rival service, then it makes sense to lower the price slowly, so that every customer pays the maximum they are willing to pay. But if other businesses could create a similar or rival service (which is usually the case) then it makes sense to lower the price faster, in order to generate a group of loyal (rather than fickle) customers.

GENERATING NEW CUSTOMERS, NEW SERVICES Once the price is set, that drives the numbers of people who will be in the loyal and fickle customer groups, and how profitable each will be. It also sets the upper limit on how much money the business can make.

Customers in the other groups ("Unaware" to "Like") don't spend any money. Ideally the business would just ignore them and concentrate on delivering services to its loyal and fickle customers.

But that is not realistic. Customers and needs and services (and competitors) are changing all the time, so the business constantly needs to be talking to the earlier parts of the chain—bringing new customers into the fickle and loyal categories, and stopping customers already there from slipping back.

The loyal and fickle customers bring both revenues and costs into the business. The other groups bring only costs. So, to make the most money, the business has to get the right balance between spending too much and too little money on these other groups.[7] If the business spends too little money, the numbers of fickle and loyal customers will gradually dwindle as people leave and are not replaced. If it spends too much, then at best the business makes less money, and at worst it also creates a group of disgruntled customers, fed up of being pushed to buy a service they know they don't want.

Every business needs to decide for itself where the balance lies between risk and reward. But getting the balance right means (theoretically) finding the point at which an extra $1 spent at whatever point along the chain brings an extra $1 in sales. If it creates $2 more, then it is worth spending another $1 to create $1.99 in more sales. If every $1 spent on marketing only creates an additional $0.50 in sales, then it is time to cut back on marketing.

But there is an alternative, and it is the approach we saw the Coca-Cola Corporation adopt above. (See "I'd like to buy the world a Coke" box.)

Rather than spend more and more marketing dollars getting fewer and fewer extra people to drink Coke, the corporation decided to offer more services—services that each appealed to a different group of loyal customers. This is the part of marketing called segmentation. And the fundamental reason that it comes about links back to the Maslow hierarchy of needs. At the lower levels of the Maslow hierarchy, people's needs are very similar (air, water). So a single service can satisfy a wide range of basic needs (think "any color you want, so long as it's black"). But as basic needs become fulfilled and the service needs to add value at higher Maslow levels, so the business finds that the service needs to be tailored to appeal specifically to

---

[7]In fact, the balance between the number of loyal and fickle customers and the price each group is willing to pay is what drives the management of the whole Customer Chain. If there are few fickle customers and loyal customers are more profitable, it makes sense to focus on the niche market of loyal customers. If the fickle customers are just as profitable as loyal ones, it makes sense to manage the chain completely differently. Loyal customers will still be more important than fickle ones (they are likely, for example, to provide more ideas for new services). But the business will need to find ways to communicate with a broader market, and realize that the cut-off point between the last profitable customer and the first unprofitable one will be harder to identify.

different customer groups. It becomes, in effect, a different service. (The ultimate customer group, of course, is a single customer.)

The result is that the business now has multiple Customer Chains to manage (one for each service), which increases the scale and complexity of the problem. But it does not change the fundamentals of what is going on.

The business still has a set of customers who start out unaware of its service. And it still needs to move them through the stages of "Aware," "Like," and so on. What is different is that it now uses increasingly diverse ways of moving people along the Customer Chain: different messages, different media, different channels to market, *and also different services.*

When we realize this, we can see the corporation differently. It becomes a single entity, with a single Customer Chain—it is just using multiple resources (including different services) to encourage its customers along that chain, and some of those resources are called services. The common factor uniting those apparently different loyal customers (different because they are buying different services) becomes its corporate identity, brand values, or corporate values. This has become increasingly important for businesses in recent years, and it will become important again in Chapters 8 and 9 when it becomes part of the core of developing self-reinforcing advantage.

When the business is delivering more than one service, competitive advantage comes not just from being able to manage the individual Customer Chain for each one, or even to link them all together through a set of shared values. Competitive advantage also comes from developing multiple services around the same core.

This is, for example, what the Hollywood movie industry does. Movies are initially released for a (relatively) small number of people to watch in cinemas. These are the loyal customers—they usually leave home specifically wanting to see that film, and they pay the most for the privilege. Next the film may be released as an in-flight movie before moving to pay-TV channels. DVD and video rentals and sales create more revenues over several years. Finally, the film is released to terrestrial or free-to-view television.

Now, as we know, some movies go straight to video, so the steps in the chain do not always need to be the same. But what is always happening is that the studio is releasing the movie in whatever formats enable it to extract the maximum possible value from beneath the demand curve. This is the same as we see below, but the core service has been broken out into multiple modes of delivery:

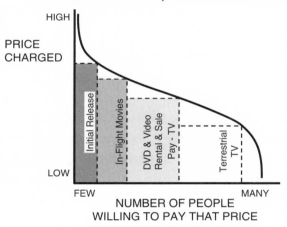

**DEMAND CURVE, HOLLYWOOD STYLE**

In fact it goes even further than this. Merchandising of toys, soundtracks, and T-shirts is another way to provide (and extract) more value to more customers, all based around the original service. In fact every sequel is also a spin-off from the original idea.

Realizing this, we see that the original movie was itself just one way of creating loyal and fickle customers out of the total set of resources that the business controlled. The business *is* its values and its skills/resources. Taking this to the next level is something we shall return to in Chapter 8 with the "Teflon Effect." But for now, this concludes our understanding of what it takes to satisfy customer needs.

Next we need to look at *how* a business can use resources to achieve all this. And that is the subject of Chapter 3.

- What is the balance between fickle and loyal customers in *your* business?
- How is it changing, and what can you do to increase the number of loyal customers in the future?
- What are the unmet needs of your loyal customers that could be turned into new services?
- Would those new services also appeal to fickle customers? If not, how could they be converted into services that would?

## SUMMARY

This chapter has been about marketing. Satisfying customer needs involves all of what we normally call sales, marketing, advertising, market research, public relations, and so on.

New techniques for *how* to achieve this are being invented all the time. But in order to satisfy customer needs successfully, *what* a business needs to do can be boiled down to just three things: understand the customers' needs, choose a combination of customers and needs to focus on, and bring the customers and the service together.

These are the fundamentals of marketing. This is all the business needs to do to achieve success in building this part of the first layer of business advantage.

The better the business is at achieving these three things, the more advantage it will have. And the more it remembers to focus on just these three things, the less time it will waste on other activities, and the easier it will be to get done the essence of what needs to get done.

That does not mean that an understanding of the latest marketing techniques is irrelevant. What it does mean is that trying to choose between them when the business has lost sight of the fundamentals presented here is like trying to choose what to take on vacation if you don't know whether you are traveling to Greenland or Greece.

Being clearer about *what* the business needs to achieve frees up more time for working on *how* best to achieve it. And it also frees up more time for understanding which marketing activities bring the business strategic advantage, and what steps to take to maintain that advantage.

Doing a good job of *understanding* the customers' needs means realizing that they all have five fundamental groups of needs, ranked according to the Maslow levels. The features of the service match against different needs on different levels. Understanding the precise needs better (especially by watching how customers *use* the service) enables a business to focus the service and its features better. The more value a business can provide, by satisfying *more* needs on more and higher levels, and by identifying the needs that are becoming *newly* important, to *more* customers, the more potential that business has to make money.

Once the customers' needs have been understood, the next step is to choose a set of customers and needs to focus on. This means choosing the combination that offers the best opportunity to build a sustainable business. And that means combining value to the customer with value to the business and the ability to do a better job than competitors. Strategic positioning relative to competitors who offer similar services can be the deciding factor in making this choice. But ultimately what matters is that the customer need exists and that the business is able to do a better job than whatever competitors exist. The size of this sustainable or defensible need is what determines the size of the business.

The third and final step is to bring the chosen customers (and their needs) together with the service. To do this, the business has to move those customers along a chain—from being completely unaware that the service exists to becoming fickle or loyal customers. How best to achieve this includes the whole range of skills we call advertising, PR, sales, and customer support, as well as delivering the actual service itself. What approach works best varies from business to business. But the first step is to identify distinct groups of different customer attitudes and behaviors along the Customer Chain. Then managing the chain becomes a matter of deciding which part of the chain to focus on, and finding the best way to give customers the information that will enable them to move to the next stage.

All three of these activities can become a source of long-term advantage for the business if it can become better at them than its competitors over time. In the case of managing the Customer Chain, it naturally means that the business will need to start to offer a wider range of services (to appeal to different sets of loyal customers). When this happens, the key driver of success changes from how well the business can manage the demand curve of a single service, to how well it can do so for multiple services built around a common core. This ultimately becomes the "Teflon Effect," a key part of building self-reinforcing advantage, as we shall see in Chapter 8.

For now, we have added some detail to our picture of what a business is and what it takes to build the first layer of business advantage:

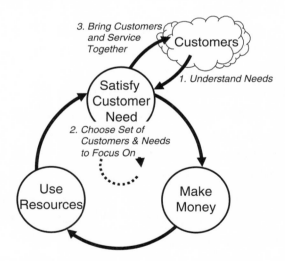

Satisfying customer needs has been expanded to include understanding those needs, choosing a set to satisfy, and then bringing customers and service(s) together through the Customer Chain.

How to do all this, by "using resources," is what we shall look at in Chapter 3.

# Using Resources

*I keep six honest serving-men*
*(They taught me all I knew).*
*Their names are What and Why and When*
*And How and Where and Who.*

—RUDYARD KIPLING, THE ELEPHANT'S CHILD

WE NOW KNOW that the foundation stone of any business is the set of customer needs it aims to satisfy. Chapter 2 told us how to understand these needs and how to choose a set of them to service. It also told us how to get the customers to recognize the value that the service brings, and how to improve that value over time.

The second part of the minimum activities a business needs to carry out in order to be successful, the second step in building strategic advantage, is actually to deliver the service. To do this a business has to "use resources."

What those resources are and how they get used will vary from business to business. So this chapter looks first at what resources are, and second at how to use them. It looks at what it takes to do a better job at this part of the business (better than the competition, and better over time) and closes by showing how the choices made in this area determine the balance of risk and reward for the business.

## WHAT ARE RESOURCES?

If we ask a steel manufacturer what are the key resources that are used in its business, we will probably get answers such as "iron ore, coal, and lime-stone," as well as "a good blast furnace, an oxygen furnace, and a continuous casting machine." Ask a car manufacturer the same question and the answers might become "pre-formed steel, plastics, and electronics," as well as "flexible factories, strong design and advertising, and a large dealer network."

Business resources, in other words, can be a variety of things, ranging from basic raw materials (such as oil and gas), to a group of these materials organized together to form some larger thing (like a furnace or a factory), to items that only really exist in people's minds (such as good advertising and design[1]).

Pretty much anything can be a resource—skill level, attitude, brand image, morale—and the picture is complicated by the fact that what one business sees as an input resource is often the output result from another business.

Ask a rental car agency what its key resources are, and the answers might turn out to be "reliable cars, friendly staff, a recognized brand, and an outlet at every major airport." Ask the airlines, in turn, and they might say that their key resources are their take-off and landing slots, the quality of cabin crew training, and a fast turn-around time once the aircraft has landed. The planes themselves are necessary resources, but the competition flies the same makes and models, so what makes the difference to the business is more the quality of the engineering departments that maintain the planes, or the safety records of the pilots who fly them. Anything, in fact, that maximizes the amount of time that each plane spends in the air, earn-ing revenues.

So, all businesses have a mix of resources that range from raw materials, to an engineering department, to the friendliness of staff. "Resources," in other words, can be pretty much anything you want them to be.

---

[1] A photograph can exist on a piece of paper, but it becomes an effective piece of advertising or design only if it has an effect or meaning in someone's mind.

The purpose of this chapter is *not* to define (down to the last paperclip) the full list of resources that are needed to run any one particular business. The purpose of this chapter is to understand what using resources means to *all* businesses. So, what this chapter will do is show how to identify and combine the resources that have the most impact on business performance, whether they are basic raw materials, concepts that exist only in people's heads, or something in between.

One standard classification that helps us to identify key resources is the differentiation between tangible resources and intangible ones.

Cars, iron ore, and planes are all tangible resources that can be touched and held. It is relatively easy for two businesses to count and measure whether one business has more or faster or bigger of these than the other. Intangible resources are things such as safety records, morale, and brand image. These are generally more difficult to count and measure.

But many resources, such as friendly staff and flexible factories, seem to fit partly into both groups. The number of staff I can touch and measure— their friendliness is more difficult. The number and size of factories I can measure—how flexible they are is more difficult to define.

So the value of making this distinction between tangible and intangible does not come from being able to decide which category a particular resource belongs to. It comes from remembering to look for the intangible resources, precisely because they are less visible than the tangible ones.

It comes, first of all, from reminding us that it is not necessarily the staff or the factories that are important to the business, but rather their *friendliness* or their *flexibility*. This helps us to understand better what really makes the difference to the success of the business. And that, in turn, helps us to focus on improving what really matters.

The second benefit of looking for the intangible resources is that because they are difficult to see, touch, and measure, they are also difficult for competitors to copy. This means they are often the things that bring most competitive advantage. Again, forcing ourselves to define precisely what we mean by them, and how to measure them, helps us to understand what really drives the success of the business, which, again, helps us to focus on what matters.

Resources, in summary, can be anything that helps to make a business succeed. This varies significantly between different businesses, and it can also vary inside a single business (or seem to), as different people have different views about what it is that drives their success.

*A STANDARD SET: THE MCKINSEY SEVEN S MODEL* At a detailed level, the resources used by each business are different. But at a high level, the consulting firm, McKinsey, has identified seven key resources, both tangible and intangible, that are the same across all businesses.

This is the McKinsey "Seven S" model, which came into widespread use after it was described by Tom Peters and Robert Waterman in their books *The Art of Japanese Management* and *In Search of Excellence.*

It contains a list of seven items or resources that (in English at least) all begin with the letter S.

They are: Strategy, Structure, Systems, Style, Staff, Skills, and Shared Values.

All of these seven factors are quite different from one another. Some, such as strategy and structure, are "hard" items that can be defined precisely. Others, such as style and shared values, are "soft" and more difficult to define.

But all seven items are closely linked to one another. The skills of the organization, for example, are provided by its staff. Their behavior then defines the style and shared values. Those shared values determine which strategies will be acceptable to the business. The strategies determine which skills will be needed, and hence which staff. And so on.

For this reason, the seven Ss are usually drawn at the six interlinking points of a hexagon, with the seventh S at the center.[2]

What McKinsey found, and the reason this became such a widespread and well-known tool, is that not only do these seven concepts represent the

---

[2]It does not really matter which S goes in the middle, but putting Shared Values there reminds us that businesses are driven by people, and that their personal values come out in everything the business does.

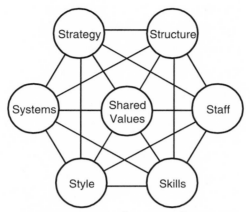

*THE MCKINSEY "SEVEN S" MODEL*

key resources of any business, but also that for the firm to be successful, all seven of the Ss need to be in alignment with one another: they need to *match*.

If the working style of a particular member of staff does not fit with the generally accepted shared values, then there will be friction and things will not get done as quickly or as well as they might. If the business systems make it harder to apply the skills of the organization to the benefit of its customers, then those customers will begin to go elsewhere. And so on.

In order to be successful, all these resources of the firm—its chosen direction and what it does to get there—need to align, support, and enhance one another. This is the subject of the next section (and there is more on aligning the business in Chapter 5).

---

**WHERE SUCCESS COMES FROM—THE "NINE S" MODEL!**

Drawing the seven Ss as a hexagon or snowflake shape is pretty to look at, but it does not actually give us any more *information* than if we simply listed them and said "they are all connected." And it certainly does not tell us how to align them all to *create* success.

To do that, we need to think through more carefully how they link together, practically, in the "real" world.

Starting with the staff, it is clear that they determine the skills the business has. They also determine the shared values, which determine management style. Together these three things then determine the [intended] strategy of the firm. And the strategy then determines what organization structure and business systems are needed. It also determines the skills that the business needs, which then feed back to affect what staff are hired.

We can draw this as a picture:

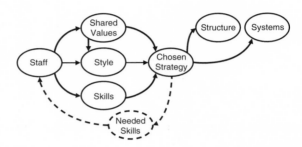

We can say that *all seven Ss* then come together to define the *actual strategy* of the firm—the way the business *actually behaves* as it interacts with customers, suppliers, investors, and competitors in the world around it.

This is always different from the strategy that was planned. And whether or not the firm is successful then depends on how well this actual strategy interacts with the firm's environment (or its *surroundings*, if we want to stick with the initial 'S' theme).

Success then depends on the interaction between the actual strategy (the seven Ss) and the surroundings of the business:

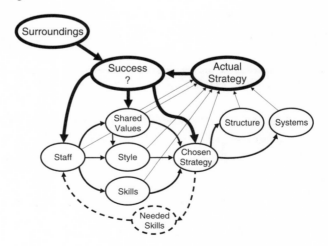

The amount of success that the business has then feeds back into the seven Ss that helped create it.

Individual members of staff will suddenly find themselves being promoted or let go. The shared values and the chosen strategy of the firm will be confirmed as being right or wrong. The current style and skills of the firm will be reinforced or challenged, and so on.

In this way behaviors and beliefs, the mental models of what drives success, become embedded within successful firms.

But the reality is that success did not come from the specific strategy, skills, systems, or shared values *in themselves*. Success came because the combination of all seven Ss, the actual strategy, *matched with the business environment at that time*. So if the business environment changes, then the seven Ss will need to change as well if the business is to continue to succeed.

Success comes when the way the business *uses resources* matches with the business environment. How it uses resources is determined by its mental models of what those resources were and how best to combine them. So, over time, what we can say is happening is that *the business environment* (the economy) is selecting and rewarding those businesses that have the best *mental models*—the best understanding—*of how the business environment works and how a business can best fit with that environment.*

That business environment, as we shall see, is made up of customers, suppliers and employees, lenders and investors, *and other businesses.* And creating a simpler, more accurate understanding of what a business is and how it interacts with that environment is *what this book,* and especially Chapters 6–8, *is all about.*

There are *nine Ss* that matter, not seven. The missing two are surroundings and success. And if the surroundings or business environment change then the business will need to change its seven Ss in order to be successful again.

Exactly how to do this, how to fit better with the environment, is looked at again in Chapters 6, 7, and 8. But for us, now, the next step in *this* chapter is to understand how to get the key resources of the business to work together to form a business.

——— **MAKING IT REAL** ———

- What are the top 7–10 most critical resources in your business?
- How would you measure them?

- What were the key resources 3–5 years ago?
- What will they be in 1, 3, 5 years' time?
- How would your top two competitors answer these same questions?

## HOW RESOURCES GET USED

*THE BUSINESS MODEL* Having identified its key business resources, the business then needs to align them as McKinsey suggests, which means it needs to get them to work together *as a business.*

The best way to show how to do this is to use an example. The example I have chosen is the airline business.

Most readers will be familiar with the way that airlines work, and we have already identified some of the key resources involved. Compared with other businesses, airlines also use a relatively balanced mixture of people *and* machinery as resources. So although this will be a simplified example, and the resources and the way they work together will be specific to this example, it should be clear how the approach would be applied to any other business.

What we are going to do is to take the list of key *resources* identified above, and show how they can be combined to work together as a *business.*

Airlines make money by selling journeys. In order to make those journeys they need planes. But the planes alone are not enough: each airline also needs routes to fly the planes on, and designated slots at each airport that allow it to take off and land. Finally, the number of trips that any one plane can make in a day depends on the time it takes to prepare the aircraft to take off again after it has landed—the turn-around time.

So, we can say that the maximum number of journeys any airline can make in a year depends on: the number of planes it has, the number of routes and slots, and the turn-around time.[3]

All this is shown in the diagram on the next page:

---

[3]It also depends on the number of seats per plane, and assumes that there are enough pilots, cabin crew, jet fuel, and so on, but let's ignore those, to keep the example simple.

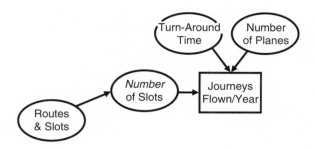

Now, if the airline sold every seat on every plane on every journey, then that would be the end of the story. But it doesn't, and so this is where the other resources are needed. They affect the number of journeys that the airline actually *sells*. (They move customers along the Customer Chain of Chapter 2.) And, roughly speaking, the balance between the number of journeys *sold* and the number of journeys *flown* each year then determines how much money the airline makes.

The *timing* of take-off and landing slots, for example, is another key resource. The number of journeys sold will depend on how many customers want to fly those routes, at those times, compared with the time slots available from the other airlines.

Another key resource is the quality of the cabin crew. This does not affect the total number of journeys *flown* each year. But it does affect the number *sold* because it affects how keen a particular passenger will be to fly with that particular airline. The same is true of the airline's safety record, which comes from a combination of the quality of training received by the pilots and the quality of maintenance carried out by the engineering department.

So, the number of journeys *sold* each year depends on: the number of passengers who want to fly those routes; the timings of the slots; the quality of the cabin crew; and the airline's safety record (which in turn depends on pilot training and the quality of aircraft maintenance).

We can add this to the bottom half of the diagram (see next page).

It might seem odd to be showing the number of customers as a resource. After all, customers are not usually thought of as being part of the business.

But the total number of tickets sold clearly *does* depend on the total number of customers who might want to travel on the particular routes the

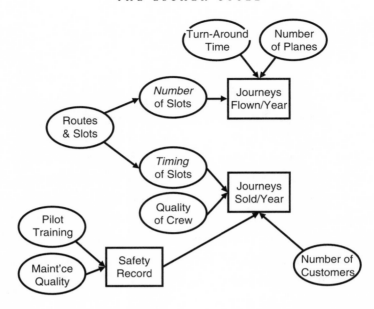

airline flies. So they are a vital part of the *total system* of resources that generates value. They might not be owned by the airline company, but then probably neither are the planes (they are probably leased). The maintenance and aircrew training is probably carried out by specialist companies, the aircraft turn-around is probably carried out by contractors, and even the pilots and cabin crew can choose to quit and go to work for other airlines (subject to their contracts of employment). And so on.

The total *business* is different from the *corporation*.

The corporation is a legal entity which has various contracts with other legal entities, under which it gains varying degrees of control over different forms of resources and tries to pull them together to create a successful business.

Chapter 2 told us that "the foundation stone of any business is the set of customer needs that it aims to satisfy." The task of the corporation is to build a set of resources *around* or upon that foundation stone, to create a *total system* that "makes money by using those resources to satisfy customer needs (today and in the future)."

The contract with customers is partly a legal contract (the part that can be written on the front and back of the ticket) and partly an emotional one (the loyalty that is generated by the advertising and frequent-flier programs of the Customer Chain).

Contracts with pilots and cabin crew, aircraft leasing companies, and so on tend to have a greater emphasis on the legal side. But the emotional part exists as well (as with airlines like Southwest). And although it is more difficult to measure, it is precisely this emotional contract that can have the greatest impact on the survival and success of the business. When times get tough, as they invariably do, it is the emotional contracts that determine whether customers remain loyal or fickle, whether suppliers continue to supply, and whether shareholders support the stock price or let it fall.

The contracts all take different forms, have different mixtures of emotional and non-emotional content, but they all exist. And it is the *total system* of contracts and resources that makes up the total business.

Whether or not that business makes money depends on how efficiently and effectively it functions in comparison with the other systems that competitors have built.

And which *part* of the total system makes the most money depends on the individual contracts that have been formed between the business and its employees, suppliers, lenders, investors, and customers. These also determine the level of risk that is taken by each part. As we shall see over the coming chapters, to be successful, to create *new* value instead of simply moving it from one place to another, the business needs to have win-win contracts and relationships with them *all*.

Ultimately, the corporation does not have complete control over *any* of the resources that make up the business system.

The *corporation* is something that struggles, with varying degrees of control, to hold the various resources together and keep the *business* alive.

It is that *total system* of resources that is the business. No customers— no business; no employees—no business; no suppliers—no business; no lenders or investors—no business.

The *business* is a different thing from the *corporation*.

Returning to our example airline, the amount of money *it* makes depends on the balance between the number of journeys made and the number of journeys sold. (This is why the percentage of seats sold on each flight is such a key measure for airlines.) As a final step we can add this to the picture:

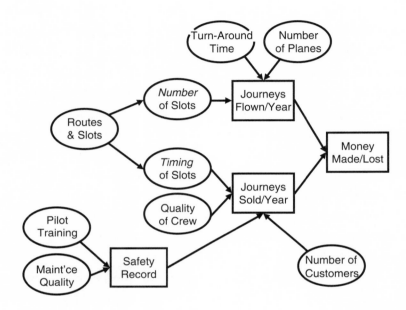

This simple diagram now summarizes how all the main resources *work together as a business.*

It shows the pressure points of the business—the key resources that make the difference in performance—as well as how to align actual strategy with intended strategy. It defines the strategy of the airline in terms of the precise operational activities that need to be carried out and the levels of performance that need to be achieved.

Extending this approach creates a powerful strategic tool. More details about this are given in the "Systems Thinking and System Dynamics" box.

But although these are powerful techniques, this is not a book about business modeling. This is a book about understanding how businesses work and how to make them work better. To achieve that, our next step is to understand where the resources in the above diagram come from.

And the answer to that is that they are all the results of processes.

The turn-around time is clearly the result of the processes that are used to refuel the plane, clean it, unload and reload the baggage, and so on. A similar situation applies to the quality of aircraft maintenance.

The planes and the slots on routes are all the results or outputs of processes to buy, rent, lease, hire, or otherwise acquire them.

The levels of pilot training and the quality of cabin crew are the result of training processes (as well as processes to hire, develop, reward, and retain them, which are not shown).

Even the number of customers in the loyal and fickle categories depend, as we know from Chapter 2, on the processes and activities that encouraged them to move along the Customer Chain.

The business model shows how resources work together to create a viable business. And if we want to improve the performance of any business model we need to create more or better resources.

The way we do this is through processes. And processes are the subject of the next section.

---

**SYSTEMS THINKING AND SYSTEM DYNAMICS: TWO POWERFUL STRATEGIC TOOLS**

This simple picture (of how the key resources of the airline fit together) shows us the *essentials* of the business. As such it is a powerful strategic tool.

It reminds us, first of all, what the key resources of the business are. These pressure points are the areas where improved performance will lead most directly to better results. (They are also the areas where poor performance will lead most rapidly to poor results.) So, it provides a strategic focus to everyday operational activities and helps us to avoid "squeakiest wheel" syndrome.

Second, it shows us how the business works as a dynamic system—it reminds us what the key contribution of each resource is *to the business as a whole*. In this example, the quality of the cabin crew affects the total number of journeys *sold* each year, not the total number *flown*. This reminds us that for this airline, the role, the purpose, the value-added of the cabin crew is not to hand out drinks and meals but to act as ambassadors for the brand image of the company. Remembering this will make a difference in the qualities the airline looks for in the people that it hires, the training it gives, the salaries it pays, and so on. By creating and maintaining this *direct link* between the strategic view of the firm and its everyday operational decisions, this resource-based way of looking at a business helps those strategic aims and objectives to be met. (For more on the differences between "strategic" and "tactical," and how to align them, see Chapter 5.) Without this link the business is likely to lose sight of the precise value that any key resource brings, and decisions will then be taken that move the actual strategy of the firm further and further away from its intended strategy—especially when times are tough.

A different airline, one with a different business model, might have a different role or focus for its cabin crew. In that case the diagram might show them feeding into the total number of journeys *flown,* or perhaps not have identified them at all at this high level. Drawing these kinds of system diagrams can help to clarify whether (and how) two companies are competing against each other. The more that companies use different resources, in different ways, the more space there is for them to co-exist. The more they use the same resources, in the same ways, the more important it is to be able to identify "What are the key resources that matter?", "How can we get better performance in those areas that matter?", and "Is there scope for us to both benefit by cooperating in the other areas?"

At the same time, two different people from the *same* business can have very different views of the business model they are working in. Someone working in the engineering department will know a lot about aircraft maintenance and why it is important, but may know very little about marketing. Someone working in marketing will be focused much more on brand. But the pilots, in their turn, will know that without them there are no flights, so *they* are the most important part of the business. This is a bit like trying to decide which organ of the body is most important. The fact is that the body needs *all* its different organs to work together in order to survive.

So, drawing this kind of business model diagram can also be a good way to get the different "organs" of the business to understand how they fit together. That, in turn, builds a picture of how the business works as a *whole* that can be better than the view that any one person has. That, in turn, can help each part to focus on the contribution it makes to the success of the whole—like a sprinter running with arms and legs in perfect synchronization, instead of with each arm and leg being controlled independently and complaining about how the others keep knocking it off balance!

All of this helps the business to make the right tradeoffs between its different priorities and still achieve its goals. *That* is what McKinsey's "alignment" of the various resources is all about.

But doing this well requires not just the qualitative understanding we can get from these pictures, powerful though that is. It requires a quantitative understanding, based on numbers.

The business model diagrams we have looked at up till now show how the resources link together as a system, but the links are not defined precisely—they are not quantified. This is called "systems thinking."

In order to be able to use these models to manage the business we need to know how big the impact of making different changes would be. Would halving the turn-around time (for example) double the number of journeys flown in a year, halve it, or increase it by about 20 percent?

By defining each link precisely and adding it as an equation in a computer model, we can turn the systems thinking picture into a quantified replica of the business. This is called "system dynamics."

As we shall see in a moment, this will give us a new level of understanding about how the business works and how to get the results we seek. But it is important to remember that the *equations are always an approximation to reality, not the other way around*. Powerful though these models are, they can never encapsulate the *whole* business.

In order to convert the simple diagram we created above into a more detailed picture of the airline business, all we need to do is add more resources and more links between them.

As we do so we are able to move from general statements like "The number of journeys flown per year is important" to being able to say that "A 5 percent increase in the cost of jet fuel would reduce the money made by the airline by $122m per year."

The result can become a model of the business that is broader and deeper, more comprehensive *and* more quantitative, than the understanding of *any single person in the business*.

That is then a powerful tool, not only for testing the likely consequences of different courses of action, but also for increasing the understanding that individuals in the business have about how it works as a whole, improving the impact of their day-to-day decision-making.

We also begin to see feedback loops that can limit the performance of the business, as well as loops that would accelerate the performance of the business, if only we realized that they were there!

But although these models can be very powerful, the map is not the territory and the equations in any model are only approximations of reality. The key to improving business performance lies not in building better models (important though that is) but in knowing how to change the numbers that go into the models.

And *that* is covered in the next section, on processes.

––––––– MAKING IT REAL –––––––

- Use the critical resources you identified in the earlier section to draw the business model for your business.
- What other resources do you need to complete the picture?
- Are there any resources that you thought were critical, but do not appear in the model?
- Draw the business models of your top two competitors.
- Are their models the same as yours, or different?
- What are the key points that bring you, or might bring you, strategic advantage? Are you competing with competitors on the basis of your ability to build or control individual specific resources (and if so, which ones), or on the basis of your ability to combine all the different resources together?

*HOW RESOURCES GET USED—PROCESSES* The resource-based view, and systems thinking/system dynamics all help us to understand how the business works as a whole. They help us to align resources and to focus on the key areas that make the most difference to the business.

For example, they help us to realize that the turn-around time is a key factor affecting the airline's performance, and that reducing that time from 60 minutes to 30 would enable each plane to make (say) six short-haul flights per day instead of five, which would increase revenues per plane from $25m (say) to $30m per year.

In other words, these ways of thinking about the business can help us to realize that cutting the turn-around time by 30 minutes would increase the airline's total revenues by up to 20 percent for almost no increase in cost, perhaps doubling the share price.

But the thing that makes the difference to business performance is not what that business *plans* to do but what it actually *does*. We could just as easily have calculated that cutting the turn-around time to three minutes would increase revenue per plane by 75 percent—that might be mathematically true, but it does not make it possible.

What makes the difference to business results is the time it *actually* takes to turn the planes around every day, day after day after day. And what determines that is the *processes* that the business uses.

In order to be able to turn a plane around in 30 minutes instead of 60, it might be necessary to use fuel tankers that can pump at twice the rate, or to use twice as many tankers. It might be necessary to change from having five cleaners armed with brooms and plastic bags to fifteen, each armed with industrial strength cordless vacuum cleaners. It might be necessary to stack all the meals and drinks inside one specially modified luggage container. And so on.

If any of these factors is not possible, or rather if it costs more to do them than the $5m extra per plane per year that the airline expects to earn, then it will not be worth making the changes.

The point is that for any airline, for any business, it is these *details*—the way that individuals "on the ground" carry out basic tasks such as loading luggage, removing garbage, and placing tray-tables in the upright position —that determine the *actual* value of the airline's turn-around time and all its other key resources. And they, in turn, then determine whether the business succeeds or fails at the strategic level.

Knowing what the key resources are tells us *what* it is important for the business to do well at. Knowing how they fit together tells us *why*. And knowing how the business does each of those things, the processes that it uses, tells us *how well* the business will perform.

Resources define *what* the business needs to be good at. Processes define *how* it does them. And success, for any business, is a combination of doing the right things *and* doing them the right way.

So, if we want to understand how to use resources, we need to understand processes.

There are many books about business processes,[4] giving detailed descriptions of things like root cause analysis, statistical process control, fishbone diagrams, and how to complete documentation to ISO 9000/1/2 standards. But this is not a book about process improvement or reengineering, so there is no space, and no need, to go into those details here.

What I want to do here is to give a flavor, a taste, a feel, for the different kinds of processes that exist within businesses—how they are different from one another and how they are the same—so that when we come to understand what it takes to do a *strategically* better job than the competition that understanding will be grounded in practical reality.

Let's start by looking at what a process is.

At the simplest level, a process is something that takes in one or more inputs, transforms them in some way (combines or changes them), and produces an output.

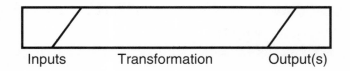

Inputs     Transformation     Output(s)

Bending a piece of wire is a process. Attaching it to a piece of wood is a process. Putting 20 of them in a box and shipping them across the country is a process. Calling them coat hangers, advertising them, and getting paid for providing them is also process—and a business.

---

[4]Probably most notably W. Edwards Deming, the Total Quality Management approach, Michael Hammer and James Champy's *Reengineering the Corporation,* and more recently the "Six Sigma" approach.

When the inputs of the process and the outputs it produces are always the same, like this, then it is easy to see how the business is a process. Indeed some industries, such as oil and gas, chemicals, paper and pulp production, plastics, steel, cement, and glass are explicitly called "process industries." They all produce items in a continuous flow.

But businesses that produce different outputs from the same inputs also follow processes. A hamburger restaurant will take the same set of ingredients, put them through unvarying processes, and produce exactly the same output every time. But a top chef could take the same basic ingredients and cook perhaps half a dozen or more different dishes with them, using different processes.

This shows us what a process is. A process is a recipe for combining inputs in a certain way. A cooking recipe tells us what the ingredients are and how to bring them together, in what order and what proportions. It tells us what actions (stirring, heating, beating) to carry out as we do so, and what tools we will need. A process tells us exactly the same things. It tells us who needs to do what, where, when, and how, in order to produce the required output. (See also the "Defining a Process" box.)

Some businesses, like good cooks, can take the same inputs and use different processes to produce different outputs. Italy, for example, has more than 150 different types of pasta. Germany has more than 200 varieties of bread, and France produces over 400 types of cheese.

---

**A NOTE ON TERMINOLOGY:**

Thinking about the ways in which the different levels of a business interconnect, as we are doing here, is often difficult. We each have a level that we are used to dealing with, but seeing the bigger picture above that level, or understanding minute details below it, can be hard.

To handle this it is sometimes useful to create a hierarchy of terms so that we know which level we are dealing with. We might, for example, say that the marketing function within a business is composed of different processes, which break down into sub-processes, and which themselves are made up of activities, and then specific tasks.

That is *not* the approach that I am taking in this book.

The first reason is that the range of levels we are talking about—from specific activities in a business, to the business as a whole, to industries, and then the total economy—is simply too large to be able to name every level. (See "The Fractal Economy" in Chapter 7.)

The second reason is that naming levels distracts us from the truth, which is that *everything* is a process. Every business is a process, which takes inputs and transforms them to produce an output: its service. The business is made up of smaller processes (Chapters 2–6), and itself forms part of larger processes (Chapters 7 and 8).

Running a television station is a process. Creating a programming schedule is a process. Commissioning a single program is a process. Making that program is a process. Filming a single take is a process. An actor speaking a single line is a process. The hour spent in make-up was a process. Bringing her a cup of coffee was a process. And so on.

So, in general I have used the word "process" to apply to all the different levels. Sometimes I have also talked about the functions or activities of a business, and what I mean here is the general idea of getting things done. But the word that *most specifically* describes this is the word "process," because it combines the *three ideas* of taking inputs, doing something with them, and creating or achieving an intended output, service, goal, or aim.

Other businesses can be built to produce different outputs from different inputs. Bridge builders and tunnel builders work in this kind of a business—the final location and design of the service they provide may be different each time, but they always apply the same problem-solving techniques and go through the same sequence of steps, from concept to finished project. Software engineering is another example. And even a creative industry such as advertising goes through the same stages for every brief, although the precise activities, the messages, and the media used may well be different each time.

And, finally, there can also be businesses that take in different inputs and produce the same output every time, like a junkyard car crusher. Military training comes to mind as another example of this, though it is not a business. Home security might be a better example, where the output is always a safer building.

The diagram below shows these and other examples.

The exact placement of individual businesses is not important, because it depends on what we mean by the "same" or "different." The key point I want to make is that all businesses are processes. Their inputs and their outputs may be the same or different each time. But what enables each business to exist, survive, and ultimately to succeed is its ability to take those inputs and produce the output that the customer wants, reliably, again and again and again. And that means that each business is a process.

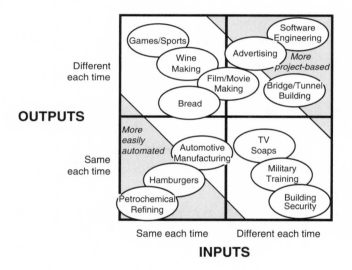

Of course each business needs people and technology to carry out the process, and the diagram also shows that when inputs and outputs are the same, the business can be more reliant on machines—it becomes easier to automate. But the more that inputs and outputs are different each time, the more project-based the business becomes and the more heavily it needs to rely on the creative and decision-making skills of people.

As we saw with the airline example, every business/process is made up of smaller processes. Some of those, such as the processes for paying or hiring employees, will exist in many other businesses. Others, such as the process for checking in at the airport, may be specific to only one or two industries, but may not make much difference to the results of the business. And others, such as the way the cabin crew behaves or the ability to prepare a plane for take-off within 30 minutes of landing, will form a critical part of the business model and become crucial to the way the business differentiates itself from competitors in the minds of its customers (and employees, suppliers, lenders, and investors).

In other words, every business will have a hierarchy of different processes, within which it will be more or less important for the business to be doing a better job than its competitors. This is what we shall look at in the next section.

### DEFINING A PROCESS

Processes are all different, but defining them can be very simple.

The writer Rudyard Kipling is probably best known for the stories that later became Walt Disney's *The Jungle Book.* But in 1892 he started work as a journalist in the north of India. Here he quickly learned the six key questions to ask to capture the essence of any news story: "What happened, where, when, and how? Why did it happen, and who was involved?"

These same six questions can also be used to define any business process: *Who* does *What, Where, When, How,* and *Why.*

- *Why* defines the reason(s) that the process is being carried out, and the outputs it is intended to produce. The ultimate *Why* is to satisfy its customers' needs, but separate processes also exist to carry out all the other fundamental activities described in this book. The better the outputs can be defined, the more likely it is that the process will produce them, and the less effort will be wasted in producing unwanted outputs.
- *What* and *How* define the activities that make up the process and the ways in which they get carried out. Like any good recipe book they list the ingredients, the tools and equipment that are used, as well as the step-by-step ways in which they are brought together. They also define measures of the process's efficiency, effectiveness, and adaptability.

- *Where* might seem trivial but should not be overlooked. It can be important, for example, where safety is an issue, or where different operating conditions force a company to carry out the same process in different ways in different parts of the world. It also defines the *scope* of the process: where it applies, and where it does not.
- *When* defines what triggers the process to start, as well as how long the process takes.
- *Who* defines the customer that the output of the process is created for, the person within the business who is responsible for the process, and the people who carry out and support the different activities.

Whatever the problem, answering these six questions is enough to define a process to create the result we want. There are no other questions, so there can be no other answers.

*A HIERARCHY OF PROCESSES* So far we have identified the key resources of the business and seen how to arrange them into a business model. To improve the performance of that business we then need to improve the number or quality of its resources. And the way we achieve that is through processes.

Some processes make a vital difference to performance. They provide, for example, the key things that convince people to buy from this particular business instead of competitors. They deliver the things that make customers loyal instead of just fickle. They define what is special about *this* particular business—and so we could call them "identity" processes.

Other processes make little or no difference to business results, but they need to get done. Taking out employer's liability insurance probably comes into this category, as does submitting statutory financial information to the government. We could call these types of processes "mandatory" processes.

In between come other processes, with a range of impacts on results. Some processes, such as preparing a plane for take-off after it has landed, might have a big impact on results, but are not quite part of the identity of the business. These we could call the "primary" processes.

Other processes might do little to improve performance, but could do a lot to *damage* it if they were not done properly. The process for hiring employees probably comes into this category. Being able to fill open positions quickly might not improve the service to the customer, but having a large number of open positions could harm it. These we could call "secondary" processes.

So, the business is made up of identity processes, primary processes, secondary processes, and mandatory processes:

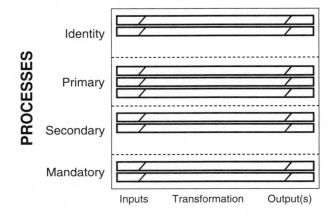

These processes form a *continuous* range of different impacts on results, but labeling them into four groups like this helps us to realize five important things.

The first is that although different businesses often *seem* to be carrying out the same process, the priority that a process has within a business can vary from industry to industry. Hiring employees is probably a secondary process for most businesses, but in sports and movies being able to hire the right player or actor can make a *lot* of difference at the box office. Successful advertising and software engineering both require the ability to manage projects—but the levels of complexity, and the types of people involved, are hugely different, so the project management processes (and the tools that get used) also need to be very different. Petrochemical refining and bread making both require processes that maintain constant temperatures, but the consequences of getting it wrong in each case are vastly different. So, the way that the same process gets carried out varies significantly between different businesses—and so do the results that it produces and the amount it costs to do so.

This fact, that other businesses carry out the same process differently, means that any business wanting to improve its processes always has a ready source of alternatives to copy from (see below). It also has implications for businesses that want to expand into other parts of the economy, and this is covered in Chapter 8.

The second thing to realize is that, even within the same industry, different businesses can place different priorities on a process. For example, a football team might find that it can make more money from selling shirts and jerseys than it does from playing games. As another example, one airline might decide to improve its aircraft turn-around time—this will affect the number and timing of the slots that it offers, which will change its attractiveness to particular customers. Another airline might choose to improve its catering processes. This will probably cost less to implement, and will improve the airline's attractiveness to a different set of customers.

The third point is that the priority that a business places on its processes (whether it treats them as identity, primary, secondary, or mandatory) affects the customers that it attracts and the results that it produces. So running the business well is really about choosing what priority to place on each process: what levels of cost to incur, what levels of output to produce.

Each process brings a mix of cost for the business and value for the customer. So getting this "value-for-money" balance right in each case is what ultimately drives the success of the total business. The fourth thing to notice, therefore, is that the balance between cost and value needs to be different for different processes. For mandatory processes, the focus needs to be on getting the lowest possible *cost* while still delivering the minimum required level of output. For identity processes, the focus needs to be first on getting the best match of *value* for the customer, and then finding a way to deliver that output for a reasonable cost (as defined by competitors).

Finally, the mix of needs that the customers have, and the costs and services that competitors provide, are both changing all the time. So running the business is really about continuously changing the value-for-money mix that each different process in the business provides. Deciding how well to carry out each one (what level of output to produce) and how much expense to incur for doing so—and then implementing the necessary improvements, is the next step.

Which brings us to the next section: process improvement.

---

**DIFFERENT COUNTRIES HAVE DIFFERENT IDENTITY PROCESSES**

Different *countries* also have different identity processes. Think of a country and what it is best known for, and the chances are that the processes it uses to do that thing are different from the processes used in other parts of the world.

France, for example, is known for its food and wine. Why? Because the processes (or recipes) that it uses are different from the processes used in other parts of the world.

Australia and New Zealand are also known for producing high-quality wines, but fifty years ago that was not the case. The improvement came when they significantly changed the *processes* they used for making wines: classifying wines by grape variety (instead of by geographic area), and developing equipment that allowed better control of fermentation.

England has its heritage and pageantry. Japan has electronics and the bullet train. Switzerland has chocolate and banking. And America clearly has the best armed forces in the world, the best fast food, and Hollywood. It also has national pride in the checks and balances of its legal and political system, a system based on the American Constitution, which itself is the result of a process[5] that can be traced all the way back to the Magna Carta in 1215.

These are just a few examples, and the reader will have others.

The point I want to make is that although we usually focus on the differences between things (bottles of wine, chocolate bars, CD players, and laser-guided missiles),

---

[5]www.yale.edu/lawweb/avalon/constpap.htm

the real difference is between the *processes* that produced them. In fact, we can now see that, strictly speaking, there are no such things as things or resources—only *processes*. What we call a resource is actually the output of one process waiting to become the input to another.

A country is a collection of processes—of money, law, food, and so on. And the way that we can tell two countries (two cultures) apart is by spotting differences in their *processes:* which ones are identity or mandatory, and how they each get carried out. (See also "A Brief History of History," in the Epilogue.)

What happens when the economies of two countries merge is that their processes begin to merge.

Customers (people) then get to choose which version of each process they really want. What type of food they want, which wine, which company's electronic goods, which computers, which currency, which movies, and so on. In every case they make a choice between higher value and lower cost. In every case they get to re-evaluate which processes will remain identity processes for their country or culture and which will become primary, secondary, and mandatory processes. This involves change and it involves choice, both of which can be difficult.

Processes are the mechanism by which culture is transmitted. So, when economies merge and their processes become more similar, then the cultures become more similar also. And this is what globalization and the anti-globalization movement are all about.

──────── **MAKING IT REAL** ────────

- What are the processes that create the key resources of your business?
- Which of them are identity processes and which are primary?
- Are they each receiving appropriate amounts of management attention and resources?
- Of the other processes that management attention is currently focused on, which are secondary and which are mandatory?
- Given that classification, are appropriate solutions being sought?

## DOING A BETTER JOB

In this chapter we are drilling down to greater and greater levels of detail. We started at the level of the total business and the fact that it needs to use resources. We looked at what those resources might be and how they combine to form a business (the business model). We learned that resources come from processes, and that different processes have different priorities— or rather that getting the right value for money requires a different emphasis between value and cost.

Now we are going to look at how a business can create advantage over its rivals by improving some of those processes. We shall then close the chapter by returning to the level of the total business, and looking at the strategic implications of all its different process improvements.

*PROCESS IMPROVEMENT* What any process does is made up of three parts: it takes inputs, transforms them, and produces an output. *How* that process gets done is also made up of three parts: the people who carry out the process, the tools or technology they use, and the activities they carry out. All three of these are interdependent, and changing any one of them can make the process better.

Again, this is not a book about process improvement, and so I will not go into detail here about *how* to improve processes. But what I do want to focus on is what the *results* of any process improvement will be: what the *benefits to the business* of carrying out that improvement will be, and why a business would want to improve one of its processes in the first place.

I personally have created and improved processes in business areas ranging from sales and marketing, finance, and HR (human resources) to strategic planning and operational service delivery. The solutions not only delivered the required results, but also were simple and robust enough to succeed in the business conditions of four different continents. Yet in every case, the reasons for carrying out the process improvements, the results created, can be boiled down to just three things.

The first is an increase in *efficiency.* This means finding ways to deliver the same results for less cost: "doing things right." It involves reducing how much it costs the process to deliver a unit of output, whether that unit is: an updated succession/progression[6] plan for the 50 key positions in the business; a ranked list of opportunities to develop new services worth millions of dollars per year; or a day's uninterrupted computer infrastructure service delivered simultaneously across 12 European countries.

The second type of improvement is an increase in *effectiveness*. This means "doing the right things"—delivering an output that is more useful, that matches more closely what the customer of the process actually wants. If the customer is an external customer, then Chapter 2 describes how to improve effectiveness. Examples of improved effectiveness for internal processes would be a manpower plan that helps to *increase* the number of productive days worked instead of just counting them, and a sales management process that helps to *improve* the likelihood of winning each bid, instead of just tracking the status of each one.

The third way that a process can be improved is by increasing its *adaptability*. This comes in at least five different forms, which are probably best explained with an example. Imagine a factory making cars on a production line:

- The first way to improve the adaptability of this process is to reduce the *total time taken* to carry it out, the total time taken to build a car. By doing this, the business becomes more adaptable because it can respond faster to new and changing customer orders.

- The second way to increase adaptability is to increase the *range of different outputs* that the process can provide. In the case of the production line, this ranges from being able to make cars with slightly different options (different colors, engine sizes, with/without air conditioning, and so on), to very different versions of the same vehicle (two, three, four, or five doors; two-wheel or four-wheel drive), to the ability to make completely different models of a vehicle on the same line—the same adaptable process.

---

[6]A succession/progression plan identifies key roles within a business and the skills and experience needed to carry them out. It identifies possible candidates to replace the people currently in each role in the event that they are promoted or suddenly leave, and so it prepares and enables the business to cope with growth and change.

- The third way to increase the adaptability of a process is to reduce the time and cost taken to make improvements to it. In a car production line, for example, splitting it into sections makes it easier and quicker to update the equipment used in one part of the line without disrupting the rest. (See also the box on process improvement on page 94.)

- The fourth type of adaptability has to do with the time taken to set up a new copy of the process: the time taken, for example, to open a new factory in China.

- And the fifth type is a combination of the previous three: the time taken to alter the process so as to be able to produce a completely new output, to deliver a completely new service. In the case of the car company, this means the time taken to set up the production line to produce a completely new design of vehicle. This affects the time it takes to design and launch new vehicles (or services), and so affects the ability of a business to respond to its changing marketplace.

This is an example of the adaptability of a process for an external customer. But the adaptability of processes for internal customers is equally important to the adaptability of the business as a whole.

For example, the succession/progression (see earlier footnote) is an internal process that enables the business to rapidly fill its key open positions. It supports the organization's ability to continue to get done what needs to get done in the face of changing circumstances. In this case a process based on electronic or Web-based data capture will be more adaptable than a paper-based one, because any change to content or format can be instantly replicated around the world in every part of the business.

So we can see that the adaptability of any process affects how long it takes for the business to go from *realizing* that it needs some new capability to actually *having* it.

The adaptability of a process will then affect the robustness of the business in coping with changes in the marketplace. How big the effect will be depends on where in the hierarchy the process is: identity, primary, secondary, or mandatory.

This means that running the business as a whole has now become a combination of two things: first, deciding how much to spend on doing each process—whether to treat it as identity, primary, secondary, or mandatory; and second, deciding how much money to spend on improving each one.

In other words, from a combined strategic and operational point of view, running the business has become a matter of deciding how to allocate money and resources across the following diagram:

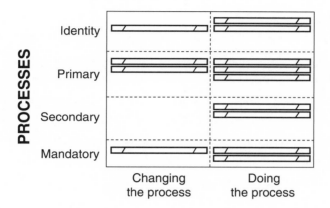

The business in this simplified example has two identity processes (right-hand side) and three primary, two secondary, and two mandatory ones. (It applies money and resources to get the right mix of value for money from each one.) And it is spending additional money on improving the value-for-money mix of four of them (as shown on the left-hand side).[7]

Deciding how much money to spend where affects the operational and strategic performance.

Every process in the business, every process described in this book, forms part of its overall competitiveness. Each one brings the opportunity for the business to be better, faster, and/or cheaper (more effective, more adaptable, and/or more efficient) than its competitors.

---

[7]Finding the right mix of cost and value for each process is covered in Chapter 7, which looks at which strategies help different businesses succeed. Getting adaptability right is covered in Chapter 8, The Escher Cycle.

Strategy, by itself, adds no value—only actions add value. So *a business can only achieve strategic success when it carries out one or more processes better and/or more cheaply than its competitors.*

*That advantage is sustainable only for as long as it can adapt/improve its processes faster than those competitors*—otherwise they can catch up.

And so process improvement is the key to achieving self-reinforcing business advantage.

This is why I have taken so much trouble to explain it step by step, and to link it clearly to the highest level, the total business.

Strategic advantage comes from doing some activity better than competitors, and doing something better than competitors comes from process improvement. So if we want to create *self-reinforcing* strategic advantage, we need to understand what generates advantage at carrying out process improvement.

*That* is the subject of the next section.

---

### A SIMPLE PROCESS FOR PROCESS IMPROVEMENT

Improving processes is a process in itself.

After all, every business is a process, and the reason it exists is to improve some *process* of its customers (relative to the performance that the customer could achieve for itself). We will come back to this in Chapter 8.

There is no need or space here to make an exhaustive review of all the different approaches that can be used to improve processes. But I do want to give readers a feeling for the types of activities involved. So I am going to summarize here a simple seven-step approach, which I have used to improve multi-country processes in a wide range of business areas, including sales, finance, marketing, core operations, and human resources.

The seven steps are:

1. *Define Purpose:* Define the purpose of the process, its customer(s), and its key measures (of efficiency, effectiveness, and adaptability).

What is the problem that needs to be fixed and what key improvements are being sought? What problems need to be avoided?

The output of this step is to know what the business needs the process to achieve, so that alternative ways of *how* to achieve that can then be looked for.

2.  *Identify Alternatives:* Look for alternative ways of achieving this purpose. It may be quicker to copy another existing solution than to reinvent the wheel or improve what exists today. Each alternative brings a different mix of advantages and disadvantages, and there is usually a balance between the time and cost to implement, and the improvement and competitive advantage that will be obtained.

    As well as working to analyze and improve the process that exists today, remember that it might be better (in approximate order of increasing difficulty) to:

    a) copy another site or office within the same company

    b) copy other businesses in the same industry (often called *competitor analysis*)

    c) copy a similar process in another industry (often called *benchmarking*)

    d) copy nature

    e) design a new process from scratch (which can sometimes also be the easiest approach)

    Although it is often quicker to copy what someone else has already done, ultimately the leading business has no one else to copy, and must create its innovations for itself.

    The output of this step is to create a few good alternatives for discussion with key stakeholders.

3.  *Get Input from Stakeholders:* Discuss the best alternative approach(es) with some of the key people who will be affected by and involved in the new process (the key stakeholders). These include the customers of the process, the people who will carry it out, and people who will be responsible for the results that it creates. Getting their feedback helps to improve the outputs of the process, how it is carried out, and the way it will be implemented.

    The output of this step is to be able to select one solution as the best.

4.  *Test It Out—Build a "Straw Man":* Choose the alternative that gives the best (not necessarily ideal) mix between efficiency, effectiveness, and adaptability, as well as the time and cost of implementation.

Build a working model of how the entire process would work, from start to finish: run it in a test site, create a mock-up (a "straw man"), a test version—do whatever it takes to give a wider set of stakeholders an in-depth understanding of how the intended process will work, as well as testing out what it takes to implement the process.

The output of this step is to be ready to make the go/no-go decision.

5.  *Go/No-Go Decision:* Based on the improved understanding of how the finished process will work, the value it will bring, how it will be measured, and how it will be implemented, decide whether to implement the new process.

6.  *Communicate:* Tell all those involved what is coming, why, where, when, and how—tell them what the impact will be for them.

7.  *Implement and Continuously Improve:* Implement the process. Make sure that it includes steps to measure its own efficiency, effectiveness, and adaptability, and to use these measurements to automatically make continuous improvements until a major improvement is needed again.

I have shown the process as having seven separate steps, but the level of activity needed at each stage can be varied according to the particular process and the business it is in. For example, steps 3, 4, and 5 might easily be combined into a single meeting. The approach is highly scalable.

It is also a lean approach, and it is fast. It recognizes that there is an S-curve relationship between effort and returns: a small amount of effort brings little improvement, more effort brings a large improvement, and then any more work brings progressively fewer returns. (See also the 80:20 rule in Chapter 5.)

It focuses on defining what needs to be achieved; looking for ways to get there fast; involving the people who will be affected (to achieve quality design and rapid implementation); and leaving future improvements to the future.

Because all of this is a process, it can itself be improved.

A business that applied this methodology to improve its processes would rapidly learn more about what each of the seven steps involved. It would learn what worked and what didn't work, *in its particular business.* It might combine some steps, or add others, or split some of them into two. If 100 different businesses started using this process, in ten years' time it would probably evolve into 100 different processes, *each one different according to the particular type of business and its experience of using the process.*

Every experience of using the process brings some new piece of information that enables the business to apply it better. And it is experience that we shall look at in the next section.

---

*THE EXPERIENCE CURVE* We have all had the experience of doing something for the first time. Whether it is riding a bicycle, fixing a broken toy, or baking a cake, the first time we do something it is always more difficult than the second, the third, or the fourth. We fall off the bicycle, we get back on, we wobble a little bit less, and soon we wonder why we ever found it difficult.

The same applies in our work lives. Using a new computer program, mending a jet engine, building a new team: the more times we do these things, the better we get at doing them—and "better" usually means more efficient, more effective, *and* more adaptable.

As the famous golfer Gary Player once said: "The more I practice, the luckier I get."

Now, what applies to individuals also applies to groups of people working together.

During the Second World War, when rapid mass production of aircraft became a priority, people noticed that the more bombers of a certain type were built, the faster and cheaper it became to build each one. When the effect was measured, the labor cost of building each plane was found to fall by between 10 percent and 15 percent each time that the total number of planes built (of that type) doubled.

In other words, if the labor cost of the 100th plane was $1,000 (say) then the labor cost of the 200th one would be around $850 (15 percent less). The labor cost of the 400th one would then be another 15 percent lower ($723), the 800th plane 15 percent lower still, and so on. The mathematical name for the shape of this curve is "exponential," and is shown on page 98.

## SAMPLE LEARNING CURVE

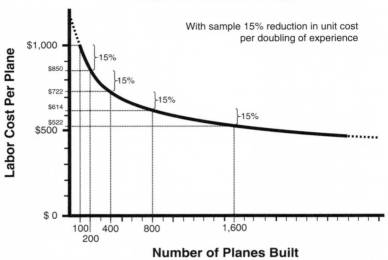

At the time, only the labor costs directly involved in building each plane were examined, and the effect was called the "Learning Curve"—essentially what was happening was that people were *learning* to do their jobs better each time, and so the labor cost per job would fall. At first this rate of learning was high, but as more planes were built, the amount of additional learning, or skill, that people got from each one was reduced—just like Gary Player hitting golf balls.

In the 1960s the Boston Consulting Group looked again at the Learning Curve in a number of different industries (television components, semiconductors, and a process industry). They found that the effect applied not only to the costs of direct labor, but to *all* the different costs involved in generating a unit of output from the business. Because of the wider scope of their findings, they called it the "Experience Curve"[8]—but the shape of the curve, and the reasons for it, are essentially the same.

The Learning Curve is just one part of the total Experience Curve for the business. It covers the labor costs in the process that directly creates or

---

[8]See the articles at www.bcg.com/this_is_bcg/mission/experience_curve.jsp

delivers the customers' service. But that process also has other, non-labor, costs, and these are also reduced as a result of the process improvements described above; after all, it is the *total cost* of carrying out any process that the business aims to reduce, not just the part that is people-related.

And what we call the indirect costs are simply costs that are associated with other processes in the business. They may not be *directly* involved with servicing the customer, but they are just as essential to success—otherwise why does the business do them? As we saw above, the only difference between a quality identity process and a quality mandatory one lies in the different emphasis in value for money. Every process in the business faces a constant redefining of what that mix is. And every process has its own improvement cycle and targets for reducing both people-related *and* non-people-related costs.

So, every part of the business—sales, marketing, finance, whatever— *every process described in this book,* goes through a cycle of learning and process improvement which improves the total cost/value mix of each one. (How it improves the value part we shall see in Chapter 6. How to assess the ideal balance we shall see in Chapter 7.)

The cost impact of all these different effects, all these different improvements, in all these different processes, is the Experience Curve for the total business.

The size of the effect, the speed at which costs fall, is driven by three main factors.

The first is the number of times the process is carried out. Every time a process is carried out, experience can be gained in how to do that process better. Where a high degree of human skill is involved (as in building an aircraft in the Second World War) we call this learning. Where little skill is involved, the improvement comes through the deliberate activities of process improvement described above: better tools, automation, simplified workflow—indeed anything that makes it easier to create the desired output and more difficult to make mistakes. All processes involve a combination of people, workflow, and technology, so all improvements involve a combination of these factors.

The second factor that drives the Experience Curve is what we commonly call "economies of scale." The inputs that are used in carrying out the process can be bought more cheaply when they are bought in bulk, or when there is a long-term contract to provide them. (Part of the reason for this is that it enables the supplier business to gain its own Experience Curve cost reductions.) The other savings are in the items that are not used up in carrying out the process, such as machinery and buildings: the so-called fixed costs. Since their costs can now be spread across a larger number of services, the cost needed to deliver each unit is lower. (These economies of scale apply just as much to indirect costs such as marketing, or the cost of having a finance department. See Chapter 5.)

And the third effect is specialization. When the same service is delivered a large number of times, people can specialize at particular tasks (or sub-processes). This was the innovation that enabled Henry Ford to mass produce the world's first affordable motor car. It reduces the dead time of switching from one task to another, and gives each person more experience at carrying out a smaller number of activities. This in turn compounds and accelerates the process improvement effects described above.

Together, these different dynamics combine in a heuristic, semi-random (but directed) way to create the overall effect we call the Experience Curve.

As the Boston Consulting Group says, "The experience curve effect can be observed and measured in any business, any industry, any cost element, anywhere. . . . It is so universal that its absence is almost a warning of mismanagement or misunderstanding."

This has implications both for the running of an individual business, and for the economy as a whole.

*IMPLICATIONS OF THE EXPERIENCE CURVE*  The first implication is that we should not automatically expect there to be inflation. As someone who grew up in the 1960s and 1970s, this came as a bit of a shock. But the costs of delivering any service should automatically fall each year unless:

a)  demand for the service exceeds supply, in which case prices can be raised to match the highest bidders

b) cost of raw materials extracted from the earth (such as oil) is rising, either due to increased costs of extraction (though these industries also have Experience Curves) or again due to demand exceeding supply, or

c) the expectation of inflation causes businesses to raise prices automatically to compensate for it before it happens

Inflation does not need to happen automatically, and the fact that governments have been able to control it by controlling their money supplies proves this. Indeed many items, especially those that involve computers and electronics,[9] now cost less than they did a few years ago.

The second key implication of the Experience Curve is that different businesses have different costs for delivering the same service. Generally speaking, we would expect the company that has sold the most units to have a lower cost for delivering a single unit of service. This means that established market leaders face a double cost advantage over their competitors. First, having sold the largest number of units to date, they have the lowest unit cost, which means they make the most money by selling at any given price. And second, having the largest market share, they are also now selling the most units per year, which means that they are moving further and faster down the Experience Curve than their competitors, lowering their costs still further. (They probably also have marketing benefits; see the Winner's Competitive Cycle in Chapter 6.)

All this generates what is called "first mover advantage"—the benefits a business gets if it is first to start delivering a new service and gains a head start in moving down the Experience Curve. It also has implications for the impact of globalization.

The word "globalization" can mean many things. What I specifically want to talk about here is what happens to competitive advantage when trade and tariff barriers around a small country fall, allowing competitors from a larger economy in. You might expect that the larger business from

---

[9]For a description of how the famous Moore's Law of computing follows directly from Experience Curve improvements in the processes for manufacturing and etching silicon wafers, see www.arstechnica.com/paedia/m/moore/moore-1.html.

the bigger economy (with a lower cost base, thanks to the Experience Curve) would instantly move in and wipe out the local competitors. This has happened in some cases, but it is not inevitable. The local companies also have advantages, in terms of understanding the local culture and practice of doing business, and in understanding the nuances of what local customers want. They might also have lower costs of doing business, if salaries and other inputs are cheaper than for the incoming global company. They might even (though this is unlikely) have the global best practice processes for delivering their particular service(s).

What then happens is that the incoming global company can hire local people, buy local resources, and learn how to do business in the local environment. The advantages that the local company had in terms of carrying out its processes are gradually eroded. So what the local business needs to be doing at the same time is learning from the processes of the newcomer, perhaps by buying the same equipment and machinery, by hiring their managers, through Joint Ventures, or by whatever means are appropriate.

This is what the Chinese government made sure would happen in China. By allowing foreign firms in only as part of Joint Ventures, it ensured that the Chinese people would learn to be producers of services, not just workers and consumers of services produced by foreign-owned corporations.

In this way the two different businesses can move towards competitive parity, based on their knowledge of how to operate the best processes.

But that is not the end of the story. The inevitable logic of the Experience Curve continues to operate, and there is one advantage that the local company has still not been able to match.

No matter how well the local company manages to learn from the newcomer, the global business still has the advantage of size and scale that comes from operating across the world, not just one country. As we have seen, this enables it to move further and faster down the Experience Curve, and so to deliver its services at a lower cost.[10] Whether or not that cost saving

---

[10]Strictly speaking, how possible it is to achieve the potential cost savings will depend on the specific business and country, and the extent to which the same processes can be used all around the world.

is significant to the business as a whole will depend on what kind of business it is (see Chapter 7). But the saving does exist. And the only way for the local company to match it, if it wants to, is for it to become a global business as well.

In the short term, going global benefits a business by bringing in more customers and revenues—it creates an additional return on the knowledge that already exists within the business. But in the long term it brings advantage in the only thing that really matters: opportunities to improve knowledge of how to deliver services, with the best mix of cost and value. As experience accumulates over time, it brings a strategic cost advantage that (almost) any business would be reckless to ignore. And *that* is why the thing we call globalization has such "unstoppable" momentum.

## COMBINING THE EXPERIENCE CURVE WITH THE DEMAND CURVE

Becoming global connects a corporation with every customer in the world who might potentially benefit from its services (see Chapter 2). As well as bringing in short-term revenue gains and long-term strategic cost reductions, this also positions the business to maximize its cycles of learning and innovation.

We shall look more closely at this in Chapter 8, where it becomes essential to creating self-reinforcing advantage. But to give you a taste, let's look at how the two fundamentals that we have looked at so far—cost and value—are *linked together* within the business.

The revenues a business earns from its services depend on the value that those services bring to customers. As we saw in Chapter 2, some people will be willing to pay a high price for a service, more will be willing to pay a lower price, and we can draw this as a bell curve or Demand Curve shape. Next to this, the Experience Curve shows how the cost of delivering a service falls the more times it is provided. (See diagram on next page.)

Let's put both these pictures together, and think about what happens to both cost and value when a business launches a new service.

The first time a new service is provided, the cost of delivering it is relatively high, because the business has no experience. If it wants to make money from this one-off

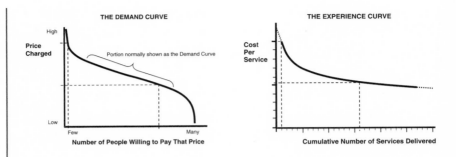

transaction, the business needs to find one of the small number of people who the Demand Curve tells us will value the service a great deal.

Once the first service has been delivered, then the business knows how to deliver the next one more cheaply. So the price can be reduced, and more customers may now be willing to pay for it. The cycle then repeats. Each time the business delivers its service, it learns how to do so more cheaply. It can then lower its price, which makes the service more attractive to more people, which reduces the cost, and so on.

If the business follows this step-by-step approach, lowering the price gradually over time following the Demand Curve, then launching the service can be a relatively low-risk procedure—the business can be fairly sure of making money at every step of the way. This approach also gets each customer to pay the maximum amount of value that the service represents to them.

But there is an alternative approach. Knowing that the cost of delivering the service will fall, a rival business might decide to launch an identical service at a lower price. In the short term that might be lower than the cost of delivering the service, but more customers would buy it. So the business would move faster down the Experience Curve, cutting costs, making money, and in the long term locking out the more expensive, more cautious competitor.

Effectively, the second business is buying market share. It is giving up some of the value that it could have earned from the (small) group of initial customers in return for a larger share of the much larger group of customers that it expects will exist in the future (they also represent the long-term market for the service). In this way making money involves thinking not only about the size of a payment, but also about its *timing* and probability, and we shall look more closely at this in the next chapter.

Both these approaches to launching a service come with different mixtures of risk and reward. But in general it makes sense to reduce the price slowly when there is a small market, or where there is little or no competition. And it makes sense to have a low price from the beginning in cases when the market is expected to be large or when competitors could easily offer a similar service.

In summary, we can see that there is a feedback loop between the business and its customers that involves both the value that the service brings and the price the business charges, *and* the amount it costs to deliver the service and the total number of services that the customers buy. Any business that wants to launch a new service needs to think through how those interactions might pan out over the long term, not just the first few customers.

The price of a service does not depend on the cost of providing it. (Think strawberries and cream at a Wimbledon final, or advertising at the Super Bowl.) But how much it costs to provide a service *does* depend on how many customers value the service, at what price, because of the Experience Curve.

Chapter 8 will show us how to create self-reinforcing business advantage, by examining the *ultimate* ways in which a business can benefit by interconnecting these two items: cost and value. But before it can do that, the business needs to understand the next section, which looks at some simpler ways to create value by leveraging the Experience Curve.

*MAKING USE OF THE EXPERIENCE CURVE—SIZE MATTERS* The Experience Curve is like a one-way street; a moving escalator that makes it difficult for competitors to catch up.

It applies to every process in the business, as well as to the business as a whole.

The most obvious way for a business to take advantage of the Experience Curve is for it to be the biggest in its marketplace. This gives it the most experience and places it at the lowest cost position on the curve.

But only one business in any marketplace can be in this happy position. For the other businesses there are four other ways, or groups of ways, in which a business can make an understanding of the Experience Curve work in its favor.

The first is to focus on the *rate* of improvement, rather than the absolute level of performance. Cost reduction does not happen by itself—the smooth exponential curve shown above is just a mathematical approximation of reality—so whether costs actually reduce by 5 percent each time experience doubles, or 25 percent, depends on the specific actions that are taken or not taken by the people within the business. A business that works harder and smarter at process improvement—that makes process improvement one of the processes which it is better at than competitors—can create a steeper Experience Curve and reduce costs by more with less.

One way to improve a process is by using a new technology. If this changes a large enough proportion of the total costs, then it effectively puts the business on to a completely new Experience Curve—one where *it* is now the business with the greatest experience in the new technology. This is the second approach: moving onto a different Experience Curve.

A business can also move onto a different Experience Curve by offering a service that is different from the market leader's. By getting closer to a (smaller) set of customers, the business can offer a service that they value more (see Strategic Positioning in Chapter 2). If the service is different then the process must be different and the Experience Curve must be different also. If the difference is large enough then the new position is doubly defendable against the market leader, on the basis of both cost *and* value.

This double advantage echoes what McKinsey said about success being based on alignment of *all* the different parts (the seven Ss) of the business. How, ultimately, to achieve that is what we are working towards in the Escher Cycle (Chapter 8).

Instead of accelerating the rate of cost reduction (by making process improvement an identity process) or moving to a different Experience Curve (by focusing on a sufficiently different service and process), the third way in which a business can take advantage of the Experience Curve is by taking a skill at a particular process and applying it to multiple different services. In this case it becomes what is known in the jargon as a Core Competence.[11]

---

[11]See CK Prahalad and Gary Hamel's book *The Core Competence of the Corporation.*

A process is made up of people, technology, and activities, and so any one of the three may form the core skill that the business does better than its competitors.

The result could then be like Black and Decker, who put their small electric motors into services ranging from drills and hedge trimmers to sanders and saws. (This is a "technology" example.) Or it could be like Honda, who uses its specialized knowledge of developing four-stroke engines to sell cars, lawnmowers, generators, snowblowers, pumps, and marine engines. (This is a "people" example, since it is the people who have and re-use the knowledge.) Or it could be like UPS, FedEx, and DHL, who have standardized the activities involved in moving things from one place to another to such an extent that they can now offer services ranging from supply chain management to logistics, on top of the "simple" task of being able to move any package from anywhere in the world to anywhere else, quickly and cheaply.[12]

The result is that although the business may not have the largest market share for any particular *service,* it focuses on gaining the largest *experience share* for a critical or important *process.*

Because each service benefits from (and contributes to) a shared Experience Curve, the business can then provide all the services at a relatively low cost. (Lower than if it provided only one service.) This will become important again in Chapter 8.

Another way of thinking about this is in terms of building each service from components. Different combinations of components create different services. Each component has its own Experience Curve, which benefits from (and contributes to) all the different services that use it. And even a brand-new service can start life with the accumulated experience of its different components.

The combined competitive advantage of all these different experience curves together then represents the strategic advantage of the business. And the ultimate resource of any business is *the knowledge of how to carry out its processes.*

---

[12]Visit www.dhl.com and click on "Services A-Z" for examples.

The importance of cost as a key driver of the short-term success of a business will depend (as we see in Chapter 7) on what type of business the firm is in. But in the long term, this way of leveraging the Experience Curve—taking advantage of the fact that size matters to provide a range of different services based on the same core competence, and all at lower cost than they could be on their own—will become a key ingredient in building the ultimate strategic advantage, as we discuss in Chapter 8.

For now, the fifth and final way to make use of the Experience Curve is to borrow someone else's. This is what we shall look at in the next section.

---

**KNOWLEDGE IS THE SOURCE OF BUSINESS ADVANTAGE**

They say that knowledge is power. But knowledge is also the source of competitive advantage—the ultimate resource of any business.

Or, rather, the ultimate resource of any business is its ability to *apply* its knowledge of how to carry out all its different processes. The ultimate resource is its ability to *combine* the practical with the theoretical, the operational with the strategic.

Where that applied knowledge comes from is each *experience* of delivering its services.

Chapter 2 showed us how to apply that knowledge to improve the value that the service adds. This chapter shows us how to reduce the cost. Chapter 7 will show us how to balance the business priorities between these two.

*The ultimate business advantage will come from gaining the maximum experience of delivering different services, and converting that into the lowest possible cost (through the Experience Curve) . . . which then gives it the maximum opportunity to develop and sell new services.*

That is what we are heading towards in Chapter 8.

---

*SOURCING STRATEGY—THE "MAKE OR BUY" DECISION* As we know, different businesses often contain the same or similar processes. So, if two or more businesses were to pool their activities, their combined experience would drive down costs faster than either one could do alone.

This, essentially, is how new businesses are born. The reason that logistics and transportation businesses exist as separate entities is because it is cheaper for other businesses to use them than it is for them to own and manage their own fleets of ships, aircraft, trucks, vans, or trains. The same applies to generating electricity, making light bulbs, office furniture, stationery, carpets, and so on. And what makes it cheaper to buy from someone else than to make your own is the Experience Curve.

Combining or sharing experience drives costs down, and that is the priority for secondary and mandatory processes. So it makes sense for businesses to outsource some of these processes and pay other businesses to carry out the processes for them.

Outsourcing simply means paying another business to carry out a set of activities or processes that the business used to do itself. In reality, when this approach is successful, it is not so very different from what we call purchasing —except that maybe the contract is more tailored to the specific needs of the customer, rather than the customer choosing from a standard set of services offered. If the outsourcing arrangement does not work out, and the business decides to take over direct control of the activities/processes again, then this is called insourcing.

The downside of outsourcing is that it can also increase risk. Not only can an outside supplier turn out to be unreliable, but the fact that service levels need to be defined in a contract makes them intrinsically less flexible than a process that the business controls itself. (Unless the supplier business explicitly focuses on making the process more adaptable than the original business had time to do itself.) Whether the increase in risk is worth the savings in cost then depends on the business, the specific process, and the contract terms that are negotiated.

But it is not only secondary and mandatory processes that can be outsourced—primary and identity processes are often outsourced, too. For example, advertising plays a key role in shaping the identity that customers perceive in a business, but advertisements and whole advertising strategies are routinely crafted by agencies that are "outside" the business.

In these cases, the reason that the business uses an outside supplier is not to gain access to lower costs, but to gain access to higher expertise— expertise that the business does not have a sufficient volume of activity at to be able to generate the required level of competence or value.

The fact that experience improves effectiveness as well as efficiency will be discussed again in Chapter 6. And ultimately it is not the classification of a process as mandatory or identity that determines whether it makes sense to outsource or insource, but simply what results the business is likely to get if it outsources the process, and what results it is likely to get if it doesn't. In other words, which approach is closer to the mix of risk and reward that the business wants?

Although buying services from outside can help a business to carry out its processes more efficiently *and* more effectively, there is a downside to outsourcing too much in this way. The downside is that there is nothing left for the business to do. The downside is that if the business can buy a great service from an outside supplier, so can its competitors. When a business outsources a particular process, it loses the ability to use that process to con- tribute to its overall competitive advantage. Or, rather, its competitive advantage changes from how well it *carries out* that process, to how well it *negotiates terms,* and works with the supplier to *adapt* the service to its changing needs.

For example, the airline we discussed above might have decided that turning-round its aircraft was not a core part of its business. It might there- fore have asked a supplier or suppliers to carry out those activities for it. This would allow the people within the airline to concentrate on the activi- ties that they are best at. But it would also allow the supplier(s) to sell the same service to competing airlines, and the airline would then lose its com- petitive advantage. An exclusivity clause in the contract might prevent this, but what is to stop another business from starting a similar service? Whether it makes long-term sense for the airline to turn planes round itself, or to use a supplier, ultimately depends upon the Experience Curve. The Experience Curve is the ultimate exclusivity clause.

So this means that success for the business now also depends on its ability to choose which processes (expertise) to buy, and which processes (experience) to keep in-house.

Each alternative is just a different way to use a (different) set of resources to achieve the target levels of cost and value from that process. And each one comes with its own contractual arrangements and its own set of risk, reward, hassle-factors, and uncertainty.

In this way *it no longer makes sense to think of "inside" or "outside" the business*—they do not exist. The business is not choosing whether to carry out each process inside or outside itself. It is choosing between different forms of contractual agreement as the best way to achieve the levels of value and cost that are needed.

This is essential to understanding how to choose the right strategy (Chapter 7), and then to understanding strategic diversification and how to create self-reinforcing advantage (Chapter 8).

So, making good choices between insourcing and outsourcing becomes a part of the competitive advantage of the firm: choosing the approach that will give the mix of efficiency, effectiveness, and adaptability that (ultimately) best matches what the customer needs. And driving it all is the Experience Curve.

Whatever choices are made will define the *operational* risk and cost for the business of delivering the service. These combine with the *market* risk and reward that is inherent in the customer needs that the business has chosen to service (and which drive the rise and fall in demand for its services). And together the *operational* risk and the *market* reward create the *financial* risk and reward that we shall examine in the next chapter.

---

**KNOW YOUR CORE PROCESS: "WOULD YOU LIKE CASH BACK WITH THAT?"**

As the world changes, businesses need to focus more and more on the key difference that they make: the processes at which they have the most experience.

For example, in the UK over the past ten years, retail banks (High Street banks) have found themselves under threat from supermarkets that offer banking services. It started from "cash back" with purchases, and rapidly led to supermarkets offering their own checking accounts, insurance, investments, and so on. When it began, supermarkets in the UK were rapidly expanding the number of their outlets, while changes within the banks' own industry meant that more and more of their branches were being closed down.

So, the reason that supermarkets could *begin* to offer this new service was first that they could carry out the process (handing over cash in return for a credit card transaction).

The reason that it *took off*—the reason that millions of people changed their behavior from getting cash from the bank and spending it at the supermarket to doing both in the same place—was first that it saved the supermarkets money (by reducing the amounts of cash that they had to bank), and second that the supermarkets were doing a *better* job at the process called "having a location that is easy and convenient for customers to visit."

At that time, some people predicted the death of retail banks. But the core value that they *really* add is actually very difficult for supermarkets to copy. It has to do with expertise in:

1)  back office transactions, technology
2)  relationships with the rest of the financial industry
3)  understanding and dealing with financial regulation
4)  combining all of the above to create more financial services

Although the banks seemed to be under threat, what was really happening was that a part of their business model that had for them become a secondary process (having a physical location that is convenient for customers) was now being outsourced to supermarkets.

The reason it seemed worrying was because the outsourcing was being driven by the customers, rather than by the banks themselves.

But the identity and primary processes of those banks had not changed, and they were still difficult to copy, and not threatened.

Once the banks realized this they could stop worrying about the change. Some even saw it as a new and perhaps better way to convert their core expertise into services for customers: they provided the financial parts of the service, while the supermarket provided the parts to do with location and branding.

In this way both parties won, by doing what each was best at and cooperating with others to carry out the rest. Competitive success then became more clearly based on both the ability to carry out the identity and primary processes, *and* the ability to coordinate the overall system. We shall come back to this in Chapters 7 and 8.

In this specific example, some customers have switched over to supermarket banking, while others have stuck with the traditional approach. Both sets of customers are now getting a service that is more tailored to their specific needs.

We can interpret this as outsourcing or as industries converging, but what is *really* driving the change is the Experience Curve combined with the different needs of different customers.

In all of this, the core of what the bank does and what it is best at does not change—in fact it becomes *clearer.* But *how* that skill is expressed in the world *does* change, and what that means for the future is discussed in Chapters 8 and 9.

——— **MAKING IT REAL** ———

- What methods does your business use to take advantage of the Experience Curve?
- What methods *could* it use?
- What methods do your top two competitors use?
- What is the truly critical knowledge that your business has that enables it to carry out a certain process better than anyone else, and around which the rest of the business is built?
- What steps are you taking to ensure that you maintain that advantage?

# SUMMARY

This chapter has drilled down from a very high level (the total business) to a very detailed level (how to improve an individual process), and then it has gone back to the top level again as it looked at the overall effect of process improvement (the Experience Curve) and its strategic implications for the business.

It has shown that the key resources of the business can be anything from raw materials such as coal, to specialized equipment and the skills of staff, to factories and distribution networks, to intangible concepts such as brand image and friendliness.

It showed how the business works as a total system, by linking the individual resources together in a business model. This revealed the key pressure points, where a difference in performance will make the greatest difference to results.

Every resource is created as the result of processes. So a business that wants to get better results than its competitors needs to have better processes.

What those processes are and how to improve them is the subject of the whole of this book.

We saw that different processes can be ranked as identity, primary, secondary, or mandatory for different businesses. But they all are essential, and they all need to get done somehow.

What is different between each one is the balance of emphasis between cost and value.

Providing better *value* was described in Chapter 2.

Providing lower *cost* depends on the Experience Curve, and five ways to take advantage of that were described.

The Experience Curve is the key driver of success at using resources, but the Experience Curve is just an approximation to reality.

What is really going on is that people are learning and inventing new ways to get done whatever needs to get done in the business. The Experience Curve summarizes that effect. But *realizing* that the effect is there helps us to look for more ways to make it happen better and faster. This is exactly what happened with aircraft production in the Second World War. And it is exactly what will happen when we come to look at the overall effects that drive the creation of self-reinforcing business advantage in Chapter 8.

To sum up this chapter, we have now added more detail to the second part of our picture of the least a business needs to do, and what forms the first layer of its strategic advantage. Using resources has been expanded to include:

- identifying the key resources of the business

- combining them into a business model

- prioritizing each process into a heirarchy, and assigning activities to suppliers and employees either "inside" or "outside" the firm to get the desired mix of cost and value, risk and reward from each one.

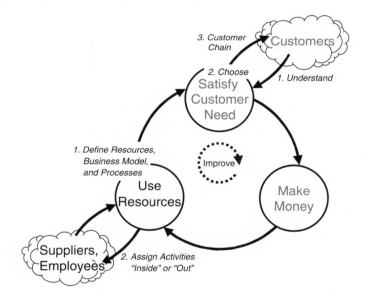

Choosing a set of customer needs defines the business's future *market* risk and *market* reward. Choosing a business model and how the processes within it will get carried out defines the *operational* risk and reward of the business. These two factors combined create the *financial* risk and reward for investors in the business, and this is what we shall look at in the next chapter.

# CHAPTER 4

# *Making Money*

*In God we trust—all others pay cash.*

—TRADITIONAL

THE PREVIOUS TWO CHAPTERS have looked at what it takes for an organization to *use its resources* to *satisfy customer needs*.

But being good at these two activities alone is not enough to create a successful business. For that to happen the organization also needs to *make money*. If it does not, then its resources will shrink away to nothing, and no customer needs will get satisfied.

This chapter looks at the third of the three minimum activities a business needs to carry out in order to be successful—the third of the activities that together form the first layer of strategic business advantage. This chapter looks at what it means to *make money,* and how a business can do that well.

For some readers *making money* will be seen as the highest purpose of any organization. For them this chapter needs no introduction. But what they probably do not realize is that all the size and complexity of finance and accounting can be boiled down to just *four* basic ways in which any business can make more money. This chapter reminds us what they are.

For other readers the main aim of their organization will be seen as something different: providing the best service, or extending the range of human achievement, for example. For them making money will be just a means to an end. But this chapter is important for them too, because by understanding the *essence* of what it takes to make money they will learn how to have the *most impact* on this part of their business from the *minimum actions.*

Understanding how to make money does not help the business to satisfy a single customer's need. Nor does it make the business any better at the key skills needed to do so. What making money does do is act as a balance between these two activities. It determines which business is most able to pay to *improve* them, to survive and grow. And as such it forms a critical part of building self-reinforcing business advantage.

We start by looking at traditional accounting.

## THE TRADITIONAL APPROACH

*PROFIT AND LOSS* What do we mean when we say that a company is *making money*?

The conventional response is probably to think in terms of profit and loss and the P&L account. But, as the accounting scandals at Enron and WorldCom showed us, whether or not a company is making a profit actually tells us very little about whether or not it is *making money.*

But governments still place legal requirements on companies to produce these accounts, and financial markets still move on announcements of profit and loss results. So we shall start by working through an example of how profit and loss works. This will introduce the basic ideas and also reveal the limitations of the approach.

As a simple example, let's imagine a young entrepreneur who has decided to start up a business, using a hot dog stand.

Let's assume that he buys the stand for $1,000, works five days a week selling an average of 200 hot dogs per day for $1.50 each. The buns and frankfurter sausages cost him $0.20 per hot dog. Onions, sauces, napkins, and cooking gas cost him $1,000 over the year.

After one year, has he made any money, and if so, how much?

We can think about this in two parts: first, how much money came into the business, and second, how much went out.

Looking first at the *satisfy customer needs* part of the business, we can find the total amount of money that came in. The entrepreneur worked 260 days selling 200 dogs per day at $1.50 each, which makes a total of $78,000. This sales figure can also be called turnover or revenue.

How much money went out of the business? The resources used were hot dogs and buns (260 days × 200 dogs/day × $0.20/dog = $10,400), as well as $1,000 for onions, sauces, napkins, and cooking gas. The entrepreneur also paid himself a combined salary and pension of $60,000, so that the total costs or expenses were $71,400.

If we subtract the money that went out of the business from the money that came in, we find that the amount left over, the amount of money that the business has made, is $6,600. The jargon word for this can be profit, earnings, or income.

In a set of company accounts this would usually be laid out in columns, as shown below. Note that the cost figures are shown in brackets, because a simple "−" sign is easy to miss when you are in a hurry.

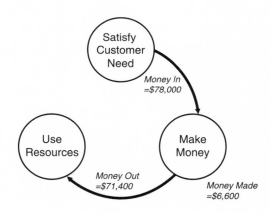

Money In:

Sales, Revenue, or Turnover:                                          $78,000

Subtract:

Money Out:

Costs, Expenses:

| | | |
|---|---|---|
| Hot Dogs & Buns | ($10,400) | |
| Onions, Sauces, Napkins, & Cooking Gas | ($ 1,000) | |
| Salary & Pension | ($60,000) | |
| Sub-Total Expenses: | | ($71,400) |

Equals:

Money Made:

Profit, Earnings, or Income                                          $ 6,600

    (before depreciation, interest, & tax)

This all seems very simple and straightforward. And it is.

But notice that when the entrepreneur chooses how much salary to pay himself he is also choosing how much profit the business will make.

This idea that profits can be altered by human decisions is an interesting and important one, and we shall look at it in more detail in the next section, where we consider the final expense that still needs to be taken into account: the cost of the hot dog stand.

---

### VALUE, COST, AND THE CREATION OF WEALTH

We know from Chapter 2 that customers will not normally buy a service unless the value of that service to them is greater than the price.

This means that the customer makes a "profit" too!

In a so-called "win-win" transaction between a customer and a business, something incredible happens: new wealth, new value is created in the world.

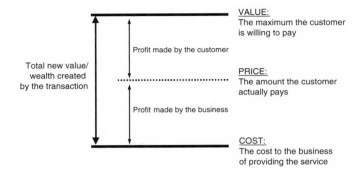

The business sells a service for a price which is greater than the cost it took to produce it. So the net value of the business has increased. And customers get a service that is worth more to them than the price they paid, so their "net worth" has increased also.

Which of the two parties—customer or business—gets the larger share of the new wealth created depends on the price. Or as we learned in Chapter 3, it depends on the contract between them.

This may be easier to see if we think about the suppliers who provided the resources that the business used. They needed to sell their services at a price that was higher than their costs, and lower than the value the business would later get by converting them into a new service.

Trade (win-win trade) is what increases the total amount of value or wealth in the world.

At its heart, making money is simply about selling a service for more than it costs to produce. Or, turning this around, it is about buying resources for less than the new value they will be used to create. The rest of this chapter is really about understanding *how to measure that* better, so that we know better how to increase it.

And it is important to realize that this basic *balance between cost and value* applies just as much to each activity carried out within the business as it does to the business as a whole. It matters when buying sausages and onions, just as it matters when hiring an advertising agency, a logistics partner, or a new chief executive. This will become important again when we look at how to choose the right strategy for the business in Chapter 7.

*AMORTIZATION/DEPRECIATION* It looks as if the hot dog vendor is *making money,* but there is one more item that still needs to be taken into account: the hot dog stand.

The cost of the stand was $1,000, and if we subtract this from the $6,600 profit we calculated before, then that gives a figure of $5,600 for the money made during the year.

But next year, the entrepreneur will still be using the same hot dog stand. Given that it is expected to last for five years, wouldn't it be better to charge $200 against each year that the stand is used, rather than charge the full amount to just the first year?

In fact this is standard practice, and is called depreciation or amortization. It is used to allocate or assign some types of costs into later sets of accounts.

A so-called "cash flow" occurs when the entrepreneur pays for the hot dog stand, and this can be allocated or spread over a number of different entries in the accounting books for different months or years. These would be called book entries.

When cash flows are assigned from future time periods to book entries in earlier ones, this is called accrual. A business might have used telephone and electricity during a month that it does not have to pay for until next quarter. In its accounts for the month it accrues the amount it expects to pay. At the same time the phone or electricity company is accruing an amount for the revenue they expect to receive.

The aim of all this accrual accounting is to get an accurate representation of all the revenues and expenses that relate to *one specific time period,* irrespective of whether or not there was a cash flow into or out of the business during that time.

In our entrepreneur's case, this means that the profit for this year (before calculating interest and tax) is $6,600, less $200 for the hot dog stand, which equals $6,400.

Money In:

Sales, Revenue, or Turnover:                                      $78,000


Subtract:

Money Out:

Costs, Expenses:

   Hot Dogs & Buns                         ($10,400)

   Onions, Sauces, Napkins,

    & Cooking Gas                         ($ 1,000)

   Salary & Pension                         ($60,000)

   Sub-Total Expenses:                                   ($71,400)


Equals:

Money Made:

Profit, Earnings, or Income                                      $ 6,600

   (before depreciation, interest, & tax)


Depreciation                                                    ($    200)

Profit, Earnings, or Income                                     $ 6,400

   (before interest, & tax)


Profit before interest and tax (PBIT) is the most commonly used reference point for comparing companies' earnings. Once interest and tax have been paid, the figure becomes "profit after interest and tax." Some of this amount may then be paid to shareholders in the form of a dividend, and the remainder ("retained earnings") is the amount by which shareholders funds (the value of the business) have increased during the year.

So, all this looks as if it answers the question of how much money the business has made. But reality is that it is just somebody's *opinion*. What if five years is actually just the *average* lifespan of a hot dog stand, with anything from two to ten years being quite common? Should we then take a conservative approach and amortize/depreciate at $500 per year (two-year life), or an optimistic approach and charge just $100 per year (ten-year life)?

Or what if someone argues that five years *is* the average lifespan, but the market resale value of one year-old stands is $400, and therefore $600 should be charged in the first year, followed by $100 per year for the next four years?

All these are perfectly reasonable approaches, but the effect on the calculated profit can be significant, as the following table shows:

| | OPTION 1* | OPTION 2* | OPTION 3* | OPTION 4* |
|---|---|---|---|---|
| Revenue: | $78,000 | $78,000 | $78,000 | $78,000 |
| Salary & expenses: | ($71,400) | ($71,400) | ($71,400) | ($71,400) |
| Profit before depreciation: | $6,600 | $6,600 | $6,600 | $6,600 |
| Chosen depreciation amount: | ($200) | ($500) | ($100) | ($600) |
| Profit Before Interest & Tax: | $6,400 | $6,100 | $ 6,500 | $6,000 |

*Notes:

Option 1 assumes five-year life, equal depreciation each year

Option 2 assumes two-year life, equal depreciation each year

Option 3 assumes ten-year life, equal depreciation each year

Option 4 assumes five-year life, "accelerated depreciation" in first year

Whatever your opinion on which is the best approach to use, the point is that it is just that—your *opinion*. And your opinion might change, depending on whether you were a manager whose bonus depended on how much profit was made, or an accountant trying to reduce the tax bill of the corporation.

Using depreciation and accrual to decide what proportions of different costs to assign to a particular time period seems a reasonable approach—but it is a slippery slope towards ever-greater complexity.

Extend the example to even a medium-sized corporation and you suddenly find yourself with an awful lot of items that need to be counted, tracked, depreciated, and accrued, month after month, year after year. This creates work that costs the business money, but adds nothing to the quality of the service that the customer is buying. And it means that a significant proportion of the expenses that appear in the company accounts are just somebody's *opinion.*

Picking two well-known companies at random, Microsoft, in its 2001 annual reports and accounts, states the figure for "depreciation, amortization, and other non-cash items" as $1.5b. This is around 13 percent of its $11.7b operating income for the year—more than an eighth. General Electric, in its 2001 financial year, stated "depreciation/amortization of plant, property and equipment" as $5.4b, with amortization of "intangibles" an additional $1.7b. The combined total of $7.1b represents 36 percent, over a third, of GE's $19.7b pre-tax profits for the year.

In other words, using profit and loss to measure how much money a company is making gives us a result that can vary by hundreds of millions of dollars, depending on the *opinions* of fallible human beings.

Clearly the profit figure is no longer a *measure,* but rather an *indicator* of whether or not a business is making money. If a corporation is making money then it will probably also show a good profit figure. But just because it shows a good profit does not necessarily mean that it is making money.

To truly know what it means for a business to make money we need a new way of thinking, a new paradigm, and we will find it in the next section. We start by looking again at the purchase of the hot dog stand.

## THE SHAREHOLDER VALUE APPROACH

*THE TIME VALUE OF MONEY* We know that the hot dog stand cost $1,000 and was expected to last for several years. We don't know whether the entrepreneur paid for it out of his savings, or whether he borrowed money and if so from whom. We also don't know whether the manufacturer insisted that the stand should be paid for all at once, or whether it accepted payment spread over several months. Let's look at these alternatives in more detail.

Let's assume that the manufacturer offers a credit scheme that gives customers the opportunity either to pay $1,000 on delivery, or 36 equal monthly payments of $40 (a total of $1,440). What we are effectively saying is that from the manufacturer's point of view $1,000 today *is the same as* $1,440 spread over three years.

The entrepreneur knows that this represents an interest rate of nearly 30 percent, similar to what his credit card would charge. He knows that his bank is offering lower rates, and will lend him $1,000 in return for either $35 per month for three years, or $23 per month over five years. This effectively means that from the bank's point of view, $1,000 today is the same as $1,260 spread over 36 months or $1,380 spread over 60 months. (The interest rates are around 17 percent and 14 percent, respectively.)

What we see is that a sum of money today can be thought of as *equivalent* to a number of different amounts of money in the future.

Or a number of cash amounts in the future can be thought of as *equivalent* to a certain amount today—the "present value," to use the jargon word for this.

What determines the size of that present value is the size, number, and timing of the future payments, and the interest rate that is applied. Let's look at this more closely in the next section.

---

**AMORTIZATION/DEPRECIATION IS ALWAYS CALCULATED ON THE WRONG AMOUNT**

The fact that money has a time value—$100 today is *not* the same as $100 in five years' time—puts another nail in the coffin of amortization/depreciation.

Depreciation/amortization is calculated on the headline price of the item: in the case of the hot dog stand, $1,000.

But the total amount that the business *actually* pays for the stand will depend on which loan alternative the entrepreneur chooses.

And if he pays for the stand out of savings, then the total impact will still not be $1,000 because he will also lose the interest he *would* have earned if he had left the $1,000 in the bank.

The profit and loss account ignores all this, and uses a $1,000 figure that is just about the only amount that will *never* actually be paid by the business. Depreciation is a fiction.

---

*CALCULATING PRESENT VALUES*  Assume you have $100 to invest, and you find a bank account that pays 10 percent interest. In a year's time you will have $110. So if I offer you the choice between $100 today and $110 in a year's time, it does not matter which you pick—they both have the same value to you.

If we want to work out what any investment will be worth in "n" years' time, we can apply a simple formula:

$$FP = PV \times (1 + i)^n$$

This may look complicated, but it is easily understood by anybody who has a savings account, or a checking account that pays interest.

What it says is that the future payment "FP" is equal to the present value "PV" of the investment, increased by *i percent* (where "*i*" is the interest rate) for each of the "n" years we leave the money in the bank.

If we want to work out what the present value of some future amount is we simply switch the formula around, to give:

$$PV = \frac{FP}{(1 + i)^n}$$

This says that the present value (the equivalent value today) is equal to the amount of the future payment "FP," divided by the interest rate factor "*i*" according to the number of years into the future that the payment will be made "n."

So, suppose we want to be able to decide whether we would rather have $110 in a year's time or $120 in two years.

$110 in a year (assuming 10 percent interest) is equal to:

$$PV = \frac{\$110}{(1 + 10\%)^1} = \frac{\$110}{1.10} = \$100 \text{ today}$$

And $120 in two years (assuming 10 percent interest) is equal to:

$$PV = \frac{\$120}{(1 + 10\%)^2} = \frac{\$120}{1.21} = \$99.17 \text{ today}$$

Now we can choose that we would rather have $110 in one year than $120 in two years. (This leaves out the issue of risk or probability, but we will come to that in a moment.)

More detailed calculation examples are given in the "Worked Examples" box, but the key ideas are:

- the value of a sum of money depends not only on its *size,* but also *when* it occurs, and the *interest* rate that could be earned
- the way to compare the relative sizes of different sums or different times in the future is to work out their equivalent value today, their present value

In other words, we need to be thinking not so much that "time is money" as that "*timing* is money."

This is a very different way of thinking about making money from the Profit and Loss approach. The practical implications for business are *huge.*

Imagine that you run a business that has been offered a contract worth $150m, spread over five years. Payments are to be $10m at the end of each of the first four years and $110m in the fifth year. (This is shown in the "Worked Examples" box.) Because you know about the present value of money, you can calculate that this is *exactly equivalent* to a present value of $100m.

Now imagine that your customer changes the offer from $150m over five years to $110m *all paid at the start of the contract.* Your competitor thinks in terms of profit and loss, and sees the fall in revenue from $150m to $110m, a reduction of 27 percent. Goodness knows what this does to his profit figure. He naturally refuses the business.

But you know about the time value of money, and so realize that the *present value* of the revenue figure has just gone *up* by $10m, from $100m to $110m. Assuming that it covers your costs, you accept and invest the money (either in your own business or in a bank) to generate the returns you are looking for.

This is a change to our way of thinking that can probably have more impact on our day-to-day lives than the realization that the earth is not flat or that it orbits around the sun. And it is a change in thinking that many businesses and governments have still not yet recognized and understood.

Given that modern accounting regulations are based on ways of thinking about the world that date back as far as 2100 B.C. in Babylonia and China (accruals and depreciation/amortization), and thirteenth century Venice[1] (double-entry bookkeeping)—times when people believed that the world was flat, and marked maps of unexplored areas with the words "Here be dragons"—it is hardly surprising that they are in need of reform. Thankfully discussion of such reform is beyond the scope of this book.

How well our mental models match the way the world actually works determines how successful we can be.

The next section examines what this new way of looking at the world will mean for understanding how much money our entrepreneur is making.

---

**WORKED EXAMPLES OF HOW DIFFERENT AMOUNTS IN THE FUTURE CAN HAVE THE SAME PRESENT VALUE**

Imagine you have $100 (or $100m) to invest, and have selected a bank account that pays 10 percent interest per year for up to five years. If you decide to invest it, the money you get back will be $10 (or $10m) per year for each year that you leave the money invested, with $110 in the last year.

You can either keep the $100 today, or invest it for 1, 2, 3, 4, or 5 years and get back $10 each year, plus our original investment back at the end.

We can summarize this into a table:

| YEAR: | 0 | 1 | 2 | 3 | 4 | 5 |
|---|---|---|---|---|---|---|
| Having | $100 | | | | | |
| is the same as | $0 | $110 | | | | |
| and the same as | $0 | $10 | $110 | | | |
| and the same as | $0 | $10 | $10 | $110 | | |
| and the same as | $0 | $10 | $10 | $10 | $110 | |
| and the same as | $0 | $10 | $10 | $10 | $10 | $110 |

---

[1]Double-entry bookkeeping, the core of modern accounting, was invented in Venice around 1200–1300 A.D. The date is vague because the first book on the subject was not published until 1494, two years after Columbus sailed to America, and around fifty years before Copernicus (1543) showed that the earth orbits the sun.

To check that the present value of each row is exactly $100 we can use the formula for calculating present values:

$$PV = \frac{FP}{(1 + i)^n}$$

The present value (the equivalent value today) is equal to the amount of the future payment (FP), divided by the interest rate factor according to the number of years into the future that the payment will be made.

You can check for yourself that this gives the following table of present values:

| YEAR: | 0 | 1 | 2 | 3 | 4 | 5 |
|---|---|---|---|---|---|---|
| Having. . . . . . . . . . . . . . . . . . . . . . . $100 | | | | | | |

is the same as

| | | | | | | |
|---|---|---|---|---|---|---|
| Present Values: . . . . . . . . . . . . . . . . . $0 . . . . $100 | | | | | | |
| Present Values: . . . . . . . . . . . . . . . . . $0 . . . . . $9.1 . . . . $90.9 | | | | | | |
| Present Values: . . . . . . . . . . . . . . . . . $0 . . . . . $9.1 . . . . . $8.3 . . . . $82.6 | | | | | | |
| Present Values: . . . . . . . . . . . . . . . . . $0 . . . . . $9.1 . . . . . $8.3 . . . . . $7.5 . . . . $75.1 | | | | | | |
| Present Values: . . . . . . . . . . . . . . . . . $0 . . . . . $9.1 . . . . . $8.3 . . . . . $7.5 . . . . . $6.8 . . . . $68.3 | | | | | | |

To check that the total present value of each row is exactly $100, start at the bottom right-hand corner and work backwards: $68.3 + $6.8 = $75.1. Then $75.1 + $7.5 = $82.6, and so on.

Notice how the further into the future any given amount occurs (whether $10 or $110), the less it is worth to us in today's terms. For example, $110 in one year's time is worth $100 today, whereas $110 in five years is worth only $68.3 today.

**INTERNAL RATE OF RETURN**  We already know that, after investing $1,000 upfront in a hot dog stand, the entrepreneur expected his business to generate net *cash* each year of $6,600. And we know that from a profit and loss point of view the resulting profit might be anywhere from $6,000 to $6,500 (because of the different depreciation amounts). Let's see how a time-value approach would look at this.

If we work out the present value of $6,600 per year over the next five years using the 10 percent interest rate, we can find the present value of all the returns from the business. (For details, see the "Present Values of Entrepreneur's Cash Flow" box.) Subtracting the $1,000 present value of the initial investment, we find that the *net* present value of the entrepreneur's business is $24,019.

In other words, by investing $1,000 in the business today, we expect to generate future cash flows that are the equivalent of $24,019 invested at 10 percent interest.

This is why it makes sense to borrow the money!

But the entrepreneur did not have the option to borrow at 10 percent interest —the rates he was offered were 14 percent, 17 percent, and 30 percent. The same box shows that at those rates the business would be equivalent to, or worth, $21,658, $20,116, or $15,075, respectively. *The value of the business depends on the equivalent rate of interest at which it is expected to generate cash flows for investors.*

**PRESENT VALUES OF ENTREPRENEUR'S CASH FLOWS AT DIFFERENT BORROWING RATES**

| | YEAR: 0 | 1 | 2 | 3 | 4 | 5 |
|---|---|---|---|---|---|---|
| Invest | ($1,000) | | | | | |
| In order to get back | $6,600 | $6,600 | $6,600 | $6,600 | $6,600 | $6,600 |
| Present Values at **10%** | ($1,000) | $6,000 | $5,455 | $4,959 | $4,508 | $4,098 |
| Net Present Value* | **$24,019** | | | | | |
| Present Values at **14%** | ($1,000) | $5,789 | $5,078 | $4,455 | $3,908 | $3,428 |
| Net Present Value* | **$21,658** | | | | | |
| Present Values at **17%** | ($1,000) | $5,461 | $4,821 | $4,121 | $3,522 | $3,010 |
| Net Present Value* | **$20,116** | | | | | |
| Present Values at **30%** | ($1,000) | $5,077 | $3,905 | $3,004 | $2,311 | $1,778 |
| Net Present Value* | **$15,075** | | | | | |
| Present Values at **100%** | ($1,000) | $3,300 | $1,650 | $825 | $413 | $206 |
| Net Present Value* | **$5,394** | | | | | |
| Present Values at **660%** | ($1,000) | $868 | $114 | $15 | $2 | $0 |
| Net Present Value* | **$nil** (The PV of future sales & costs exactly balance the PV of the investment.) | | | | | |

*Note: Net Present Value = the sum of the present values of future cash flows generated by the business, minus the present value of the investment.

There are several other points worth noticing.

First is that each amount of $6,600 is worth less today (its present value is lower) the further into the future it occurs. This means that it *makes sense* for stock markets to have a relatively short-term view—a million dollars of revenue this year is worth more than a million dollars in two or five years' time.

Second, notice how the present values fall faster as the interest rate increases. The higher the interest rate, the truer it becomes that "a bird in the hand is worth two in the bush." The higher the interest rate, the more sense it makes to have a short-term view.

Thirdly, we see that the higher the interest rate, the lower the net present value of the business. (This is part of the reason why stock market prices generally fall when interest rates go up: investors use a higher interest rate or "discount" rate in their net present value calculations, because they can now earn higher returns elsewhere. Combine that with the lower sales that business expects when its customers have to spend more money on interest payments, and interest rate rises hit share prices with a double whammy.)

The net present value of the enterprise is still greater than zero at interest rates of 14 percent, 17 percent, and 30 percent, which means that it would still be worthwhile for the entrepreneur's to borrow money at those rates. In fact, as the table shows, it would still be worth his while—the enterprise would still *make money*—if he borrowed the $1,000 at 100 percent interest.

If we want to find the interest rate at which it would no longer be worth borrowing money to finance the business, we need to find the rate at which the *net present value* becomes *zero*.

This turns out to be 660 percent. At this rate the cash generated by the business ($6,600 per year) *only just* covers the interest repayments on the $1,000 investment. So the cash generated by the business is exactly *equivalent* to the $1,000 investment. At any interest rate higher than 660 percent the business will no longer *make money*.

So, the business is effectively generating a rate of interest—a "rate of return" on the invested $1,000—of 660 percent. This rate is known as the "internal rate of return" or IRR.

It looks as if we have found a way to answer the two questions we asked earlier and define not only *whether* a business is making money, but also *how much* money it is making:

- A business is *making money* if the effective interest rate that it generates is greater than the interest rate that it pays on the money tied up in the business.[2]

- *How much* money the business makes is defined by the internal rate of return. This is not a number of dollars per year, like the profit figure, but a *percentage return* per year on the money that is invested in the business.

We can put all this into our diagram, as follows:

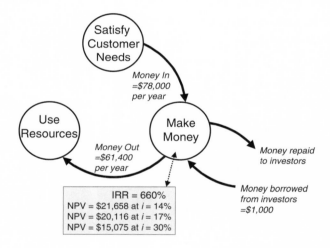

A business *makes money* if the net *rate* at which its service generates cash is greater than the *rate* it repays cash to lenders and investors.

---

[2]Note that at this stage we are not making any differentiation between money lent to business by banks and money invested in the business by stockholders and shareholders.

> ### INVESTOR CONFIDENCE IS WHAT MAKES OR BREAKS BUSINESSES
>
> The time value of money shows us that, ultimately, lenders and investors will always be willing to put cash into a business *if* they believe that they will get back the return they want at *some point* in the future.
>
> This is what funds start-ups: the confidence that negative cash flows today will turn into strong positive cash flows tomorrow. And this is also why businesses fail—not because they had a bad year, but because no investor can be found who believes that the business will one day give them the return they want to make on the money that needs to be put in today.
>
> The ultimate financial risk, then, to any business is *investor confidence*: confidence that customers will continue to buy the business's service(s), and that competitors will not render its way of using resources obsolete.
>
> If those two parts of the business are strong, then investor confidence should also be strong, and the business can continue.

*THE SHAREHOLDER VALUE APPROACH*  So far we have realized that:

i)  cash flows have a different value depending on *when* they occur

ii)  the way to compare them is to calculate their *present value,* and

iii)  the rate at which the business is generating a return on the money invested in it is given by the internal rate of return: the rate at which the present value of all future cash flows becomes equal to the present value of the money invested

Now we are going to use this way of thinking to show us how much the business is worth to different investors.

We know that on day one the business owns a single asset worth $1,000. But we also know that the entrepreneur has found a way to work that asset to generate $6,600 cash per year.

The earlier box, "Present Values of Entrepreneur's Cash Flows," shows that this is equivalent to investing $15,075 in a bank at 30 percent interest per year. So, people who want to generate a return of at least 30 percent on their investment would be willing to invest up to $15,075 in the business. In other words, for them, the business would be worth up to $15,075. (If they could buy it for less, then the return they earn would be higher than 30 percent.)

Someone who wanted to earn a 17 percent return on his or her money would be willing to invest up to $20,116.

Someone who wanted to earn a 14 percent return on his or her money would be willing to invest up to $21,658.

In all cases, *the value of the business is equal to the net present value of its future cash flows* at the chosen interest rate, or "discount" rate, as it is known.

If we change the size or timing of the future payments, or the level of discount rate, then the present value of the business will change.

All this is called the "Shareholder Value Approach."

It is a *pure financial/mathematical approach* that involves no need for human opinions or discussions about depreciation/amortization, accruals, and deferrals.

*Mathematically* the value of the business today is *exactly equal* to the net present value of the cash flows it will create, into and out of the business.

This forward-looking approach is in direct contrast to the backwards-looking approach of profit and loss.

Under the profit and loss approach, the value of the business today is equal to the sum total of all the profits (and losses) it has accumulated over the years since the day it was founded. (Those profits are held in the form of the different assets of the business.)

But under the shareholder value approach the business is worth the cash flows that those assets can be used to generate.

A typewriter company may have built up 100 years of profits—but if a rival business invents the word processor, then sales of typewriters will fall, and the value of the typewriter business will fall ... not because its assets are any different from what they were before, but because the size of the *expected future cash flows* are different.

The assets of the business are only useful insofar as they can be used to deliver a service to a customer. And if they can no longer be used to make typewriters (because the customers all want word processors) then the value of the business falls to whatever the individual assets can be sold for. If those assets are cash, then the value is unchanged. If the assets can be used by other businesses to make other services, then they are worth whatever those businesses are willing to pay for them. If the assets can only be used to make typewriters that nobody wants, then their value is zero.

Under the shareholder value approach, *the assets of the company are worth the present value of the cash flows that different businesses can use them to create.*

A business that owns a pile of sand and does nothing with it is worth a pile of sand.

But a business that owns a pile of sand and *combines* it with other resources to make something useful can be worth as much as Pilkington, or Duralex, or Intel.

This is not a book on accounting policy, but it is important to have spent this time looking carefully at what it really means for a business to *make money.* Because the way that we perceive the world determines what we do within it, which then determines the results that we achieve.

If I believe that the Earth is flat (as any fool can see, simply by looking out of the window) then I *know* that there is no point in sailing west from Europe across the Atlantic, because I *know* that I will simply sail off the edge of the world. But if my mental model is that the world is round, then I *know* that by sailing west I might just win fame, fortune, and the love of beautiful women.

And in the same way, if we *truly* understand what it means to *make money,* then we can understand better what the business needs to do in order to make *more money.*

And that is what we shall examine in the next section.

---

### BETTER TO BE APPROXIMATELY RIGHT THAN ABSOLUTELY WRONG

It might seem that although the profit and loss approach is backwards-looking, at least its valuation is based on real historic numbers, rather than predictions about the future. But the figures in a profit and loss account are estimates, too, even though they occurred in the past.

We already know that depreciation/amortization represents an estimated cost. And no business of any size *really* knows how many units of service it has bought or sold. Customers can go bankrupt before they pay. Suppliers can deliver more or fewer widgets than are shown on the invoice. So every company's revenue, inventory, and expense figures are actually also *estimates,* even though they all *look* accurate, and happened in the past.

The only financial reality is the flows of cash into and out of the business.

Valuing a company based on future cash flows may seem to be more difficult than measuring what happened in the past, but in fact companies can get very good at predicting revenues and expenses. Most managers' jobs are about achieving precisely this: agreeing to a future set of results (their targets), and then working to make those results happen. Managers pay a lot of attention to getting this right, because that is what their rewards are based on. Financial markets, in turn, measure the ability of entire corporations to predict and then meet their future results, which is why share prices rise and fall on surprises, and why a share price can remain unmoved when the company announces profits down on last year—because the results match expectations.

Using the profit and loss approach reminds me of the joke about the man who, late one night, found his friend searching for a lost key underneath a streetlight. After helping his friend for a few minutes he asked "Are you sure you dropped it here—I can't see it anywhere." "Oh no," replied the friend, "I lost it over in those bushes." "Then why aren't you searching over there?" "Well, the light's much better here."

Using the profit and loss approach is like searching under the streetlamp because the light is better there.

Whatever the difficulties of the shareholder value approach, it is better to be approximately right than absolutely wrong.

--------

## MAKING IT REAL

- Does your business apply a profit and loss mentality to making money, or does it follow a time value of money approach?
- What about your top two competitors?
- Is the net *rate* at which your firm generates cash greater than or less than the *rate* at which it is repaying cash to lenders and investors?
- What internal rate of return does your firm apply to new contracts with external customers? Does it apply the same criteria to internal projects? Does it alter the IRR to match the risk associated with the activity?

## MAKING MORE MONEY

*ACTIONS TO INCREASE SHAREHOLDER VALUE* So far we have looked at the profit and loss approach to making money and have seen that it depends on people's opinions. Then we understood the time value of money and how it leads to the idea of an internal rate of return. And now we have seen how to use that to calculate the net present value or shareholder value of the business.

In this final section we are going to look at what actions a business can take to increase its value—in other words, to make more money—and how it can turn skill at those actions into a source of strategic business advantage.

Under the profit and loss approach there are just two ways to make more money: increase revenues, or decrease expenses. The third approach, as we have seen, is to use the accounting rules to change the profit figure. But this just changes the value of a number on a piece of paper—it does not alter the value being provided to customers, the price they are paying, or the total cost of using resources.

Under the shareholder value approach, the (net present) value of the business is equal to the present value of future cash flows, minus the amount of money invested in the business:

$$\text{NPV} = \text{PV} - \text{Investment} = \frac{\text{FP}}{(1 + i)^n} - \text{Investment}$$

This means that there are *just four ways* in which any business can increase its value. That is, there are just four ways in which any business can make more money. They are:

1. Increase the net *size* of future cash flows (that is, improve "FP" in the equation)
2. Improve the *timings* of future cash flows (reduce "n" in the equation)
3. Reduce the amount of *money invested* in the business (reduce "Investment")
4. Reduce the interest *rate repaid* to lenders/investors (reduce "$i$")

We can see how these relate to practical actions and cash flows in the real world by adding them to our diagram of the business:

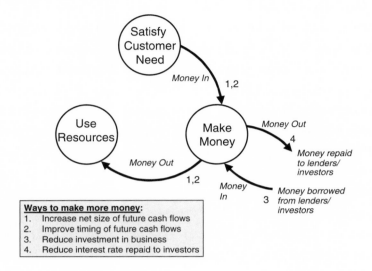

There are two sets of money coming into the firm. One is called revenue and comes from customers in return for the services they receive from the business. The other is called capital and comes from lenders and investors in return for certain rights and repayments that we shall discuss in a moment.

There are also two sets of money going out of the business. One is called expenses, and is paid to employees and suppliers. The other is called interest or dividends and is paid to lenders and investors.

It is the balance between these two sets of money coming *in* and going *out* that determines whether or not the firm is *making money.*

Let's examine them one by one, to understand the precise actions the business can take to make more money, and how to turn them into strategic advantage.

*MANAGING REVENUES AND EXPENSES* The first two ways to make more money have to do with managing revenues and expenses.

The first action is to increase the net size of future cash flows, which means either increasing revenues and/or reducing expenses. This is exactly what the profit and loss approach tells us to do, and depends on actions taken in the *satisfy customer needs* and *using resources* parts of the business (Chapters 2 and 3).

The way the business converts this ability into strategic advantage is by becoming better at predicting the financial impacts of changes in the *satisfy customer needs* and *using resources* parts of the firm. The more accurately the business is able to predict the costs and benefits that will come from different courses of action, the better it can plan, and the better it will be able to create the results it wants. Skill here comes simply from gaining greater experience in these two processes, as discussed in Chapter 3 and in Chapter 6.

Selling more services is no good if the customers never actually pay their bills, so the *second* action is to improve the *timings* of future cash flows. This means getting customers to pay earlier, and paying the business's own suppliers later.

Again, this is closely integrated with the actions taken under the *satisfying customer needs* and *using resources* parts of the business, and depends on the contract terms which the business has with customers and suppliers. The timings of payments can also be improved through activities within the finance function, such as credit control, accounts payable, accounts receivable, and factoring.[3] Care also needs to be taken because pushing too hard to improve cash flows can damage the customer relationship, and delaying payments to suppliers can result in resources being cut off. This is why the three basic activities *together* form the first layer of strategic advantage.

Again, getting good at these activities comes from experience (see Chapters 3 and 6).

Cash flow management is hugely important to almost all businesses, but the profit and loss approach to making money gives us no clue as to why

---

[3]Factoring involves selling customer invoices to a factor company that pays perhaps 80 percent of the face value immediately, chases the customers on your behalf, and pays most of the remainder once the bill has been paid. The business gets good cash flow and can focus on its core business. The factoring company focuses on what it is good at, and is paid a few percent of the invoice value in return for its services. This is a form of the outsourcing described in Chapter 3.

this should be. The time value and shareholder value approaches, on the other hand, make it immediately obvious that managing the timing of cash flows does not simply put more money in the bank, but directly impacts the value of the business.

The third and fourth ways to make more money have to do with managing the capital invested in the firm.

REDUCING CAPITAL EMPLOYED   The third way for the business to make more money and increase its value is by reducing the amount of money invested in the firm (in a way that keeps the forecast revenues and expenses the same).

Good cash flow management, as just described, helps contribute to this. Other simple activities could also include:

- reducing the size of stocks and inventories (perhaps by Just In Time manufacturing)
- buying used equipment instead of new (assuming it works just as well)
- selling an asset (such as a warehouse) that is only partially used by the business, and leasing back only the portion that the business actually needs
- closing down factories in expensive countries (such as the USA and Europe) and opening up cheaper ones in Mexico, Eastern Europe, or China

All these items are clearly linked to the *using resources* part of the business, Chapter 3. They are not pure financial activities, merely the financial results of actions taken in the *using resources* part of the firm.

In essence, this approach involves looking at the different resources in which the capital of the firm is invested, to understand which services they are used to provide and what financial returns they generate. In this way the business is divided into a number of different smaller businesses, each with its own resources, and each producing its own internal rate of return, its own return on capital employed.

Each part can then be examined to look for new ways in which those resources might be used to deliver new services: for example, by opening shops in airports and stations, or by selling advertising on the sides of buses and taxis.

Resources that then still produce a return that is lower than the effective interest rate paid by the business can then (potentially) be sold off, and the money either returned to lenders and investors or reinvested in the types of assets that generate the highest returns. In this way the average return produced by the business grows.

Managing the performance of the total firm then becomes a matter of managing its portfolio of different resources (see Chapter 5). Getting strategic advantage from this process is a matter of experience (see Chapters 3 and 6).

One word of caution: changing the mix of services (and resources) not only changes the returns the business generates, but also the risks it takes. This might not be what lenders and investors want, as we shall discuss in the next section.

REDUCING THE RATE AT WHICH CAPITAL IS BORROWED  The fourth and final way to increase the value of the firm is a *pure* financial approach. It does not involve changing the services that the business offers or the resources that it owns or uses. The action is simply to minimize the interest rate at which money is borrowed from (and repaid to) lenders and investors. How is this achieved? By raising the money that the business needs at the lowest rates possible.

There are two main types of capital that can be used to raise money for a business, and these are called debt and equity. Broadly speaking, debt means loans and equity means stocks and shares. Each comes in many different forms, and together they provide an infinite range of possible combinations of risk (to the lender and to the business), ownership and control, size and duration of the loan, and size and timing of repayments to the lender or investor. The different combinations are known as investment instruments.

A detailed discussion of these is beyond the scope of this book. But, in general, the lowest interest rates charged for capital will be the ones that bring the lowest risks to the investor or the lender. This probably means that there is a well-defined repayment schedule, that the size of the amount borrowed is small compared with the size of the business, and that the contract includes the right to sell a specific asset owned by the business if it should fail (i.e., a mortgage). These are characteristics usually associated with loans/debt.

On the other hand, the form of capital that provides fewest *guarantees* of returns (and hence most risk) is equity. So this is generally the form of capital that is most expensive—although a loan to a start-up could easily provide a higher risk, and a higher return, than an equity investment in an established business.

Different investors want different mixes of risk and return from investing their capital in businesses, and there is a huge range of different forms of debt and equity that can be arranged.

There are two ways in which a business in this situation can create strategic advantage by raising money at the lowest rate possible.

The first is simply by being a low-risk business: having a high credit rating. This comes usually from being large or well established, or by operating in a type of business considered to be low risk. Unfortunately (for investors) the apparent risk and actual risk can be very different, as Enron and Barings Bank have shown. But that is the first way to raise money at low rates. It also comes simply from being a well-managed, reliable business, in terms of competence at the activities described in the other chapters of this book.

The second way is to manage the mix of debt and equity that the business uses.

We know that different investors want different mixes of risk and return from investing their capital, and there is a huge range of different forms of debt and equity that can be arranged.

By treating its investors and lenders as customers, the business can apply what we learned in Chapter 2 by:

1. Understanding lender/investor needs

2. Choosing the set of needs that it can best satisfy

3. Managing the "Customer Chain" for lenders and investors

These are the activities of what is known as investor relations, and as we know from Chapter 2, doing them well can bring the business another source of strategic advantage.

The more the business has investors and lenders who want *exactly the mix of risk and reward that it can provide them,* the more the business is creating "Loyal" investors/lenders (see Chapter 2), and so raising its capital at the lowest rates possible.[4]

The box on Bowie Bonds gives an example of this, and Chapter 7 will show us how to identify the mix of risk and reward that best suits different businesses. And, we will then close this chapter with another, final look at our entrepreneur.

---

**BOWIE BONDS**

A classic example of how businesses convert market returns into investment instruments is the so-called Bowie Bonds.

In 1997, Prudential Insurance paid $55m for bonds that promised to pay 7.9 percent interest over ten years. The money to pay that interest was "guaranteed" by sales of music albums—specifically the royalties from 25 albums that David Bowie recorded before 1990.

Why did they do this?

Well, David Bowie is an established artist, and presumably his albums have a fairly good track record of selling a certain number of copies each year. This means that David Bowie, as the owner or "equity" holder of the royalties, can expect a fairly steady and reliable income stream over the ten years. (See the solid line in the diagram below.) The equivalent for any other business would be its market forecast.

By paying $55m to buy these bonds, Prudential Insurance is tapping into that income stream, setting up a reliable supply of cash over the next ten years. (Presumably

---

[4]The best mix of capital for a business also depends on the tax treatments that governments define for different types. Repayments for some types of capital are made from profits *before* tax, whereas others are paid *after* tax has been paid. This effectively makes the first type much cheaper than the second—but that's another story.

this will be useful for paying out against the insurance claims it expects during that time.) At the same time, Prudential also gets to earn a good rate of interest on its money, with a low risk that the repayments will not be met. The risk of default is higher than if they had lent their money to the government, but the interest rate is higher, too: at that time

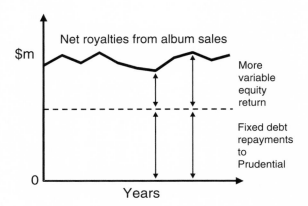

ten-year US Treasury bonds were paying only 6.37 percent. Prudential decided that the extra returns were worth the extra risk.

What David Bowie gets is a loan of $55m in cash without having to wait ten years for it.

He can also be fairly confident that he will have enough royalties coming in each year to cover the repayment schedule.[5]

His downside has two parts. The first is that the volatility of his remaining equity has now increased. What was a fairly steady and reliable stream of royalties has now been split into one part that is absolutely certain (the loan and repayment schedule) and another part that is more uncertain (the royalties that will be left after Prudential has been paid). If he wanted to, Mr. Bowie could probably find another investor willing to buy the rights to these remaining royalties, either as debt or equity. But their relatively high unpredictability means that he would probably either raise too little money or face

---

[5]The fact that the money is in the form of a loan, and not subject to income tax, will also be significant to him, but that is outside the scope of this book.

too high a risk of being unable to meet the payments to make it worth his while. So he continues to own the equity part himself.

The second downside is that he has created a commitment (to Prudential) that he did not have before. Although the probability that he will not be able to keep that commitment is low, it does exist, and if it happened its consequences would be significant.

All of this is precisely what happens in any business, but much simpler.

Any business has a forecast set of revenues and expenses, which will rise and fall depending on the activities of the business, competitors, customers, and so on. Those future cash flows can be sold to investors and lenders (each of whom want different combinations of risk and reward) by issuing different forms of debt and equity instruments.

In David Bowie's case, we can imagine that if he had wanted to raise just $15m, not $55m, then the risk of not meeting the repayments would have been lower, so the interest rate could have been lower also. If he had then decided to raise another $15m, then the risk and the interest rate would have both been slightly higher . . . and the new bond would probably have been bought by a different investor. Another $15m bond would have raised a different amount. And in each case the equity holders effectively own the cash that is left over after the debt interest has been paid.

And as the expected returns from the business change over time, so the risk of not meeting the repayments will change, and the forms of capital that are appropriate will change also. At the same time the mixtures of risk and return available from competing financial instruments in the marketplace will change, and so the relative attractiveness of the risk/returns offered by the business will change again.

Matching the size and timings of future assets and liabilities for a business is called balance sheet management.

--------- **MAKING IT REAL** ---------

How closely does your business manage:

- the size of revenues and expenses?
- the timing of revenues and expenses (cash flow)?
- capital employed?
- rate of interest paid?

Where is the greatest need for improvement?

- What are the key resources in which the capital of your business is invested?

  Which generate higher/lower returns?

  For resources generating low returns, what other businesses would use them more effectively?

  Is it feasible to use the resources in a similar way, or sell them to those businesses?

- Does your business have loyal or fickle investors?

  How could it increase the proportion of loyal investors? Who would they be?

---

*INTEGRATING THE FIRST LEVEL OF STRATEGIC ADVANTAGE* Let's look again at the entrepreneur who wants to buy a hot dog stand.

He knows he has a good business plan. And he knows that although his actual sales and costs and the money he makes will rise and fall over the years—depending on market conditions—the risk that his revenues might one day not cover his costs is low.

But he also knows that the likelihood that *any* of this will happen is currently zero, because he does not have a hot dog stand.

So, he decides take out a loan. The lender sees the business plans, and so knows what the predicted revenues and expenses will be. There is a low probability that the business will be unable to meet the repayments, so the risk to the lender is small, and a low interest rate is agreed.

From the lender's point of view, her sum of cash (which has a 100 percent probability of zero growth unless she lends it to somebody) has been converted into a loan that has a high probability of earning the agreed rate of interest, plus a low risk of being lost altogether. In other words, the lender has exchanged "guaranteed zero growth and no risk" for "probable low growth, and some risk."

From the entrepreneur's point of view, a business plan that has a zero probability of happening (unless it gets funding) has been converted into an opportunity that has a high probability of making him slightly less money than if he'd bought the hot dog stand himself, and a low probability of losing the $1,000 it would have cost him.

Both parties, both people, have exchanged one mix of upside, downside, and probability/risk for another combination *that they value more*.

*A business is a probability and interest rate converter.*

It forms contracts with lenders/investors, customers, and suppliers/ employees. Each contract is a combination of upside, downside, timing, and risk/probability.

Running any successful business is partly about finding a win-win-win overlap and *alignment* between the financial aims of these three sets of stakeholders.

This is what *making money* is all about, and businesses that make this their core activity are called banks.

In this way we see that all three parts that form the first layer of strategic advantage are intrinsically and intimately linked.

A successful business is a successful combination of making money, using resources, and satisfying customer needs. That is the first layer of advantage.

Improving the balance and alignment *between* these activities will add further layers of advantage.

Getting that balance right internally is what we shall look at in Chapter 5, and maintaining it over time is the subject of Chapter 6. Together these form the second layer of advantage.

Getting the balance right in relation to the external environment of the business forms the third layer of strategic business advantage, and is what we shall look at in Chapter 7.

## SUMMARY

A business *makes money* if the net *rate* at which its service generates cash is greater than the *rate* at which it repays cash to lenders and investors.

Despite all the tangled complexity of finance and accounting, there are *just four ways* in which any business can make more money. Accountants, financiers, and experienced businesspeople will know more ways than I have had space to show here for *how* to achieve these things. But *what* needs to be done always boils down to these *four* fundamental things.

The first two are to increase the size and improve the timing of the future cash flows of the business. Both are intrinsically bound up with the skills in *satisfying customer needs* and *using resources,* but they are also supported by a new activity: cash flow management.

The third method is to reduce the amount of capital that is tied up in the firm. Capital released from resources producing low rates of return can either be returned to lenders and investors, or reinvested in resources that produce higher rates of return.

The fourth and final method is to minimize the interest rate at which the business borrows money. This is achieved by becoming a well-managed, low-risk business, which reliably delivers the results it promised. That enables the business to borrow from lenders and investors who want exactly the mix of risk and reward that it can provide.

In these ways, the activities of the first layer of strategic business advantage —satisfying customer needs, using resources, and making money—are separate, and yet are intimately linked and bound up with one another.

And we understand that every successful business is a system that makes money by using resources to satisfy its customer needs.

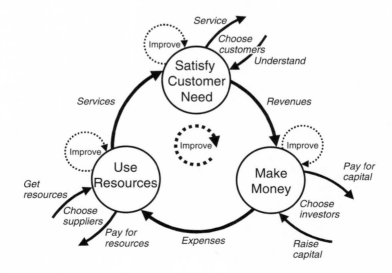

Balancing the three activities together better than competitors will bring further advantages, and this is what we shall look at in the next three chapters.

We begin with Chapter 5, which considers activities that will explicitly balance and align together the three core activities we have reviewed so far.

LAYER 2

# THE LEADERSHIP PERSPECTIVE:
# BALANCING THE SYSTEM

# CHAPTER 5

# *Today . . .*

*Balance is beautiful.*

—MIYOKO OHNO

IN THE FIRST SECTION OF THE BOOK we looked at what a business needs to do to satisfy customer needs, use resources, and make money. Whether that business is a convenience store, an airline, or a hot dog vendor, the same activities always need to get done—it is *how* they get done that varies between the businesses.

This has shown us not only the minimum a business needs to do in each case, enabling us to focus on what matters most, but also how to create the first layer of strategic business advantage.

But what if someone else, a neighbor or someone on the other side of the world, has the same idea and decides to start a business in competition with us? What if they then carry out exactly the same activities in the very same way?

We need a new source of business advantage: the second layer. This will come from being able to balance the three core activities against each other, integrating them to improve the efficiency and effectiveness of the business as a whole. That is what this chapter and the next will look at.

This chapter looks at optimizing the business at a single moment in time ("today").

Chapter 6 looks at optimizing the business over time ("and in the future").

There are, as we have seen, three core processes or activities that make up the first layer of strategic advantage. So there are also three balancing or coordinating activities—one to align each of the three basic processes with the other two.

The first activity involves improving the balance between *satisfying customer needs* and the rest of the business, by actively managing the mix of customer needs that it supports.

The second activity looks at better balancing how resources get used—how the activities of the business get carried out—which is through people. So the second part of the chapter looks at organization structure or design, and how different forms can help or hinder the business in achieving what it needs to do to succeed.

This leads us to the third balancing activity: balancing the priority between *making money* and the rest of the business. Every activity in the business gets done through people. Even if there is intensive use of machinery, it is *people* that drive and optimize that usage. And so it is *people* that determine the final balance between cost and value that every activity in the business achieves. The key tool for balancing making money in the business is therefore the measurement and reward system. It determines the balance at each step between the cost of carrying out an activity and the value it produces for the business.

One final word before we begin. Balance and alignment do *not* mean here a static or unmoving balance, like two weights balanced on a set of scales, or two arguments that cancel each other out. The balance that forms the second layer of strategic business advantage is a *dynamic* balance that changes over time.

Balancing a business is like balancing a bicycle. Without balance you cannot move forward. And the better your balance, the faster you can go and the more fun you can have.

Being able to achieve this balance, aligning the different parts in a way that optimizes the business as a whole, is the point at which *management* becomes *leadership*.

## PORTFOLIO MANAGEMENT:
## THE PARETO CURVE

We know from Chapter 2 that different customers want different things, and that over time this leads the business to offer a mix, or a portfolio, of different services. Each service sells for a different price, costs a different amount to produce, and brings a different amount of money into the business.

The first part of leadership is choosing what mix of customers' needs the business should focus on satisfying.

Let's imagine a business that sells ten services, or groups of services. Some of them will be more popular than others. So if we drew a diagram of the revenue per month or per year that came from each service or group of services, it would probably look something like this:

### Pareto Curve

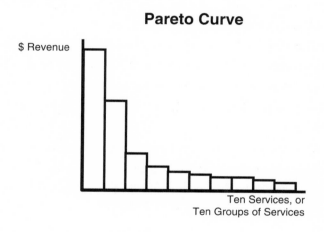

This shape is called a Pareto Curve, after its discoverer, Vilfredo Pareto. He was an Italian economist and sociologist (originally trained as an engineer) who lived from 1848 to 1923. One of the things he was interested in was the distribution of wealth between people in different societies. What he found, in country after country, was that 20 percent of the people owned 80 percent of the wealth. Although he developed complex mathematical formulas to calculate and explain this distribution, his work is most simply summarized as "the 80:20 rule."

This law that he discovered applies to many natural phenomena: 20 percent of tornadoes cause 80 percent of damage, 20 percent of vehicles create 80 percent of pollution, 20 percent of golfers or tennis players win 80 percent of tournaments, and so on.

Although the ratio is not always *precisely* 80:20 (sometimes the tail of the diagram is shorter or longer, in which case the ratios might be 70:30 or 90:10), the rule is useful because it helps us to achieve more with less: it enables us to focus our limited resources where they will have most impact.

If 80 percent of the election result depends on a particular 20 percent of voters/districts/states, then concentrating our energy on that 20 percent will make us more likely to win than if we applied the same effort to each. If I am learning to play jazz trumpet, then memorizing just 20 percent of all possible triads (the major triads) will enable me to play along with about 80 percent of all blues tunes ever written.

We can use this law to help us manage our business mix, to help us find a group of services that gives a better match to the business's customers, resources, suppliers, investors, and lenders.

What we generally find is that 20 percent of services generate 80 percent of sales revenues.

Redrawing the above diagram for a business that offered 100 services, and smoothing the curve, would look something like this:

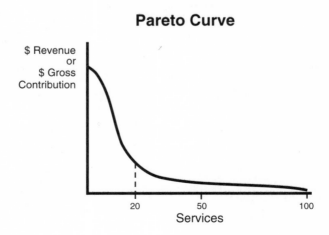

## Pareto Curve

Each of these services has costs or expenses that are *directly* associated with the specific service. (The business also has what are called "indirect" costs, which are shared between services and are often called overheads.) If we subtract the *direct* costs from the revenue for each service, then we have what is called the gross contribution that each service brings to the business. This also follows the Pareto shape: about 20 percent of the services provide 80 percent of the contribution. So the above shape could show the revenue figures or the gross contribution amounts.[1]

This shape comes up remarkably consistently, and I have personally seen it come out of data for the oil, frozen foods, and wholesaling industries. To make a quick check with data from your own business, take a *sample* of one in ten, one in twenty, or even one in 100 services.

I have also seen an example from the IT services industry where *half* of all contracts signed with one key client during a year brought in just *1 percent* extra revenue. This would not have been a problem, except that it costs about the same amount of time and money to sell and sign a contract for $100,000 as is does to sell and sign one for $10m. (It certainly does not cost a hundred times more.)

So, to understand the true financial contribution of each service, we need to understand the indirect or overhead costs of the business. These can be items such as head office costs, the contracts department, finance, human resources, and so on, that do not seem to be directly linked to any one particular service.

But the fact is that these costs *are* directly *generated* by the existence of the service lines. Double the number of services and you need (approximately) twice the number of service line managers. You then need more people in the human resources department, because there are more staff members to recruit, retain, train, and rehire. The finance department will

---

[1]But note that the 20 percent of services that provide 80 percent of revenues are not necessarily the same services that provide 80 percent of the gross contribution.

also have to increase costs to track and analyze sales and expenses for twice the number of services. Double the number of services and you need (approximately) twice the amount of market research. Call centers will need to be larger, because there will be a larger number of inquiries and complaints. And so it goes with building space, telephone calls, stationery, heat, light, and so on.

What usually happens to these indirect costs is that they are then *allocated* across all the different service lines in proportion to the gross profit that each one generates. This is shown by the dotted curved line in the diagram below.

The services that generate the largest contribution are arbitrarily assigned the greatest share of the indirect costs, because this seems "fair." The result is that every service line *seems* to have the same percentage net contribution margin; even the small-revenue services *seem* to be making money for the business.

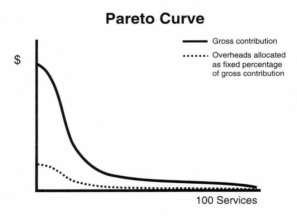

**Pareto Curve**

But this is exactly like the allocation of depreciation/amortization that we saw in Chapter 4. It is arbitrary. *Reality* is that it costs about the same amount of money to sell and sign a contract for $100,000 as is does to sell and sign one for $10m; it costs *about* the same amount of money to manage or carry out market research for a top-selling service as it does for a low-selling one. And so a better approximation is that the overhead cost generated by each service is the *same*. That is shown by the *horizontal* dashed line in the next diagram.

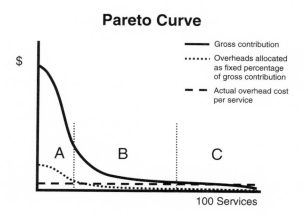

**Pareto Curve**

This means that the top-selling services (A) are actually bringing much *more* money into the business than we thought, while the low-selling ones (C) are making little or no contribution.

*FINANCIAL TRIAGE*  We can now divide the services that the business provides into three main groups:

- Services that lose money, or nearly do (C)
- Services that make much more money for the business than was realized (A)
- Services that bring a small financial contribution to the business (B)

A business consisting solely of the services in category C would be loss-making: it has around 5 percent of the gross contribution of the total business and 40 percent of its indirect costs (since it has about forty out of 100 services).

A business that only offers the services in category B would be moderately profitable, with around 15 percent of the contribution of the original business and 40 percent of the indirect costs.

And a business that provided only the services classed as category A would be very profitable indeed, with around 80 percent of the contribution of whole business and only 20 percent of the overhead costs (twenty out of 100 services).

This does not mean that the business should automatically cut all category B and C services. Some customers may buy their category A services from this business explicitly because they value the ability to buy all services in all three groups from the same place. In this case category C services act as a kind of marketing expense for the business, and cutting them would reduce category A sales as well.

But by understanding how the different services *truly* generate costs within the business (not just allocating costs according to revenues or gross contribution) a very different picture of financial performance then emerges. That is then the first step to improving the overall business mix, and hence to improving the overall business.

As we know from earlier chapters and will learn further in Chapter 7, different businesses need to place a different emphasis on the three core processes of satisfying customer needs, using resources, and making money. But as an example, we could use this simple triage analysis as a way to improve the business mix in the following three ways.

The first priority is almost certainly to *reduce* the prices of services in category A. This may seem surprising, but we now know that these services are making far more money than we realized before, so cutting prices would still make more money for the business than we believed before. And it would also *strengthen the strategic core* of the business that these high-selling services represent. By (carefully) reducing prices in this category, customer loyalty can be increased in the key services that matter most, and market share can be taken from competitors. This leads to further cost savings through the experience curve effects described in Chapter 3, improving financial performance again.

The second priority would be to cut services in category C. As long as cost-generation has been understood properly, these services offer the business the chance to significantly reduce costs while losing very little revenue. To achieve this the business needs not only to stop providing the services, but also to take active steps to remove the costs associated with them.

Managers can often be resistant to the idea of cutting their services, even loss-making ones, and category C *may* well include the star performers of tomorrow. But although price increases and new ways of delivering the service may be suggested as alternative steps, these still divert resources and management time to services that are not core to the business. So the question always has to be asked "Will this really bring more value to the business than applying the same resources elsewhere?" and "Why was this not done before?"

The third priority is category B, and the preferred action for services in this category is probably to do nothing, at least at first.

Some category B services might have the potential to move into category A, but that will only become important once competitors are also successfully managing categories A and C. Category B services can also help to accelerate Experience Curve effects (Chapter 3), which we know will be important in creating self-reinforcing business advantage.

This approach can be applied not only to the services that the business sells, but also to the customer groups that it sells *to*, and the different channels (customer chains) that it sells *through*. In effect these are just different ways of slicing up the underlying customer needs that the business is servicing.

## THE BALANCED BUSINESS

Chapter 7 will show us how the priority that needs to be placed on each of the three core functions—satisfying customer needs, using resources, and making money—varies for businesses operating in different parts of the economy. But the ideal business might balance its three core functions by managing its portfolio in the following way.

It would start from a strong core of category A services. These provide a lot of value to a lot of customers, and the experience that the business gains from delivering them enables it to become very efficient at using the resources involved. As a result, the business can make a lot of money.

But category A is a small number of services, so this still leaves a lot of customer needs unfulfilled. The business can greatly increase its appeal to customers by providing services in category B. These do not make as much money for the business, but if they use some of the same resources as category A then they can both benefit from and contribute to the Experience Curve effects. They also help to prevent competitors from becoming strong.

In a well-managed business the only services in category C are experiments: new service lines or product launches that are expected to move into category B or A, but which are rapidly axed if they do not perform according to expectations. Or they can be a form of marketing, bringing in more customers for the services in category A.

- Of the services or groups of services in your business, how many are in each category—A, B, and C?
- What is your total revenue under each of the categories?
- How big is the indirect expense that is allocated between the services?

  How does that compare with the total profit or free cash flow of the business?

  What method is currently used to allocate this cost to different services?
- What would be the effect on financial performance if the costs of, say, a quarter of the services in category C could be removed?
- What would be the effect on sales if prices for category A services were reduced to reflect their actual overhead costs?
- What mix or ratio of services in categories A, B, and C would best suit your business?

## ORGANIZATION STRUCTURE/DESIGN

The second core function is *using resources,* and the way that every activity of using resources gets carried out within the business is through people.

The way that leadership affects this is through leadership style, and the way that this is encapsulated is in organization structure and design. This covers not only the management reporting structure, but also "soft" factors such as culture and style: "The way we do things around here."

This section looks at different types of organization structure and how they can make it easier or more difficult to carry out each of the activities that the business needs to succeed. It looks at how organization design can enable the business to use resources in a way that is more effective at satisfying customer needs, more efficient at making money, or more adaptable at changing over time.

The best design is whatever helps to achieve the particular combination of *making money, using resources,* and *satisfying customer needs* activities that the individual business needs to accomplish. This means that there is no single ideal organization structure that is best for all businesses. And that structure will change over time as business conditions change.

Imagine we have a business for which we have defined the core activities that bring the first layer of strategic advantage. Now we want a group of people to implement those actions. If we had a "telepathic organization," where everybody knew exactly what needed to get done and the part they each needed to play, then we wouldn't need an organization structure: all the right things would simply happen.

This may seem completely hypothetical, but colonies of ants and bees operate like this. Each insect has its own role: there are no performance reviews, no pay increases, no management review meetings, promotions, or hierarchies. Each colony simply goes about its business of making more colonies by using its resources to add value in the ecosystem,[2] today and in the future. The need for organization has been replaced by instinct.

Unfortunately, or perhaps fortunately, human beings are not like that. We cannot operate telepathic organizations. So the business needs to add a

---

[2]We all know the useful roles that bees play in pollination, making honey, beeswax, and so on. The roles that ants perform, including enriching and aerating the soil, are perhaps even more important, and we are less aware of them mainly because we have not found ways to harness them directly to our own benefit. The parallels between business and nature will be extended in the Epilogue.

further activity, called management or organization, in order to get things done. This adds cost to the business, compared with the telepathic ideal, as well as distortion and delays in communication and in making decisions.

So, before continuing with this section, let's remind ourselves what an organization is for—only then will we be able to judge what makes a good one and what makes a bad one.

Organization structures are needed for several reasons. First, to communicate what needs to get done, because people are not telepathic. Second, to help to make it happen, because (unlike ants) people do not always do what needs to be done, even if they know what it is. And this leads to the third role, which is to measure the results of what has been done, as well as gather information about the wider world. Finally, as the business situation changes over time, the fourth role is to choose between alternative courses of action—here the organization structure determines not only who it is that makes these decisions, but also what information they have when they do so.

This cycle then repeats, and so the four roles of organization are:

- to *decide* what needs to be done
- to *communicate* what needs to be done
- to *implement* what needs to be done, and
- to *measure* what has been done, as well as what others are doing.

A good organization design will be one that matches the relative priorities of these four roles *to suit the particular business,* whilst at the same time introducing as little as possible of the downsides: namely cost, information distortion, and delay.

So the first challenge of a good organization structure is to enable the business to get done what needs to get done.

This changes over time, and so the second challenge is to change what needs to get changed.

And all of this takes place within a particular cultural context. It depends on the skills, attitudes, and psychologies of the people involved. (The head of product development at Google, for example, once had *160* engineers reporting *directly* to him.) And it depends on the vital intangibles we call management approach or leadership style.

We can therefore summarize the three challenges of organization as being:

- getting done what needs to get done
- changing what needs to be changed
- managing the "human factors"

Once again, there is no one best solution to this problem—only what seems like a thousand "good enough" combinations within a zillion possibilities.

What does all this mean for our hot dog entrepreneur?

*FOUR SIMPLE MODELS OF ORGANIZATION* For the hot dog entrepreneur, the organization structure is simple: there is only one person and he does everything.

This *is* the telepathic organization described above. All decisions are automatically taken in the fullest possible knowledge within the business of what the situation is, what the objectives are, and what it's going to take to implement any decisions—there is no other person in the business who knows a critical piece of information that the decision-maker does not.

This gives the business strength in its ability to make decisions and change. But the weakness of this structure is that the entrepreneur is less good at some activities than he is at others, so some parts of the business will not be carried out as well as they might be. (Human factors in the one-person organization reduce to the psychology and motivations of the individual entrepreneur.)

Every organizational form has its own strengths and weaknesses in relation to the three key challenges of doing, changing, and managing the human factors. And as a way to discuss how different forms can optimize different parts, and so might be suitable for businesses in different situations,

I want to look now at four standard models of organization, adapted from Charles Handy's 1976 book *Understanding Organizations.*

As we look at how the entrepreneur's business might grow and evolve through these four types, remember that how well the organization performs against the three key challenges will depend not only on the way in which the particular organization works, but also on the quality of the decisions that the business makes.

Those decisions, in even the largest global corporation, will be made by people: leaders with individual strengths and weaknesses, just like the entrepreneur.

How good their decisions are will depend on:

- how well they understand the *situation*
- how well they understand the *aims* of the organization, and
- how well they understand the *implications* of their decisions: what it will take to successfully implement their decisions, as well as what the unexpected results might be.

The organization structure can help with this by bringing the right information to them in the right form at the right time. Or it can hinder it.

But ultimately the decision-makers will also need to hold all of this information in their heads. That means that the best leaders will be the ones who can hold a "map" in their heads of all the most important features of how their business works. That map will need to combine breadth and depth, but it also needs to be simple so that they can communicate it, and their decision-making, to other people.

A structure for that map is what this book provides.

***THE POWER CULTURE*** As his business grows, the entrepreneur will probably want to hire people to work for him. He might want them to operate more hot dog stands or manage the finances, deal with suppliers, conduct market research, or come up with new product ideas. Whatever roles he wants them to take on, it is likely that initially he will want them to operate as a tight-knit team, while he retains close control of everything they do. We could draw this organization structure as a spider web, with the spider, or entrepreneur, in the middle:

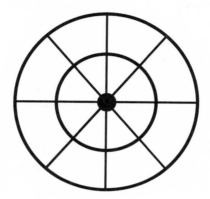

This is called the "power culture." The entrepreneur is at the center of the web, and has direct links to all the people in his organization. The different strands that radiate from the center are the different groups of activities that need to be carried out (sales, purchasing, finance, and so on). People closer to the center of the web have more day-to-day contact with the entrepreneur. The business is still small enough that everyone can talk to everyone else, and direction clearly comes from one place.

Effectively, this structure separates the roles of the organization—the center *makes* the decisions, the outer rings *implement* them, the strands communicate the decisions and measure the results.

This reduces the total decision-making capacity of the organization (to just one person), but *increases* its focus and alignment. Because all relevant information is channeled into the head of the person at the center, the decisions made are always based on good overview of the different aspects of the situation, and therefore are more likely to be consistent with one another. This makes the power culture good at both doing what needs to be done, *and* at changing what needs to be changed. (The inevitable tension between the two is automatically balanced as part of the decision-making process.)

The strength of businesses with a power culture is therefore that they can be focused, fast-moving, and adaptable. But the fact that all the information is in the head(s) of the one or few people at the center is also a weakness. Effectively those key individuals *are* the business. When they succeed the business succeeds. But when they leave or die or their mental map of the world does not match reality, then the business fails also.

Under this organizational form the human factors are handled by treating everyone in the business as subordinate to the person at the center. Whether this works depends on the cooperation (explicit or implicit) of the people in the outer rings. In the 19th century the British Empire was able to rule 250 million Indians with fewer than 100,000 soldiers and administrators. But in general this kind of organization structure is most likely to be found in smaller businesses, or in businesses where there is a low amount of change and/or complexity in *how* things get done (leaving the center able to decide *what* needs to get done).

*THE ROLE CULTURE* As the entrepreneur's business grows, so the number of people within it grows. Part of the benefit of coming together as an organization, rather than working as individuals, is that people can do what they do best, or what they enjoy the most (which is usually the same thing). As people focus on doing their own job well, so they tend to spend more time with the people they can learn most from—the people in similar roles. This is good for the business as it increases efficiency, but as people become more specialized they lose the overview of what is happening in the total business, and how it is the three core functions working *together* that create success.

When the business grows to the point where the entrepreneur can no longer keep track of everything, formal management structures and reporting lines reinforce this trend. This leads to the creation of formally separate business activities or functions such as marketing, finance, human resources, and operations. Where there used to be a single, integrated business there is now specialization and differentiation.

This way of organizing is called the "role culture," and is drawn like the diagram shown on the next page.

Instead of just a single, central source of power, there are now several: one for each of the business functions. These are the pillars of the temple.

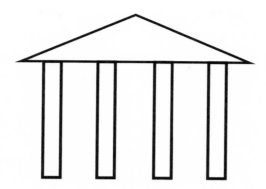

The overall coordination and direction of the business still requires a cross-functional view, which is contained in the roof of the temple. This is the executive board, a team of leaders from each of the different functions, the only part of the business that contains the cross-functional information necessary to be able to direct change in the business. (The entrepreneur now sits at the apex of the roof.)

The amount of power that each function has will broadly depend on the degree to which activities in that function bring competitive advantage to the business (see Chapter 7). This effectively means that different columns have different sizes, and different businesses will certainly have different numbers of columns. (In some businesses, for example, sales and marketing will be separate columns; in others they will be combined.) The organization chart for this business would duplicate the picture above: reporting lines would be in clearly defined functions and information would mainly flow up and down within the functional hierarchies, only crossing between functions at the top.

This is very similar to the power culture, except that there is now a team at the center instead of an individual, and the links between the different strands (now functions) have been cut. In fact, you can convert this temple back to the web shape by imagining that the "roof" shrinks down to a single point and that the columns roll around so that they all radiate from the center.

The strength of this organizational approach lies in its functional specialization, which brings greater efficiency and effectiveness to each part of the business. In theory, strong parts make for a strong whole, but if they are not coordinated well, if they are not *balanced,* then the business as a whole can be weaker. Whether that happens depends on the cooperation of the team at the top. But functional specialization tends to build career paths that remain within a single function. As a result the team members have a limited understanding not only of how the other functions work, but also of how to coordinate them to make the *business as a whole* successful. If this happens, then the focus of the top team will tend to be less on driving the business as an integrated whole, and more on responding to individual functional "fires," because that is what they understand.

The weakness of this organization, therefore, lies in responding to change. Successful change requires the ability to coordinate the total business, not just individual activities. If senior managers are pure specialists in their own functions then they will inevitably find it difficult to understand or communicate with other members of the top team, no matter how hard they try to work together.

*THE TASK CULTURE* The integration and alignment of the whole business can be improved by pushing the cross-functional view back down into the organization, so that managers at lower levels learn to balance more than one viewpoint at the same time.

This adds cost and delay (since it is more difficult to balance two views than just one), but it creates a more robust organization, one that is better placed to face simultaneous change on multiple fronts. It also produces senior managers who reach the top with previous experience of what it takes to balance the different needs of the whole business on a smaller scale.

The way to achieve this is by dividing the business up into several smaller businesses, or business units, and aligning people in all levels of the functional organization to support one or more of those specific units.

We can draw this by taking the functional columns of the temple in the role culture and adding a set of horizontal lines that represent the business units. The total organization now has the form of a matrix or net:

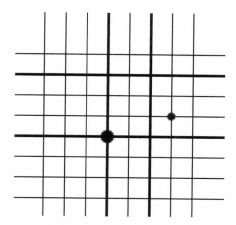

Each of the vertical lines is a business function, as before: marketing, finance, operations, and so on. People who work in the same vertical line share information and tools in order to improve the efficiency and effectiveness of that function, just as in the role culture.

Each of the horizontal lines is a business unit, and contains all the functions needed to run a successful business. (That business might, for example, be a part that is focused around a particular set of services, a particular group of customers, or a particular geography.) People who work in the same horizontal line bring their different skills together to achieve a common goal.

Where two lines meet, the person or team is being asked to carry out a particular activity or task in support of a particular goal. Hence Charles Handy calls this the task culture.

The roof of the temple is not shown, but continues to exist and now stretches around two sides of the organization. Again, the different threads of the organization will have different degrees of importance and power within the organization. A highly customer-oriented business would tend to show stronger horizontal alignments than vertical ones. Sometimes, as shown here, there will be groups from both sides that have more power, probably representing the key customer groups and whichever internal activities are most important to the business. As customers' needs change, and as the activities the business needs to be good at change, so the organization will experience changes in the balance of power (which will probably lag behind the changes in the external environment).

For our entrepreneur's growing business this form of organization might mean, for example, that a manager from one functional area (vertical line—"purchasing") is assigned to support a particular geographic area (horizontal line—"Midwest"). Or it could mean that someone responsible for running one key activity ("hiring") is assigned to a part of the business that focuses on a particular group of customers ("corporate events").

Combining viewpoints in this way strengthens the business by placing cross-functional balance deep within the organization.

The weakness of this structure is that as the organization grows, it becomes more and more difficult to maintain a clear focus. Each business unit has a different focus, and so has different support needs from, say, the finance or the marketing functions. The efficiency and effectiveness of these functions is then reduced, because they are being asked to do multiple things, and compromise means that none of them gets what they want.

The performance of the individual business units may still be better (which, after all, is what matters) but as the customer needs of different units diverge, the business finds it harder to balance the competing viewpoints. And if "doing what needs to be done" becomes harder, then so does "changing what needs to be changed": should decisions be optimized to benefit a particular business unit (horizontal line), a specific function (vertical line), or the corporation as a whole? It may even become harder to judge which outcome would produce which result. (For more on the relative priorities of different functions in different marketplaces, and on balancing efficiency and effectiveness, see Chapter 7.)

One solution to this problem is to bring more information to the decision-maker, which means involving more people in the decision, and leads naturally to the endless telephone conference calls that we all know so well. Since it is impossible to know in advance what information is going to be useful (if we did, the meeting would already have taken place) the result often seems to involve too many people, rather than too few. But the value of these calls also lies in building the shared knowledge and understanding that replaces central directives in the task culture, building cross-functional robustness deep into the business. In other words, conference calls solve the human factors challenge.

*THE PERSON CULTURE, OR NETWORK CULTURE* The task culture is a step back closer to the holistic viewpoint of the original entrepreneurial organization, but retains at least some of the functional optimization that the role culture brought to the business.

But as people try to balance the different priorities they are asked to maintain and as they talk to other people who are doing the same, so the functional and business-line alignments within the organization become weaker and more blurred. The question arises, "Is my primary focus and loyalty to my function, my business unit, the corporation, or to myself, my career?" The degree to which this is felt will be different for different people in different parts of the organization. But for some, the organization structure dissolves, and we are left simply with a network of individuals.

Charles Handy draws this as a cluster or galaxy of individual stars (he does not draw the lines that I have shown to link individuals) and gives examples of architects, families, and small consultancies as organizations that typically operate in this way:

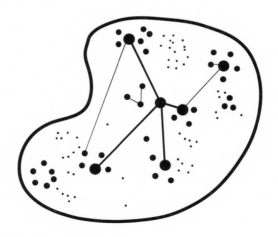

© *CHARLES HANDY*

Film or television producers would also find this a useful way to think about organization. They have a project that they want to accomplish, and doing so involves a wide variety of people in a wide variety of roles. They need make-up people to do make-up, lighting people to do lighting, writers to write, directors to direct, actors to act, and so on.

Two other groups of people who place themselves *explicitly* in the role of acting as hubs in the network are agents and headhunters.

The organization chart for a business that operates like this may show little relation to reality—people's influence depends less on their position on the organization chart, and more on their position in the informal networks that determine what actually gets done.

In a sense we have now returned to our starting point, the individual entrepreneur. But now there are many entrepreneurs, and instead of the whole world as their marketplace, each individual now has the corporation as an "internal marketplace" for his or her skills.

*PULLING IT ALL TOGETHER* Each of the above models of organization summarizes a complex combination of structure and culture, policies and procedures, politics, psychology, and people. And to an extent, every business probably contains pieces of all four models.

The key idea is that different organizational approaches optimize different things, so the business needs to understand where its priorities lie and choose an approach that supports those objectives. This means that the approach that works best in one part of the business is likely to be different from the approach needed in another. When it comes to organization, one size does not fit all. This is, after all, one of the reasons why we have different businesses, different organizations: *to do different things.*

What matters is that the organization structure/design is something that helps the business to get done what needs to get done and change what needs to change, all within the context of handling the specific human factors.

Interestingly, the research of Christopher Bartlett and Sumantra Ghoshal into what it takes to make a good global manager has tended towards the same conclusions.

Bartlett and Ghoshal carried out "in-depth case studies of more than twenty large worldwide companies," and found that what companies needed was not just one type of individual, but a combination of skills: a "network of specialists."[3]

The four types of managers they discovered and described were:

- *The Country Manager:* "play[s] the pivotal role . . . in meeting local customer needs"

- *The Business Manager:* "further[s] the company's global-scale efficiency and competitiveness"

- *The Functional Manager:* "transfer[s] specialized knowledge while also connecting scarce resources and capabilities across national borders"

- *The Corporate Manager:* "not only leads in the broadest sense . . . [but also] identifies and develops talented business country and functional managers"

The first three clearly match the core activities that form the first layer of strategic business advantage: satisfying customer needs, making money, and using resources. The fourth matches our second layer of advantage, leadership.

| Making money | = | Business manager . . . efficiency and competitiveness |
| By using resources | = | Functional manager . . . transfers knowledge . . . resources |
| To satisfy customer needs | = | Country manager . . . meeting customer needs |
| Today and in the future | = | Corporate manager . . . leads in the broadest sense |

We should not be surprised. We have defined the least a business needs to do to be successful. The simplest way for any business to get that done is just to make one person responsible for each of the activities, to turn each activity into a role.

---

[3]"Managing Across Borders," Harvard Business School Press, 1989, and "What Is A Global Manager?" Harvard Business Review, 1992.

The overlap may not seem perfect, but that is because we have come at the answer from different directions. Bartlett and Ghoshal have looked through the lens of what twenty or so specific companies happened to be doing at the end of the 20th century. We have derived from first principles what is the least a business needs to do to be successful.

Bartlett and Ghoshal found that successful global companies needed "country managers." That was because the businesses they studied faced different conditions in different countries: differences, perhaps, in customer needs, distribution channels, financial laws, and/or competition. If they had looked at another set of companies who sold private jets or luxury yachts, for example, they would have found that country managers were less important. These businesses would still need somebody to be responsible for *satisfying customer needs,* but the needs (and the managers responsible) would now vary by region, or by corporate/private clients, rather than by country.

The country manager is a symptom, not a cause, and if Bartlett and Ghoshal had been looking at the USA 100 years ago, they would have been writing not about the new global businesses but about the new *transcontinental* businesses. Instead of having country managers the key idea would have been the need for state managers.

But countries and states are human inventions. Having managers to run them is a symptom, not a cause. And as globalization continues we are likely to find that businesses of the future have as much need for a manager in every country as they do for a manager in every US state today.

The same applies to the other roles, and what matters is that *someone, somewhere* in the organization, is responsible for the activities it takes to make the business successful. *Somebody, somewhere* in the organization, needs to be responsible for *satisfying customer needs,* someone for *using resources,* someone for *making money,* and someone for combining the viewpoints, and *changing over time.*

For some businesses, at some times, it will make sense to assign a separate person to each of these roles. For others, it will make sense to combine two or more roles into a single job.

As any anthropologist will tell you, there is and has been a huge variety of organization types in which human beings can work together successfully. What matters is less what the organization structure or culture is (or how we draw it on a piece of paper), and more that at least *someone, somewhere* is responsible for getting each of the essential activities of the business done.

In order to define the outputs of what each role is and to be able to measure how good a job the individual is doing, the final part of defining *how* a business can get done *what* it needs to get done is to define a system for measurement and reward. That is what we shall look at next.

———— **MAKING IT REAL** ————

- What organization structure(s) do(es) your business officially have?
- What structure(s) reflect(s) the way the organization actually works? (The way that information moves and decisions get made.)
- What priorities does the business have, in terms of efficiency, effectiveness, and adaptability?

  What structure(s) best match(es) those priorities?

  Has the organization structure/design ever prevented the business from achieving what it needed?

- What changes or workarounds, if any, would make it easier for the business to achieve what it needs to?

## MEASUREMENT AND REWARD

Strategic business advantage comes when a business carries out an activity better than its rivals.

What those minimum activities *are* is what this book describes. And as we have seen, "better" can mean providing more value, lower cost, or a combination of both.

"What gets measured gets done," and so the single most important tool that any business has, not only for *defining* the balance of cost and value that it needs, but also for *achieving* that balance, is its measurement and reward system.

This is the third part of leadership: getting people to focus on what really matters.

If the strategy or business plan is to focus on retaining *existing* customers, but sales people are paid commissions for winning *new* ones, then there is going to be a gap between action and intent—between actual strategy and intended strategy. If the customer pays the business based on the number of non-defective *parts per thousand,* but the business pays the manager based on the *total number* of non-defective parts delivered, then again there is going to be a mismatch between what the business needs and what the business gets.

As Lou Gerstner of IBM puts it, "People don't do what you e*x*pect but what you *in*spect."

This section looks at the two parts of measurement and reward, in reverse order: reward first, and then measurement.

REWARD  As we know from Chapter 3, the resources that the business can use to achieve its results are a combination of "internal" employees and "external" suppliers. The approaches used for rewarding each of these are usually thought of as very different, so there is likely to be something that each can learn from the other.

Both employees and suppliers can be paid in terms of the basic *inputs* they provide to the business, or in terms of the *outputs* and results they help the business to create. Input measures might be the number of hours worked or the number of phone calls made. *Output* measures could be the number of new customers signed up, the amount they spend, or the company profits for the year.

But that is not the whole story.

If we think about businesses that buy advertising on the Internet, we know that some simply pay for the ad to appear on a certain page for a certain length of time. Others pay according to the number of people who actually visit the page and *see* the advertisement. Others pay for "click-throughs": the number of people who see the ad and then click through to their own site. And some, including the Amazon.com associate scheme, for example, only pay when the person sees the ad, clicks through, *and actually buys something* during that same visit.

What is happening in each of these different forms of agreement is that the advertising service being bought is bringing the business closer to its final aim: *a customer purchase.*

The closer it comes, the lower the risk to the business, and the higher the reward it can afford to pay the advertiser. This is why companies buy targeted mailing lists: to increase their hit rate.

The same applies to all employees and suppliers.

Movie actors, for example, can receive a fee per day on set (low risk, low reward), a fee per picture, or a share of the box office receipts.

In this way the business has again become a risk and reward converter. But instead of managing the risk between customers and investors, as it did in Chapter 4, this time it acts as an intermediary between those same customers and its suppliers and employees.

As we know from the Maslow hierarchy in Chapter 2, people have a variety of needs, and so money is by no means the only thing that will motivate an employee or supplier to work for the business. A good measurement and reward system will therefore provide a *mix* of rewards that is tailored to suit the individual.

For an employee that might mean flexible working hours, tickets to sporting events, or a cow for their smallholding (as a colleague of mine once received!). For suppliers, these non-money items could include the credibility that comes from being associated with a particular customer, a guaranteed minimum order quantity, or longer contract period.

Not only do these non-money items broaden and strengthen the total value that the employee or supplier gets from working with this particular business, but their value to that employee or supplier can often far outweigh the financial cost to the business of providing them: another example of win-win creating new value in the world.

As in Chapter 2, the maximum that a business will be willing to pay for a service will depend on how much cost and risk remains before that input can be converted into an output for the end customer, as well as how much that end customer is willing to pay.

And, again, the actual price paid will depend on how many other employees/suppliers are available who can provide the same service, or better.

That covers the reward part of measurement and reward. What about measurement?

*MEASUREMENT: THE "BALANCED SCORECARD"* Ultimately, in any business, what gets measured gets done.

W. Edwards Deming, the so-called "father of Total Quality Management," is widely credited as being a key factor behind the Japanese industrial success in the second half of the 20th century. Although his approach goes far beyond mere measurement, the core of it is statistical process control: controlling the outputs of processes by measurement and statistics.

Simplifying greatly, this says that:

1.  In order to be able to improve the outputs of a process you first need to be able to measure those outputs.

2.  The next priority is to standardize the process, to make it reliable, repeatable, and consistent, so that outputs and results are the same every time.

3.  Finally you can adjust the now-reliable process to improve levels of quality to what you want.

4.  Once that has been done, simply repeat the "plan, do, check, act" cycle for continuous improvement.

Deming achieved his success by focusing primarily on Japan's manufacturing processes. These come under Chapter 3, "Using Resources." But all the minimum activities needed to achieve a successful business are processes, and so the approach applies to each of them, as well. And since the total business is a process, it applies to the business as a whole, as well.

In 1992, Robert S. Kaplan and David P. Norton published an article in the *Harvard Business Review* called the "Balanced Scorecard—The Measures That Drive Performance."

Having worked extensively with "twelve companies . . . at the leading edge of performance measurement," the conclusion they came to was that successful companies need to define goals and measures in *four* areas:

- The customer perspective—how do customers see us?
- The internal business perspective—what must we excel at?
- The financial perspective—how do we look to shareholders?
- The innovation and learning perspective—can we continue to improve and create value?

These clearly match *directly* against the four parts of our simple definition of the least a business needs to do to be successful: satisfy customer needs, use resources, make money, and adapt into the future.

In other words, just as with organization structure, what researchers have found to be best practice in the modern world *exactly* matches with what we would expect, with one set of measures for each activity.[4]

This means that it is shortsighted to define the purpose of a business only in terms of making money (see also Chapter 7).

Specific measures that are important to each of the four parts of the business have been discussed in each of the relevant chapters, and are summarized together in the "Sample Scorecard Measures" box.

These measures define the health of any business. But because they are generic they are only a starting point. If everybody measures the same things (because what gets measured gets done) then there is no advantage to be gained. If you want your business to do *better* you need to do *different*, which also means you need to *measure* different.

---

[4]Strictly speaking we would expect to see an extra set of measures covering the activities described in this chapter—but these would be difficult to separate out from the other measures described.

A detailed discussion of this is beyond the scope of this book, but in brief it depends on:

- Focusing on the areas of performance that matter most to the individual business (see Chapter 7)
- Focusing on the key measures that make the difference for your particular business model (see Chapter 3)
- Having the right number of measures: too few and performance in key areas can slip, too many and the business will have difficulty adapting to changing market conditions, as it gets locked into delivering the measures that mattered last year rather than the measures that matter now
- Including "danger signal" or "early warning" measures to monitor events the business wants to avoid (for example, a rise in "churn" rate of customers leaving the business each month might show up long before the actual number of customers changed)

What gets measured gets done, and what the business chooses to measure depends on what its managers believe is important. In other words, it depends on their "mental models." In this way, competition between similar businesses is really about competition between different ways of thinking about the world. And here, having the simplest and most accurate mental model can also bring competitive advantage.

**SAMPLE SCORECARD MEASURES**

The list below covers most of the key points raised in each of the relevant chapters. As is pointed out in the main text, it is important *not* to measure everything, but instead to pick the measures that matter most to the individual business and the part of the economy that it is operating in (see Chapter 7).

1.  Customer Perspective: (Chapter 2)
    - Total revenue (as a measure of the total value received by customers)
    - Market share:
        - Share of customers' total spent on our type of services
        - Share of loyal customers' total spent on our type of services

- Ratio of revenues from loyal and fickle customers
- Percentage of customers classified as "know," "like," "use," and "trust"
- Cost to move a customer from one group to another
- Numbers of services and percentage of sales from services in the different life-cycle phases of introduction, growth, maturity, regeneration, and decline

2.  Internal Business Perspective: (Chapter 3)
    - Efficiency:
        - Cost per unit of service delivered
        - Cost per unit of service delivered by different channels
    - Effectiveness:
        - Price charged per unit of service delivered
        - Error rate (customer-defined, e.g., defects per thousand)
    - Adaptability:
      Time and cost to:
        - Introduce new processes, sites, services, channels to market, etc.
        - Close down existing processes, sites, services, channels to market, etc.

3.  Financial Perspective: (Chapter 4)
    - Free cash flow generated per year
    - Net present value:
        - Actual generated over past 1–5 years (for example)
        - Forecast over next 1–5 years (for example)
    - Internal rate of return on capital employed (forecast and actual)
    - Risk (does this match the returns?):
        - Percentage difference between actual cash flows and previous forecasts
        - Percentage difference between best case and worst case forecast NPV
    - Credit rating (as measure of overall investor confidence)

4.  Today and in the Future: (Chapters 5–8)
    - Focus: percent of services, channels, customer groups, investment instruments that account for (say) 80 percent of sales
    - Amount of business in each of the groups: A, B, and C
    - Ability to define future market space, confidence levels in critical success factors identified in future blueprinting—accuracy of previous blueprints

- Ability to define how much money is being spent/will be spent on all four phases of the audio cycle
- Ability to quantify the winner's competitive cycle for the business
- Top priorities for strategic diversification understood and being applied
- Percentage accuracy[5] of past predictions of what this month's *key* measures would be, as forecasted 1, 3, 12, 24 . . . months ago

Deciding what *level* of performance is good enough for each measure depends on a combination of:

- last year's performance
- competitors' performance
- where the business needs to be in order to reach its long-term goals (see also Chapter 6)

The results can again be plotted as a spider chart (see Chapter 2). This gives a good combination of qualitative and quantitative, overview and detail results. When the target performance level is set as a circle half-way out from the center, and anything *inside* the circle shows under-performance and anything *outside* the circle is over-performance, the results can look something like this:

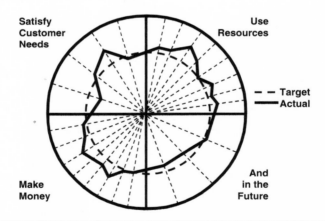

---

[5]The point here is not to try to predict the future with 100 percent accuracy, but to test how well managers truly understand what drives their business. Short-term forecasts measure items more directly under managers' control. Longer-term forecasts measure how well they understand the environment or larger business processes of which the business is a part (see Chapters 7 and 8).

—— **MAKING IT REAL** ——

- What is the relative importance of each of the four areas to your business (see Chapter 7)?

- What levels of performance do you need to achieve in each area this year?

- What levels of performance are needed to ensure future success (see Chapter 6)?

- What might "bite" you?

## SUMMARY

The second layer of strategic advantage comes from activities having to do with what we call leadership.

The first part of leadership is choosing what mix of customers' needs the business should focus on satisfying. This is achieved through portfolio management.

The second part is to exercise a particular leadership style by means of an organization structure and design.

And the third part of leadership is to get the people in the organization to focus on what really matters. And the way that is achieved is through the measurement and reward system.

*PORTFOLIO MANAGEMENT* Running a successful business is about making trade-offs. It is about choosing sets of customers, needs, services, resources, suppliers, processes, investors, and investor instruments that match each other well enough for the business to survive. The mix also needs to change over time as competitors change the value that they provide to customers, suppliers, and investors.

The Pareto Curve shows that 20 percent of a business's services generally create about 80 percent of its revenue, and 80 percent of the total contribution to the money it makes. Allocating the remaining indirect costs according to gross contribution is easy, but provides the false picture that every service is making the same percentage contribution to the business. When indirect costs are instead allocated according to how they are *generated,* we get a new, more accurate, picture of the contribution that each service line brings.

By using "financial triage" we can identify and strengthen the services that form the core of the business, and take action to make them (and the business) more competitive. We can identify the service lines that are losing the business money, and take steps to stem that flow. And we can identify, understand, and better manage the other services, which broaden the appeal of the business.

This approach can be applied not only to the services that the business sells, but also to the customer groups that it sells *to,* and the different channels (customer chains) that it sells *through.* In effect these are just different ways of slicing up the underlying customer needs that the business is servicing.

ORGANIZATION Organization is the means by which the business gets done what it needs to get done, and changes what it needs to change. The fact that different businesses need to achieve different things means that they all need a different organization structure: there is no single ideal form.

We can judge how well an organizational form might suit a particular business by examining how well it matches the particular mix of the four roles it needs to carry out:

- to *decide* what needs to be done
- to *communicate* what needs to be done
- to *implement* what needs to be done, and
- to *measure* what has been done, as well as what others are doing

The power culture, the role culture, the task culture, and the person culture are four different ways to solve, and to think about, the trade-offs that always exist between getting done what needs to be done, changing what needs to be changed, and managing the human factors of the business. In any real-life business, all four forms probably exist side by side, and the important thing is to find the form that best helps the business to do what it needs to.

As we know, the minimum activities a business needs to be successful are to:

1. make money by

2. using resources to

3. satisfy customer needs,

4. today and in the future.

So it should be no surprise that these four actions match almost exactly the four roles identified by Bartlett and Ghoshal as best practice in modern global companies.

These are the basic activities that any business needs to carry out, and the simplest way to get them done is by making one person responsible for each role.

MEASUREMENT AND REWARD  What gets measured gets done, and so the single most important tool that any business has, not only for defining the balance of cost and value that it needs, but also for achieving that balance, is its measurement and reward system.

Measurement and reward covers suppliers *and* employees, and both will have a variety of different needs that can be used to identify rewards. They will also have different attitudes about how much risk and reward they want to get in return for investing their time and energy in this particular business. By carefully understanding these differences, a business has an opportunity to minimize its own risk and maximize its financial value.

A successful business is a combination of making money, using resources, satisfying customer needs, and adapting into the future, so any measurement system needs to track performance in all four of these activities. Chapter 7 will help us to understand the relative importance of these parts to different businesses, but all four are necessary elements of the whole.

Defining too many measures for the business constrains performance. So, as with the rest of this book, optimum performance comes from defining the minimum needed to achieve success.

This concludes our look at what it takes to balance the three core functions of the business at any one time. The next chapter looks at how to maintain that balance, in a changing environment over time.

# CHAPTER 6

# . . . *And in the Future*

*We march backwards into the future.*

– MARSHALL MCLUHAN

CHAPTER 5 INTRODUCED the second layer of strategic business advantage. It looked at the first three activities involved in leadership:

- Choosing which portfolio of customers' needs to service
- Providing personal leadership, implemented through an organization structure
- Measuring and rewarding what matters most to the success of the business

This chapter looks at the other part of leadership: leading the business successfully over time. It shifts the focus from optimizing what is needed today to building what will *become* necessary to achieve success in the future.

In that future, as we know, the business will still need to carry out the same fundamental activities. What will change is the *level of performance* it needs to achieve at each one if it is to remain successful.

One way that the business can do this, as we saw in Chapter 3, is by continuously improving each process.

But leading the business this way is a bit like playing soccer or football the way that five-year-olds do: all chasing the ball around the field together.

This chapter is about taking the business to the next level of performance. It shows the business how to look up, and run to where the ball is *going to be,* instead of where it is now.

The first section discusses general issues before describing a simple yet powerful approach to identifying and building the levels of performance that will be needed. The chapter then looks at the wider process of business innovation, before closing with a review of the different ways in which businesses in general can expand and diversify.

## THROUGH A GLASS, DARKLY

Leading a business into the future involves balancing two things. One is that the future is what you make it. The other is that the future is unknowable.

The future *is* what we make it. But we all have limited resources and limited foresight, so there will always be surprise events that threaten the survival of a firm that focuses only on what *it* wants to create. Even the mighty Microsoft can be surprised by a Netscape. A business that focuses *only* on creating what *it* wants to achieve will eventually be blindsided by something.

At the other extreme, if the future is unknowable, then it seems to make sense to build a business that can adapt to whatever that future turns out to be. This is a "sense and respond" approach. But responsiveness costs money, and a business that can react seamlessly to the "once-in-a-100-years" disaster is spending too much on responsiveness for all of the other ninety-nine years. A business that responds to *every* pull that it senses will be torn apart. So there has to be *some* element of choice about what sort of future the business wants to create so that it can know which pulls to respond to and which to ignore.

So, success in leading a business over time requires a balance between the two: planning for the future and responding to events.

Managing a business over time is like driving at night on a mountain road. The farther ahead you can see, the faster and more safely you can drive. By watching for signs, you can prepare for twists and turns in the road before you reach them.

*THE COMBINED FIVE FORCES AND PEST MODELS* Two traditional tools that a business can use as "headlights" to view the road ahead are the Porter Five Forces model and the PEST analysis.

The Five Forces model, introduced by Michael Porter, can be used to identify the external pressures generated by other businesses and customers. The PEST model captures the drivers that come from other, non-business, sources. Together these two models can be used to list all the external drivers and long-term trends that might affect the future of the business.

PEST stands for the **P**olitical (legal), **E**conomic (environmental), **S**ocial, and **T**echnological factors that might affect the business. These impact different businesses to different degrees at different times. Clear examples of each that have been important in recent years are safety legislation, the opening up of China, recession, emissions regulations, the aging population, and Internet technologies.

The Five Forces analysis focuses on pressures from other businesses and customers:

1. *Industry rivalry* refers to factors to do with businesses in the same industry (i.e., providing similar services through similar ways of using resources).

2. *New entrants* are companies that have recently started to offer services that compete to satisfy the same customer needs, possibly in different ways.

3. *Substitutes* are services that customers might buy *instead of* the service offered by the business doing the analysis. These are often the most difficult to spot.

4. The impact of *customers* on the business usually depends on whether there are few of them or many, and on whether spending patterns (needs) are static or changing.

5. The same applies to *suppliers:* are there many or few of them that can provide the quality that the business needs, and how is this changing?

Each category might contain intense pressures on the business, or none at all, depending on the nature of the firm.

Together, the four PEST categories and the Five Forces can summarize onto a page all the key external drivers affecting the future of the business.

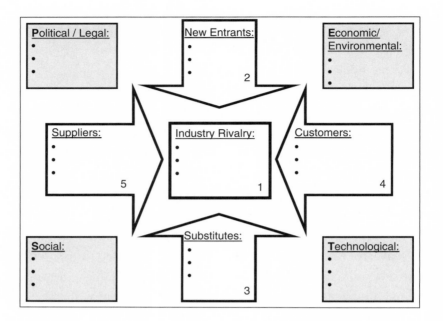

But they say nothing about what the business is going to *do* about these drivers. And deciding what to do, as we shall now see, is more difficult than it might at first sight appear.

***THE SWOT ANALYSIS*** One common way to convert this understanding of external trends and drivers into a plan for action is to classify each external driver as an opportunity or a threat, and to compare these with the internal strengths and weaknesses of the business. (Although we know, of course, from Chapter 3 that there is no "inside" or "outside" the firm.)

The result is called a SWOT analysis, for Strengths, Weaknesses, Opportunities, and Threats.

Where a strength matches an opportunity, so the thinking goes, the business should advance. Where a threat meets a weakness, the business needs to prepare to defend or retreat.

Let's work through an example.

The table on the next page shows a simplified example for the convenience store we saw in Chapter 2. The store believes it has a number of strengths in the way it operates, including its wide range of fresh fruit and good location in a busy area. Weaknesses include a relatively narrow range of specialty breads and an old-fashioned storefront.

Opportunities that have been identified include an increasing trend towards healthy eating and the fact that people are increasingly "cash rich, time poor." Threats include the fact that the local neighborhood is considering introducing a new bylaw to restrict the ways that businesses in the area can operate, and that a specialty bakery has recently opened up on the other side of town.

If we tabulate these and work through the table we should get a clear picture of what the business ought to do.

We mark a "+" sign where a strength matches an opportunity or helps to neutralize a threat, and a "−" where the opposite happens. Where the two elements do not affect each other, we put "=." The overall position of the business in relation to each opportunity/threat is totaled at the bottom of each column. This is then a signal for action.

| | OPPORTUNITIES | | | THREATS | | |
| --- | --- | --- | --- | --- | --- | --- |
| STRENGTHS | HEALTHY EATING | CASH RICH, TIME POOR | MORE... | POTENTIAL NEW BYLAW | NEW BAKERY | MORE... |
| Wide Range of Fruit | + | − | | = | = | |
| Good Location | = | + | | = | + | |
| More ... | | | | | | |
| WEAKNESSES | | | | | | |
| Narrow Range Specialty Bread | − | − | | = | − or ++ | |
| Old-Fashioned Storefront | = | − | | + | = | |
| More ... | | | | | | |
| Total | = | − − | | + | = or +++ | |

Key: "+" advantage, "−" disadvantage, "=" neutral

Let's review the opportunities and threats one by one.

The wide range of fruit that the store stocks will help it take advantage of the trend towards healthier eating, but its location makes no difference. The fact that it does not stock many specialty breads means that there is an opportunity being missed, and the old-fashioned storefront is irrelevant. Overall this opportunity is currently neutral for the business.

The store's strong range of fruit does not help it address the fact that people are becoming more cash rich, time poor—in fact it takes up space that could be used to sell them what they value more, which is ready meals. Its good location and easy accessibility will help sales to rise. But again the weaknesses in the range of bread and the old frontage make it difficult to take advantage of this opportunity. Overall this seems not to be an opportunity for the business after all.

The fact that the store has a wide range of fruit is irrelevant to the potential new bylaw, and may even turn the good location into a disadvantage. The narrow range of bread is irrelevant, but the old-fashioned storefront may actually turn out to be a positive. It is in keeping with the type of business that the locals want to encourage, and so it may give the store an edge compared with other businesses and in influencing the wording of the bylaw.

The fact that the store has a wide range of fruit is irrelevant to what is probably the biggest threat to the store: the new bakery that has opened on the other side of town. The store's good position will help it to withstand the threat, but its narrow range of breads clearly places it under an even greater disadvantage: bread sales will fall. The old-fashioned storefront is irrelevant.

But what if the convenience store were to change its attitude to the bakery and offer to sell its products? A win-win agreement could be reached. The bakery would get an additional outlet in a part of town where it cannot operate (because of the new bylaw). And the convenience store would turn its current weakness in this area into a strength. That would also help to serve the additional numbers of cash rich, time poor customers who want to buy healthy specialty breads. What at first glance seemed to be a threat is perhaps the greatest opportunity for the business.

This is a highly simplified example, but it is meant to illustrate two things.

First is that thinking through how a business can create future success is more complicated than simply matching opportunities and strengths.

Second is that a so-called strength in relation to one external driver can be a weakness in relation to another, or completely irrelevant to a third. And whether an external driver turns out to be an opportunity or a threat often depends more on *how the business chooses to respond* to that driver than on any intrinsic property of the external trend.

Strengths, weaknesses, opportunities, and threats are all *value judgments*. If we use these terms or concepts then we automatically prejudge the situation: we restrict our options for action because we effectively assume that the way the world will work in the future is the same as the way it worked in the past.

In June 1812 Napoleon's empire was at its height, and covered most of Europe. The Russian economy had been weakened by trade embargoes, and when Tsar Alexander broke those embargoes Napoleon saw the opportunity he had been looking for to bring his old enemy to heel. The opportunity was matched by the strength of an army over half a million strong—how could he fail? And so Napoleon invaded Russia. But before the year was out, 97 percent of his men lay dead, and the stage had been set for his defeat at the battle of Waterloo just three years later.

Business history is littered with examples of companies that failed because they stuck too long to what they believed were the strengths that worked for them in the past. Even *BusinessWeek* once famously ran an article describing how around a quarter of the companies praised by Peters and Waterman's *In Search of Excellence* were in trouble *only three years* after the book was published.

Classifying items as strengths, weaknesses, opportunities, or threats prejudges the situation, and assumes that what worked and didn't work in the past will also apply in the future.

This makes the approach easy to use, because it takes our preconceptions and feeds them back to us. And it can work fine if the world is changing slowly, or if everyone else is using the same approach.

But if we truly want to lead our businesses successfully over time, we need an approach that gets us away from looking at what it took to be successful in the past, to focusing purely on what we're going to need to be successful in the future. We need an approach that asks not "given where we are now, what's the best direction to move?" but rather "where is the ball going to be, and how are we going to get there?"

I call this approach "future blueprinting."

---

**SOAPBOX**

It seems as if the only strength that can *never* become a weakness is the ability to adapt.

But strength and weakness are value judgments, so there can be *no exceptions* to this rule.

Mankind's ability to adapt *will* become a weakness if it results in us making the planet uninhabitable for every species that does not share our ability to adapt.[1]

This is already happening every time we see the solution to wiping out one stock of fish as simply to move elsewhere and catch another type. This is what is happening when our solution to ozone depletion is simply to slap on more sun block. And this is also what is happening when our solution to more and more children being born with allergies, asthma, and eczema is simply to treat them with stronger steroids, inhalers, and creams.

Every time we *adapt* to cope with the problem, we fail to fix the root cause. The root problems build up, and will bring us ultimately to one of two possible futures.

At best, we will end up struggling to control *every* aspect of a complex system that Mother Nature used to manage pretty well by herself. But it will be a version of "nature" that is far bleaker and less rich than the one we have today.

At worst, we will end up like Charles Handy's frog in "The Age of Unreason," placed in a pan of water on the stove, and thinking as the temperature rises: "this is not so bad . . . this is not so bad . . . ," until eventually we are boiled alive.

Adaptability is good, but it needs to be balanced with self-control: the ability to set limits and stick to them.

---

[1] Some of the organisms that *can* adapt as fast as us or faster are rats, cockroaches, and viruses.

In the commercial world this means we need businesses that understand that success comes from making money, by using resources, to satisfy customer needs, today, and in the future.

—————— **MAKING IT REAL** ——————

- What are the key drivers of change in your industry?
- Which are opportunities and which are threats?
- What are the strengths and weaknesses of your business?
- How do they match against the opportunities and threats?
- How would you turn the threats into opportunities?
  What skills and capabilities would you need to make that happen?
- What situation do your top two competitors face?

## FUTURE BLUEPRINTING: "PREDICT AND PREPARE"

The aim of future blueprinting is to get the business to change from a mentality of evolving from where it is now to building in advance the skills and capabilities it will need to be successful in the future: in other words, running to where the ball is going to be.

It achieves this very simply, by focusing on a specific time in the future (typically 2–5 years out) and answering four very simple, but critical, questions:

1. What is that future world going to be like?
2. What will be the key factors for success in that world?
3. What does that imply about what our business needs to achieve to be successful then?
4. What actions shall we take to make that happen?

Let's apply this to the convenience store example.

The first thing we know about what its future world is going to be like is that customers are going to be more health conscious. As a result they are likely to want to buy more fresh fruit and more special types of bread. They might also do other things—such as drink more spring water, exercise more, or take more active vacations—that might be important for this or other businesses, but which we have not considered here. The first implication for the convenience store is that it is well placed to sell more fruit. Actions it might decide to take include advertising the fruit more clearly in the window and raising prices. The second implication is that it does not have enough specialty breads to satisfy this growing customer need. One possible action is to cooperate with the newly opened bakery. Another would be to open an in-store bakery, or stop selling bread altogether, and so on.

This simple example is shown in the table below, which also shows implications of the trend towards customers becoming more cash rich, time poor.

**TABLE 1: SATISFY CUSTOMER NEEDS**

| FUTURE SITUATION IN [DATE] | CRITICAL SUCCESS FACTORS | IMPLICATIONS FOR OUR BUSINESS | ACTION PLAN |
|---|---|---|---|
| • Customers more health conscious | • Want to eat more fruit<br>• Want special breads | • We already sell fruit<br>• Not enough breads! | • Advertise fruit more<br>• Raise prices<br>• Cooperate with new bakery across town<br>• . . . |
| • Customers more cash rich, time poor | • Need to shop at handy location<br>• Buy more ready meals<br>• Pay for higher quality<br>• . . . | • Our location good<br>• Number of customers will increase<br>• Need to change range of items that we stock | • Plan for rent rise<br>• Improve store layout<br>• Stock more [products] and fewer [products] |
| • More. . . | • More. . . | • More. . . | • More. . . |

I developed this approach for a half-billion dollar IT services account as a way to explain to employees what their business plan was. They were often impacted by the action plans the business had created, and I wanted to show

how these fit into the big picture of strategic events in their customer's future. And I wanted to be able to show it all in one page.

We start by describing what the world will be like from the customers' point of view. What are the overall trends and drivers that will affect them? How will the way they carry out their day-to-day activities have changed from today? If the customers are businesses, we can include key factors from their PEST and Five Forces diagrams. If the customers are consumers then these are still relevant, but what are their broader values, aspirations, and problems?

Between ten and twenty bullet points will be enough to summarize the key points. The aim is to paint a broad-brush picture of what the customer-related part of the future business will need to fit with, *irrespective* of how the business operates today.

The second step is to add more detail, identifying what will *really matter* to customers within that environment. What key goals will they be trying to achieve? What key problems will they want to solve? What will they most need to get right? What will they most need to avoid getting wrong? In business terms, what will be their critical success factors? For consumers, what will be their "must have," "must do," "must be," and "must avoid" items?

By identifying what matters most to customers, we focus on *what would add the most value.* (Once we get this right, then the details can follow.) Some items on this list will be relevant to services that the business offers today. Others will have implications for services that it could offer in the future.

In either case, the third step is to list the implications for the firm that is making the plan, describing the changes it would need to implement to achieve success in the imagined future.

The fourth and final step is to identify the actions the business is going to take.

The resulting plan is a four-column table that shows not only *where* the business is going, and *why,* but also *how* it is going to get there.

Satisfying customer needs is only one part of the first layer of strategic advantage, so a similar table needs to be filled out for using resources and making money.

The "using resources" plan for the convenience store might look something like this:

**TABLE 2: USE RESOURCES**

| FUTURE SITUATION IN [DATE] | CRITICAL SUCCESS FACTORS | IMPLICATIONS FOR OUR BUSINESS | ACTION PLAN |
|---|---|---|---|
| • New bylaw likely to come into effect | • Must fit with new requirements | • We already fit well<br>• Some positive, some negative effects | • Lobby to influence wording<br>• Get customer signatures of support<br>• . . . |
| • New bakery will dominate specialty breads in our area | • They want small range of outlets in top locations | • Either partner with them, or<br>• Stop selling bread | • Move fast to negotiate sole-outlet agreement based on our unique value |
| • More. . . | • More. . . | • More. . . | • More. . . |

For using resources and making money, the nature of the first two columns changes slightly, as it is the business's *own* situation that needs to be described. In the "Future Situation" column the PEST and Five Forces analyses will be useful. For the "Critical Success Factors" column it is important to think from the point of view of any business that wants to compete in this space, not just the firm that is making the plan. The more the business can do this, the less constrained it will be by its own past. As before, the "Implications" and "Action" columns are both specific to the business that is making the plan.

By combining the three points of view, the business can find an overlap that creates the successful business of the future, so iteration is an important part of the process. Taking each viewpoint separately improves focus. But we know that the successful business of the future is something that will need to:

- satisfy customer needs

- by using resources, *and*

- make money, all at the same time

*So if we define what it will take to achieve those things in the future, then we have automatically defined what it will take to build a successful business in the future.*

(If necessary, the approach can easily be extended to cover the activities that form the second layer of strategic advantage.)

The result is an entire plan that can be summarized onto just a few pages, usually with 10–20 key bullet points per column.

This is a very simple approach, but also very powerful.

It identifies what the successful business of the future will look like, and what steps it will take to get us there, *from wherever we are today.*

If expectations about the future change, then actions can quickly be updated. And if very different futures are possible, then alternative plans can be created for each. (This is called scenario planning.)

Because the result ties everyday operational activities to the strategic future that the firm wants to create, it can also be used in everyday decision-making. For example, if the convenience store has to choose between two types of fruit or two types of bread because it only has space for one, then it can ask the question "which of these would provide more health benefits to customers?" More generally, the approach can be used to feed into the measurement (and reward) system of the business.

This not only makes today's activities more *effective* by aligning them with a consistent vision of tomorrow, but it also makes them more *efficient,* because the purpose has been made explicit. And yet room is left for it to remain as flexible and *adaptable* as the accuracy with which we can predict the future.

The whole process can also be scaled to become as simple or as complicated as the business wants it to be. It can be tailored to match whatever level of certainty or risk the business needs before it can make a decision. And it leaves each individual business to choose its own balance between shaping and responding to the future.

*WIDER IMPLICATIONS* Let's reflect for a moment on what just happened.

The convenience store business knew (because it had read this book) that in order to be successful, it had to build a system of three matching parts: needs, resources, and money.

Those parts had to align not only with each other, but also with the outside world—in the shape of customers, employees/suppliers, and lenders/investors.

In order to create a successful vision of what it would become, the business needed to find a way to make these three separate building blocks align, match, and overlap.

The simplest way in which they do this is when they come together to form a single service. A single service is the simplest way in which resources get used to make money by satisfying a need.

So if we want to understand more deeply how to lead a business over time, we need to understand the mechanisms involved in creating new services over time. We need to understand the innovation process.

This is the simplest, most fundamental way in which future customers' needs can be combined with future ways of using resources to create future ways of making money.

In other words, it is the simplest, most fundamental way in which businesses can successfully change and evolve over time.

This is what we shall look at in the next section.

——— **MAKING IT REAL** ———

- Pick a timescale, say 2–3 years in the future.
- What are the key trends and drivers affecting your customers, and what will their world become like by then?
- What are the key things they will then want or need (to have and to avoid)?
- What are the implications for your business, in terms of capabilities that will no longer be needed, or levels of performance that will need to be achieved?
- What alternative actions *could* your business take, when, and which give the best balance of risk and return?

- Repeat for *using resources:*
  - What are the key trends affecting the ways your business and rivals deliver their services? What will the situation be like by your chosen point in time?
  - What will be the key factors for the success of those types of business?
  - What are the implications for your business?
  - What alternative actions could it take, when, and which give the best mix of risk and return?
- What do your answers tell you about whether your business is more driven by satisfying customer needs, or using resources, or a balance of the two? (Remember this answer in the next chapter.)

## THE INNOVATION PROCESS — THE AUDIO CYCLE

Whether a new service is completely new or a slight improvement on something that exists already, it always begins its life in the same way: when two ideas meet in a person's head.

One of those ideas is an understanding (either vague or precise) of what the customer might want. The other is an understanding (either vague or precise) of how the resources of the business might be used to deliver it.

Sometimes the customer need comes first, and the business looks for different ways to fulfill that need. Sometimes the business knows what its resources can do, and looks for different customers who might find that useful. Sometimes it is the engineer who suddenly "gets" what the marketer is saying. Sometimes it is the marketer who suddenly understands the engineer. And sometimes it takes a complete outsider to understand them both.

Whichever comes first does not matter. What matters is that it is only at the instant when the two ideas come together in *someone's* head that the potential *solution* and the latent or hidden *need* combine to become a potential *service.*

The next step is then to check whether this potential service is likely to make money, both in itself and in comparison to rival services (see Chapter 2). If it is likely to do so, then it enters some form of design and development process. The precise details of this will vary from business to business. But in essence, the rough ideas about what the customer wants, how the service would be provided, and what the financial returns would be, get developed into greater detail. The results then get tested against a new set of criteria. And if the potential service passes then it moves to the next stage of development.

After a number of different stages, depending on the particular business, it will finally be launched or implemented before being sold to customers on an ongoing basis.

In other words, we can say that the new service goes through four stages or phases—understand, design, implement, and operate—that we can draw like this:

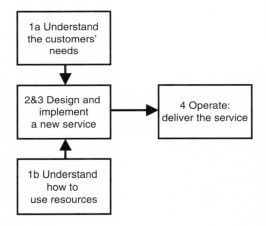

Any business that wants to be better than its rivals at this process needs to be better than them at one or more of the four component items.

The fourth part, operate, has already been discussed. This is the first layer of strategic advantage: making money by using resources to satisfy customer needs. What about skill at understanding customers' needs?

Awareness and understanding of customer needs can come from many sources, including market research, industry reports, and so on. But the best and most accurate source—in some ways the only real source—is always the customers themselves, and their interactions with similar services. This is what the business learns in stage 4: operate.

The same is true of understanding how to use resources. Businesses can gain theoretical knowledge of what it takes to provide a service from trade fairs, trade press, competitor analysis, benchmarking, and so on. But the proof of the pudding is in the eating and the best way to learn is by doing, and so the best knowledge about what it really takes to use resources to provide a service comes from actually doing so. This also is stage 4: operate.

The third part that determines the performance of the new service is the innovation process itself: the steps taken to design and implement the new service. We know that the precise activities followed will be very different in different businesses. The steps followed in a pharmaceutical company, for example, will be very different from those taken at a record company, a watch company, a hotel, or a venture capital company. But the rough outline of the process they follow will always be the same: finding or generating ideas, testing them against certain decision criteria, developing the ideas further, testing them again, and so on.

What determines the quality of the output of this process—how well the services that are developed then go on to sell—is the *questions* that are used to decide whether each potential service should move forward to the next stage. The speed and cost of development are also important, but if the wrong questions are being asked, the wrong criteria and threshold levels being applied, then the business is simply being very efficient at developing the wrong services.

The best source of information for criteria to determine whether new services progress to the next stage is the measures that track the performance of the total business. This is what we discussed in Chapter 5. And again the best source of information for what measures work best is the operate stage!

In other words, competitive performance at all the first three parts of this innovation process comes from a feedback loop of information from the operate stage.

The business explicitly uses its *understanding* of customer needs and how to use resources to create a *design* which is then developed and *implemented* into the *operate* phase. This builds *awareness* that then becomes *understanding,* and the whole cycle begins again.

Awareness, Understanding, Design, Implementation, and Operation: I call this the AUDIO cycle, and it is shown in the diagram below:

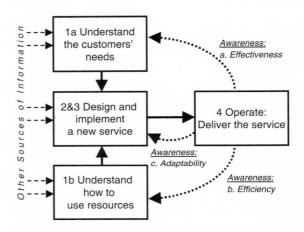

## THE AUDIO CYCLE

This process is what happens when a business designs a new service.

It is also, as the diagram shows, the process that drives the efficiency, effectiveness, and adaptability of the business as a whole.

In other words, *it is what drives the ability of the business to change and adapt over time*, as we shall see in the next chapter.

Amazon.com is a business that demonstrates the power of this cycle. It started with a simple model—a simple way of using resources to satisfy customer needs that did *not* at first *make money*—and then applied this cycle relentlessly, achieving profitability, reducing costs, improving service levels, and expanding into new service areas as it did so.

If we look back to the future blueprinting process, we can now understand better why it works. The first column of the table converts awareness to understanding. The second column converts understanding into a design for a successful business (the critical success factors). The third column (implications) defines what this particular business will need to implement as a result. And the fourth column defines the actions that will convert that implementation approach into operational reality.

Practically, the picture also shows us that successful innovation comes from bringing together people who have the three relevant points of view: the customers, the "doers," and the investors. Sometimes this can be achieved simply by involving one person from each department in the business: marketing, operations, and finance. Sometimes more specific information will be needed, in which case it might make sense to hire a market researcher, involve a key supplier, or invite someone with specialist knowledge of how to raise venture capital. Sometimes it might be necessary to involve the specific customer in the process. What will always be the same is the need to combine the three points of view into one person's head. *How* best to achieve that will depend on the specific innovation that is being sought, who has the information that is needed, and what approach will give the best mix between cost and value.

Finally, the presence of these three feedback loops introduces us for the first time to the way that success breeds success. It shows how a business can generate self-reinforcing advantage. Not only does every sale provide the opportunity to reduce the *cost* of using resources (through the Experience Curve we saw in Chapter 3), it also enables the business to learn more about *customer needs,* and to learn more about what it takes to *change* successfully over time.

Together, these three factors combine to create the "winner's competitive cycle"—a concept that will lead directly to the self-reinforcing strategic advantage of the Escher Cycle, which compounds the effects across multiple different service lines.

**SUCCESS BREEDS SUCCESS: THE WINNER'S COMPETITIVE CYCLE** We often read about "first mover advantage" or about a company with a "dominant market position." Success, it seems, can breed success, and there are several factors that can help to make this happen.

First, people tend to buy services they are already familiar with, and when people decide to try a service for the first time, they are likely to be most familiar with the business that already has the most customers. Having more customers also gives the business more opportunities to truly understand those customers' needs, which enables it to improve its marketing, which again increases the number of customers. This creates a reinforcing loop between higher market share and greater customer awareness.

Second, a business that has sold a greater volume of services will have had more opportunity to reduce the cost it takes to deliver each service, through Experience Curve effects. This means the price charged to customers can be reduced, which again increases the firm's share of the total number of services sold. This creates a reinforcing loop between higher market share and lower unit cost (price).

Lower costs mean the business can make more money. And higher customer awareness can do the same—by strengthening the firm's bargaining position with other businesses such as suppliers and distributors, or by enabling *higher* prices to be charged, simply because the firm is better known.

These higher profits can then be reinvested to create more or better marketing (which increases customer awareness) and/or in better ways of using resources (which reduces unit costs). Both of these then lead again to higher market share.

All these effects are shown in the diagram below:

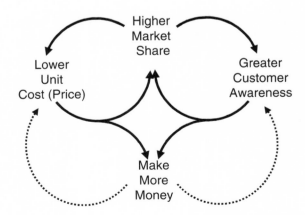

Finally, the extra money made can also be combined with the better understanding of customer needs and the greater experience of using resources to create better services. This is the AUDIO cycle innovation process we have just seen. This loop is *not shown* (it requires a third dimension, coming out of the page) but if done correctly will lead again to higher market share.

Which of the alternatives shown here would be most useful and most achievable will depend on the particular business. But together they make up the winner's competitive cycle—a reinforcing loop that accelerates the advantage of any business that manages to get ahead of its rivals, making it even more difficult for them to catch up.

Again, in the winner's competitive cycle we see the triple effects of efficiency, effectiveness, and adaptability. And it is a combination of them all that the Escher Cycle will achieve in Chapter 8.

─────── **MAKING IT REAL** ───────

- What key innovation is your business seeking to create?
- Who are the people who have the customer-related, resource-related, and money-related knowledge and understanding relevant to that level of change?
- Are they involved in the process, or is someone who understands them involved?
- What process is being used to:
  a) define the problem?
  b) generate ideas?
  c) get all the relevant knowledge into (at least) one person's head?
- What criteria are being used to decide which alternatives continue to the next stage? Are they the right criteria?
- Which of the three parts of the winner's competitive cycle currently operate in your industry, who takes advantage of them, and how could your business use them better?

## STRATEGIC DIVERSIFICATION —
## ANSOFF REVISITED

In this final section of the chapter I want to step back from the detail of specific processes for business planning and innovation to think generally about the different directions in which a business might branch out or expand from where it is today. This is called strategic diversification and we will revisit it just before we find the Escher Cycle.

The father of diversification (some have said the father of strategic management) was Dr. H. Igor Ansoff.

He said that a firm is defined by the customers or markets it serves, and the products or services that it sells.

This means that any business has just two strategic choices to make: first, whether to serve existing customers or find new ones, and second, whether to sell existing services or develop new ones.

This gives four strategies, which he named market penetration, product development, market development, and diversification:

**PRODUCTS or SERVICES**

|  | Existing | New |
|---|---|---|
| **Existing** | Market Penetration | Product Development |
| **New** | Market Development | Diversification |

**CUSTOMERS or MARKETS**

If the firm chooses to stick with its existing services and existing markets, then it can grow only by taking business away from competitors. This is market penetration. Although it seems a low-risk approach, and is sometimes called the do-nothing strategy, we know from Chapters 2–4 that it actually requires continuous improvement in all areas, so "better, faster, cheaper" would probably be a more descriptive name.

One alternative is to find new customers or markets for its existing services. This is called market development. Another is to create significantly different *new* products and services, but sell them to *existing* customers as a way to minimize risk and maximize returns from the costs of innovation. This is the product development strategy.

The fourth and final strategy is to move into selling completely new services to completely new customers, and is called diversification.

This is Ansoff's approach, and it is very powerful. But only tells us part of the story.

We know that a business is a system that not only has to use its services to satisfy customer needs, but also needs to *make money* by *using resources*.

So, remembering our diagram of the business, and the three different groups of people that it exists to satisfy:

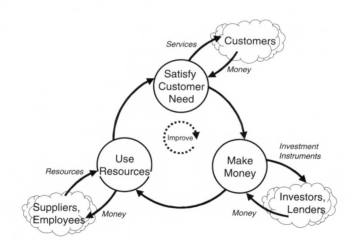

we can see that there are in fact *six* parts of the business that it can decide whether to change or not to change:

- Customers and the services provided to them
- Suppliers/employees and the contracts that define what they provide and how they are paid
- Lenders/investors and the financial instruments that are used to raise money from them

What Ansoff identified is the possibility to change customers and the services provided to them. But there are two other sets of stakeholders that the business has contracts with.

The business can also choose to change (or keep the same) the suppliers/employees that it uses and the contracts that define the exchanges that take place between them. This would give another four strategic alternatives. And indeed, deciding to switch from "existing" to "new" in these areas is what drove the major changes in process reengineering, outsourcing, strategic sourcing, and supplier management of the 1980s and 1990s. It is also driving the growth of manufacturing in China. These are definitely strategic changes, even though they do not appear on Ansoff's matrix.

Finally, the business can change (or keep the same) the lenders and investors that it raises money from, and the financial instruments it uses to do so. Getting the right balance between debt and equity comes under this heading. And securitization, corporate bonds, and mezzanine finance are other relatively recent innovations in this area. Again, they are strategic changes for the business, taking it into new areas of risk and return, but they do not appear in Ansoff's model.

In summary, we see that the alternatives Ansoff identified simply need to be repeated for all three sets of stakeholders that the business exists to satisfy, not just the customers.

This gives a total of not four but sixty-four possible combinations,[2] so listing and naming them all is pointless. But, of course, there is only *one* approach that any business needs to follow to be successful: to find a combination of services, contracts, and investment instruments that gives a win-win-win agreement between the firm and its chosen three stakeholders.

Changing the mix of stakeholders and agreements is what enables the business to maintain the balance between the three core functions over time.

So, with sixty-four possible combinations, the only question that remains is how to identify what to change and what to keep the same—

---

[2]There are four alternatives for each stakeholder, like Ansoff's matrix, and $4 \times 4 \times 4 = 64$.

which of the three core functions and sets of stakeholders matters most to which businesses. That is what we shall look at in the next chapter.

——— **MAKING IT REAL** ———

- Which of the following have changed significantly for your business during the past five years?
  - Customers and the services provided to them
  - Suppliers/employees and the contracts that define what they provide and how they are paid
  - Lenders/investors and the financial instruments that are used to raise money from them
- Which do you expect to change significantly over the next five years?
- Which have changed and which have stayed the same for your two most successful competitors?

  And where are they headed next?

## SUMMARY

Leading a business into the future involves balancing two things: that the future is what you make it and that the future is unknowable.

A common approach is to identify the opportunities and threats that seem to exist in the external environment, and then match these against the strengths and weaknesses of the business. This works well in slow-changing environments, but it prejudges the situation. A strength in one situation can be a weakness in another; a threat can be turned into an opportunity, depending on how it is reacted to.

A simpler and more robust approach is to realize that the business is a system made up of three core functions: making money, using resources, and satisfying customer needs. The combination of these three things today is what the business is today. Defining what those three parts need to become in the future automatically defines what the business needs to become.

I call this approach future blueprinting, and it works by defining (for each of the three parts):

- What is the future world going to be like?
- What will be the key factors for success in that world?
- What does that imply about what our business needs to achieve to be successful then?
- What actions shall we take to make that happen?

By finding a solution that simultaneously links and integrates success in all three core functions, actions in the three areas of the business are not only linked to and integrated with each other, but also with the future success that the business wants to create. The plan automatically defines what it will take to create a successful business in the future.

Over time what it takes for the business to succeed in each of the three core functions changes. Each one goes through a four-stage process of *understanding* what the necessary level of performance is, *designing* a new way of operating to achieve that performance, *implementing* that new way of running the function, and then *operating* it until a change is needed again.

Understanding is preceded by *awareness,* so the whole repeating sequence is the AUDIO cycle. It is the innovation process by which the whole business improves its efficiency, effectiveness, and adaptability.

This means that far from a business having four possibilities for strategic diversification, as Ansoff identified, there are sixty-four to choose between. The business can choose to alter, or keep the same, any combination of the three stakeholders of the firm and the contracts it has with them:

- Customers and the services provided to them
- Suppliers/employees and the contracts that define what they provide and how they are paid
- Lenders/investors and the financial instruments that are used to raise money from them

Changing the mix of stakeholders and agreements is what enables the business to maintain the balance between the three core functions over time.

The only question that remains is how to identify what to change and what to keep the same—which of the three core functions and sets of stakeholders matters most to which businesses. That is what we shall look at in the next chapter.

LAYER 3

# THE STRATEGIC PERSPECTIVE:
# FINE-TUNING THE SYSTEM

# CHAPTER 7

# Origins of Strategy

*I have called this principle, by which each slight variation,*
*if useful, is preserved, by the term Natural Selection.*

—CHARLES DARWIN

A T THE START OF THIS BOOK we identified two key problems facing businesses. One was getting done each day all the things that need to get done, and the other was building some form of strategic advantage that will last.

In this chapter our focus shifts from the first problem to the second. We switch from identifying the minimum activities a business needs, to understanding how those activities form the building blocks of self-reinforcing advantage. (The next chapter will show us how to put the blocks together.)

Before we begin, let's review our journey so far.

We started from the idea that strategy by itself adds no value. Only actions create value.

So we asked what was the least a business needs to do to be successful. We found that there were only three things: making money, by using resources, to satisfy customer needs. We looked at the minimum activities needed to achieve each one, and understood the first layer of strategic business advantage: operations.

Then we saw how balancing and aligning the core functions could improve the performance of the business—over time, and at a single moment in time. Again, we understood the activities needed, this time to create the second layer of advantage: leadership.

These first two sections have shown us that the core of *what* any business needs to do is always the same three things (making money, by using resources, to satisfy customer needs), and that it is *how* those three things get done that is different for different businesses, and changes over time.

Now we need to shift from looking at how well the business balances them *internally,* to how well it performs them *in comparison with other similar businesses.* This chapter looks at the third layer of strategic business advantage: strategy.

As Darwin told us, plants and animals evolve over time, and the survival of the individual and of the species as a whole depends on how well it *fits* with its environment. "Survival of the fittest" does not mean "Survival of the one that exercises the most," it means survival of the species/individual that best matches its surroundings.

So if you are a polar bear, it means that having the thickest, whitest coat is an advantage in the cold of the Arctic Circle. But put that same thick coat into the heat of a tropical rainforest or a desert and suddenly it becomes a huge disadvantage. It is not the specific characteristic of the plant or animal that is intrinsically useful or not useful, but how well that characteristic *matches* or *fits* with the environment the organism is in.

The same applies to businesses. This is what we saw in Chapter 3 with the "Nine S" model. Business success depends on how well it fits with customer needs, employee skills, supplier reliability, investor expectations, and so on.

The environment for a business is what we call the economy. Like a flock of birds or a school of fish, this is a collective entity made up of many individual units, in this case businesses. A thousand starlings make a flock, whirling together in the light of evening. A thousand (or a million) businesses make an economy, whirling under the influence of interest rates, legislation, new technologies, and global socio-political trends (among other things).

If we want to understand the behavior of a flock of birds or a school of fish, we can do so by understanding the behavior of a single animal and then using a computer to see what happens when we put 100 or 1,000 of them together.

We are now ready to do nearly the same thing with businesses.

The previous chapters have shown us how the single "animal" called a business behaves. This chapter now looks at what happens when a large number of these businesses come together to form an industry, a marketplace, or an economy.

This chapter draws a map of the economy and shows how it is different in different parts. It then shows which characteristics, like the polar bear's coat, will help a business to be more successful in each part of the economy.

In other words, this chapter tells us which strategies will make any business successful, and *why*.

**MAPPING THE ECONOMY, PART 1: SATISFYING CUSTOMER NEEDS** If we wanted to draw a map of the world, we might start by realizing that the location of every point on it can be defined by a combination of latitude and longitude. So drawing a rectangle with latitude along one side and longitude down the other would give us a two-dimensional map on which every place on the earth could be put.

How can we do the same for businesses?

Well, the world contains a huge variety of businesses—from builders to bakers, lawyers to lawnmowers, and civil engineers to software engineers— so it is not immediately apparent how to show them all together on the same map. But although the *way* that each of them goes about their business looks very different, we know that *what* they are all doing is essentially the same. They are all making money by using resources to satisfy customer needs.

So if we could draw a map based on these three things, then again we could be sure that every business would appear on it somewhere.

Let's start with satisfying customer needs.

We know that any industry contains a range of services, from mass-market, standard, or commodity to premium, specialty, or niche. The mass-market services are bought by relatively large numbers of customers and satisfy needs that are relatively low on the Maslow scale. The premium or bespoke services are more differentiated, sell to smaller numbers of people, and generally satisfy needs that are higher on the Maslow hierarchy.

We need to summarize all these different attributes into one single idea, like "latitude," and the word I am going to use is distinctiveness. This combines the concepts of different-ness and special-ness. Commodities can be differentiated, but niche services are even more distinctive. Plain vanilla is special to people (like me) who like plain vanilla, but a flavor such as Cherry Garcia is even more distinctive.

Like latitude, this concept may seem a bit odd to start with,[1] but its meaning and usefulness will become clearer as we understand how to apply it.

As an example, we can see that an individual business would probably offer a range of different services, each one with a different distinctiveness. The success of General Motors, for example, was famously founded on its creation of a series of vehicles that matched customers' changing needs over their lifetimes. Their first car needed only to be "cheap and cheerful," but as they grew older their needs diversified and became more specialized, more differentiated. In other words, the services needed to become more distinctive. Ford's range of services is roughly the same. Other car companies have ranges of services that are broader and narrower, higher or lower than GM's. We can draw some of them like this:

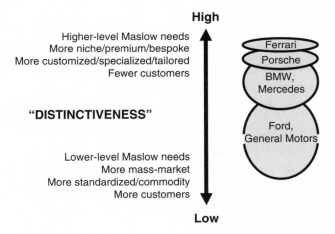

**High**

Higher-level Maslow needs
More niche/premium/bespoke
More customized/specialized/tailored
Fewer customers

Ferrari

Porsche

BMW, Mercedes

**"DISTINCTIVENESS"**

Ford, General Motors

Lower-level Maslow needs
More mass-market
More standardized/commodity
More customers

**Low**

---

[1]Latitude is the number of imaginary degrees from an imaginary line called the equator. How ridiculous!

If we wanted to, we could increase the detail of this "map" by showing individual models of car, or even specific sets of options and specifications that are available on each one. Competing models would line up quite clearly alongside each other.

Alternatively we could reduce the scale and just show industries. "Electricity," for example, would form a relatively narrow band at the bottom of this scale.[2] This would be like having a map of the world that just showed the continents.

So, this first axis of our map rates businesses according to the distinctiveness of the needs that they satisfy and the services that they provide. Although not as immediately quantifiable as latitude—because it is based on a combination of measures, not just one—it is clear that this measure:

- can be scaled up or down to higher or lower levels of detail, right down to a single specification service bought by a single customer—it ties to measurable reality
- definitely covers all the businesses in the world

### THERE ARE NO SUCH THINGS AS INDUSTRIES

Think for a moment what we mean by an industry. Whether we are talking about oil, airlines, food, hotels, television, publishing, or whatever, an industry is a group of businesses that use roughly similar processes and/or technology to create a roughly similar set of services.

Let's think about how this distinctiveness scale would apply to some other industries. Five-star restaurants, for example, would be rated as more distinctive than McDonald's. Rolex watches would be higher than Swatch, Dom Perignon above Coca-Cola, and so on.

If we show all these side by side, we realize a number of things:

[2]Industrial and domestic users of electricity buy slightly different services. "Green" electricity is a recent innovation that provides value against higher-level Maslow needs.

223

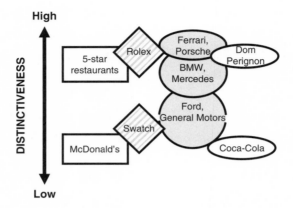

First, each of the businesses shown here is targeted around satisfying a different set of needs. The quality of the services they provide has nothing to do with whether that service is higher or lower on the distinctiveness scale than another service. Quality is purely about how well the business satisfies its chosen needs, in comparison with other businesses aiming to do the same.

Second, businesses "aiming to do the same" might well not be in the same industry. The competition for Ferrari, for example, is not the Ford Mondeo or the BMW 3-series, but the private jet and the 70-foot yacht. Using this map will help us identify the true competitors and substitutes for any service—they will clearly appear side by side.

As the president of Rolex once famously said, "Rolex is not in the watch business—it is in the luxury goods business."

This is why industries can merge, because they never existed in the first place. Computing and (tele-)communications, for example, were just two different ways of *using resources* to satisfy two different sets of customers' needs. When technology changed so that it could satisfy both needs, then the lines between the services that each type of business could offer became blurred, and the industries merged. This is in direct parallel to the discussions we had in Chapter 2 that the business defines the market, not the other way around.

Industries are a useful shorthand for thinking and talking about some business problems. But they do not really exist. And forgetting that fact can lead to sloppy thinking and mistaken conclusions. As we know, the things that are real are the customer needs being satisfied, the ability of each business to use resources to satisfy those needs, and whether or not they make money. Focusing on these is a better approach.

Finally, individual customers (as we can see from the diagram) tend to buy items that appear on about the same level of distinctiveness. This ties back to what we learned from Maslow in Chapter 2, that people look for and buy services that match the next level of needs that is unfulfilled *for them*. Realizing this can help improve marketing, for example by identifying which channels to sell through.

——— **MAKING IT REAL** ———

- How does your business compare on the distinctiveness scale against your top two competitors?

  What about other businesses in your industry?

- What services from other industries do your customers also buy that would rank alongside your services?

  Which of them offers the chance for cooperation, either directly or indirectly?

*MAPPING THE ECONOMY, PART 2: USING RESOURCES* The second core function that any business has is *using resources*. Like longitude, this will be the second axis of our map.

We know that *how* each business uses resources is different. And we know from Chapter 6 that it has to change over time.

As customers change what is desirable, technology changes what is possible, and competitors change what levels of performance are acceptable, so the business needs to:

- Understand what is happening in the world around it
- Design new ways of using resources
- Implement those new ways
- Operate the new ways of using resources . . .

. . . and repeat.

This is the AUDIO cycle (see Chapter 6), and each of these four activities gives the business the potential to do a better job than its rivals. Each of these four activities can bring strategic advantage—if the business finds a way to do them better, faster, and/or cheaper.

So the map that we can use to understand which characteristics (like the polar bear's coat) will help a business to be more successful needs to show all four of these stages:

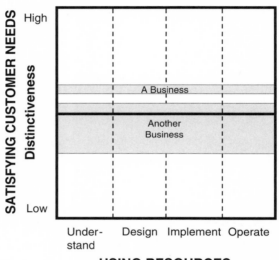

A business now appears as a horizontal band.

The height and width of the band depends on the range and distinctiveness of the services it provides.

The activities to do with actively delivering the service are mapped onto the "Operate" column. The activities to do with understanding what improvements the service might need (or how to use resources better, or how to make more money), and then designing and implementing those changes are mapped onto the other three columns. A business that wants to diversify into a service on a new level of distinctiveness will need to start with activities in the "Understand" zone for that service. Then it will design it, and so on.

Businesses used to be able to change slowly and take each of the four stages separately. But that is now increasingly rare. Businesses increasingly have people/resources working in all four phases at the same time. The numbers of people in each area will be different, but performance at each one has the potential to make or break the business.

When the understand/design phase is looking at the business as a whole rather than just a single service, as strategy and change consultants do, it is no wonder that the role of changing the business gets compared to rewiring the building with the lights still on.

The faster this rate of change through the AUDIO cycle is, the more important it becomes that the activities and processes integrate both the strategic and tactical views of the world. The faster the rate of change, the more important it is that strategic design (Layer 3) is based on a solid under-standing of operational realities (Layer 1), and that people in operations understand the strategic objectives that the business needs to achieve. That is what this book is about, and it will become an extremely important building block of the self-reinforcing advantage, as we shall see in the next chapter.

---

## WHEELS WITHIN WHEELS—THE FRACTAL ECONOMY

If we look around we can see this AUDIO chain repeated everywhere:

- The Swatch Company understood the need for the SMART car and designed it. Their design was then implemented (manufactured) and sold by Mercedes-Benz.
- Property developers understand the market demand for new offices or housing. They employ architects to design the buildings, which are then built by builders and maintained by maintenance companies, gardeners, and security firms.
- Executive producers understand the movies the public wants to watch (or like to think they do). Writers design the movies, directors implement them, and the distri-bution networks operate the delivery of the service. Box office receipts then feed back into the producers' understanding of what the public wants to watch.
- Nike understands and designs shoes, factories in Asia make them, and retailers sell them.

- McDonald's understands and designs fast food, together with the kitchen processes needed to deliver them reliably. Networks of franchisees then operate those processes. (McDonald's opened/implemented new restaurants in Russia itself.)

And so on.

| | | | |
|---|---|---|---|
| Swatch | | Mercedes-Benz | |
| Property Developer | Architect | Builder | Mainte-nance |
| Producer | Writer | Director | Distri-butor |
| Nike | | Factories | Retailers |
| McDonald's | | Franchisees | |
| Under-stand | Design | Implement | Operate |

This means that we can understand our map of the economy on two levels: once at the level of each individual business, and once at the level of the larger processes of which the individual businesses are themselves part.

Of course, those larger processes are themselves businesses—they are also part of the economy—so the economy displays a kind of fractal quality, which we will return to in Chapter 8.

——— **MAKING IT REAL** ———

- What share of your business's total expenses/resources is spent in each of the four phases of the AUDIO cycle?
- To what extent is changing the business seen as different from running the business, and what specific steps (if any) does your business take to ensure that there is good mutual *understanding* between the four AUDIO phases?

- What larger process is your business part of? What other businesses are involved?

---

*MAPPING THE ECONOMY, PART 3* We said at the start of the chapter that we could simulate a flock of birds or a school of fish by understanding a single animal and then multiplying it.

The map of the business world we have so far created uses just two of the three activities that we know define the "animal" called a business. This section adds the third: making money.

We know from earlier chapters that making money is about the balance between cost, value, and timing. And we know that every activity in the business can potentially make money for the business, according to whether the value it brings is greater or less than the amount it costs.

Maps of the earth often use contour lines to show the height of the land above or below sea level. We shall use similar lines to specify whether an activity in the business needs to focus more on cost or on value.

Let's think first about the distinctiveness axis of the map.

In both halves of the diagram, customers are choosing value for money. But in the upper half of the picture, businesses are delivering services that are customized, individualized, and tailored to the needs of a relatively small group of customers. For these businesses it is more important to get the *value* part of their service right than it is to get the cost part right. Competitiveness here is more about getting a closer match to the individual customer's needs than it is about charging a lower price.

In the bottom half of the diagram, value for money still matters, but businesses are now delivering services that are less differentiated. For them it is more important to focus on getting the *cost* part right than to get the value delivered to match closely to each customer's individual needs.

The balance between value and cost is always important, but the relative importance of each is different in each half, and we can add this detail to the map on page 230.

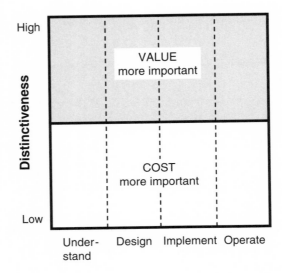

If we remember the analogy of the height contours on a map, and say that value-focus means "higher" and cost-focus means "lower," then what we are saying is that the value-cost balance of the business environment or economy looks something like this:

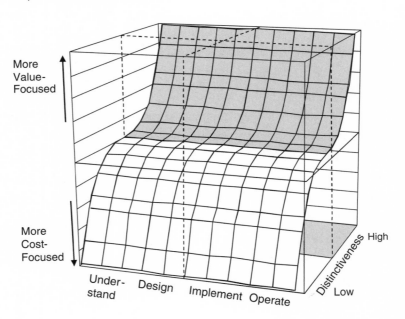

What this says is that for a business to be good at the *third* layer of strategic advantage—for it to perform its activities better *in comparison with other businesses delivering similar services*—what it needs to do is to get its cost-value balance for each activity closer to this shape than its competitors do.

Now, this is not a precise mathematical representation of the shape of "economic hyperspace." And we do not (yet) have the tools to be able to measure what the actual balance is. But the shape *is* indicative of reality. And what is important to understand is that:

- The high distinctiveness side is higher (more value-focused) than the low distinctiveness side, and

- The surface or shape that links the two extremes is not a flat slope but a *curve*. Increasing differentiation requires more-rapidly increasing focus on value. And so the curve is flatter in the middle and steeper at the edges, as shown. (This echoes the shape of the Demand Curve from Chapter 2.)

Now, let's think about the value-cost balance across the four stages of the AUDIO cycle.

We know that all four stages offer the possibility to do a better or a worse job than competitors. So when a business assigns resources to work in any of the stages, it needs to think about value for money, too. It needs to be clear about the outcome that it seeks and the balance that it wants to achieve between cost (efficiency) and results (effectiveness). Is the priority in each phase to get a good-enough result quickly, and at a low cost? Or is it more important to achieve the right result, at almost any cost?

In the first two stages of the cycle, understanding the situation and designing changes, effectiveness is more important than efficiency, value is more important than cost.[3] A business that understands its situation better than competitors has a head start in building a better solution. Or putting it the other way around, a business with a 1 percent worse understanding of

---

[3]Value and effectiveness and cost and efficiency are both two sides of the same coin. The first word in each pair describes the output or result of an activity, and the second word describes the activity itself.

its situation than its competitors will always be running to catch up—a business that understands that the world is flat when in fact it is round will always be wondering why its projects never quite live up to expectations, no matter how efficiently they are implemented.

So, in the first two phases, cost is important but the priority needs to be on getting the best value. (This is one reason why strategy consultants can charge so much.)

Once the situation has been understood and appropriate solutions designed, the business then moves into the implementation and operation phases. Here what matters most is efficiency and cost when implementing the course of action that has been chosen. Value is still important, because the quality of the implementation and operation determines the extent to which the full potential of the design is realized. But in both cases the focus needs to be on doing what needs to be done as cheaply as possible, not on defining what needs to be done.

So, in the left-hand side of the map, effectiveness (doing the right things) is more important than efficiency (doing things right). And in the right-hand side efficiency (cost-focus) is more important than effectiveness (value-focus):

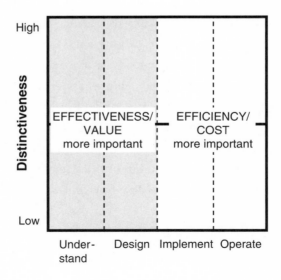

Again, looking at this shape in three dimensions we do not need to worry about the precise mathematical shape. But we *do* need to realize that:

- The understand and design side is higher (more value-focused) than the implement and operate side, and

- The slope between the two halves is again curved, not flat. This time it is because of the S-curve implied by the 80:20 rule (Chapters 3 and 5). The first 80 percent of the value from any activity requires only 20 percent of the effort, and increasing returns requires disproportionately more effort.

This time the three-dimensional shape that our map represents looks like this:

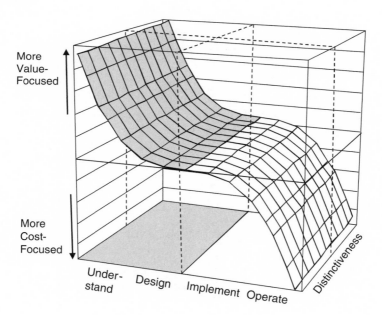

Again, what it means is that for a business to be good at the *third* layer of strategic advantage—for it to perform its activities better *in comparison with other businesses delivering similar services*—what it needs to do is to get its cost-value balance for each activity closer to this shape than its competitors do.

Putting the two perspectives and the two curves together, we find that the balance between cost and value divides into four quadrants:

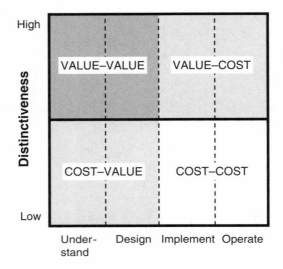

In three dimensions this represents a "competitiveness landscape" that looks like this:

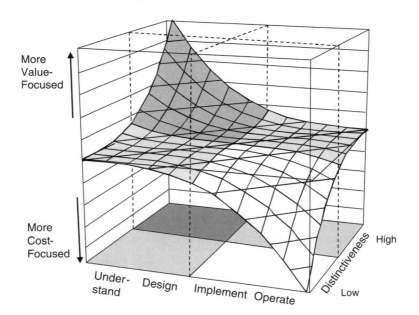

This is, if you will, a map of what quality means in every part of the economy.

- How does your business measure and manage the value-for-money mix for services with different levels of distinctiveness?

  Does it apply the same standards to both, or different standards?

  What would the effect be if that approach was reversed?
- How does your business measure and manage the efficiency and effectiveness of people involved in running and changing the business?

  Does it apply the same standards to both, or different standards?

  What would the effect be if that approach was reversed?

*IMPLICATIONS, PART 1: THE THIRD LAYER OF STRATEGIC ADVANTAGE*

This is a map of every business in the economy, and what it takes for that business to succeed.

Just as with a map of the world, there are details that it does not show. And there will be places where local reality does not match the overall smooth shape. In other words, there will be "mountains" and there will be "canyons."

But every activity in the business is part of one of the four phases of the AUDIO cycle, so this curved surface defines the optimal balance between efficiency and effectiveness for every activity within the business. It defines the balance of value for money that a business needs to aim to get from every one of its activities.

An activity that has a cost-value balance below the surface has failed to deliver enough value. An activity that lies above the surface has done more than was needed, and so has cost more than was necessary.

This is, if you will, a map of what quality means in every part of the economy.

The closer to this surface that a business gets with all its different activities, the more successful it will be—whether it does so deliberately or by accident.

Getting good at deliberately bringing performance closer to this curved shape forms the third layer of strategic business advantage.

Of course, doing a less than perfect job once in a while is very unlikely to bring down the entire business. (Although it can happen: Barings Bank, for example, was brought down by the actions of a single trader, more than 6,000 miles (10,000km) away from the head office.)

But it all adds up over time. Over time, a business that can reliably and consistently carry out all its different activities to a closer approximation of the general shape shown above will be more efficient, more effective, and will generate a larger surplus than its rivals. In this way it will become fitter for survival in its environment.

That does not make it immune from the short-term crisis—the polar bear with the whitest coat can still be hit by lightning—but it does improve the odds for survival over the long term.

And so it forms the third layer of strategic business advantage.

*IMPLICATIONS, PART 2: KNOWING WHAT TO BE GOOD AT* To be successful, a business needs to satisfy customer needs, it needs to use resources, and it needs to make money. All three of these core activities offer the opportunity for the business to do a better (or worse) job than the competition. And all three have to be in balance with each other for the business to succeed.

But we finished Chapter 6 with the question of which of the three needs to take the lead—which of the three sets of stakeholders the business should pay most attention to.

That is what this three-dimensional surface shows us. It shows us what "better" means in different parts of the economy, different areas.

What the diagram shows is which of the three core functions a business needs to be best at in different parts of the economy. In other words, as we are about to see, it defines what constitutes a successful strategy for each part of the economy.

Future generations may learn to calculate the exact shapes of the "economic-success hyperspace" surface, and then run their businesses to within 1 percent or 2 percent of it. But for us, the curves are *qualitative* indicators, and all we need to do is to get closer to the curve than our competitors.

To do that, we need to understand just two things. First, that there are four different areas or territories (which gently merge into one another). And second, that what a business needs to do well to be successful is different in each area.

In the top left-hand area, where businesses that deliver highly distinctive services are understanding and re-designing their business models or services, it is important to focus on value and effectiveness, both in *what* they do and *how* to do it. In other words, here it is important to be good at activities to do with *satisfying customer needs* (Chapter 2).

When delivering those highly distinctive services (top right-hand corner), the businesses need to get a good balance between efficiency and effectiveness—in other words, they need to focus on the activities to do with *making money* and *balancing* the overall *portfolio* of the firm (Chapters 4 and 5).

Businesses providing low distinctiveness services (bottom right-hand corner) need to focus on cost and efficiency. They will be successful by being better than rivals at *using resources* (Chapter 3).

And when understanding their markets and designing new services and new business models, these businesses need to balance effectiveness and efficiency with cost and value. This equates to a focus on the *return on investment* to be gained from these activities—in other words, Chapters 4 and 5 again.

What we are seeing is that all businesses carry out the same fundamental activities, but which of those activities is most important to success is different in different parts of the economy and different phases of the AUDIO cycle. See diagram on page 238.

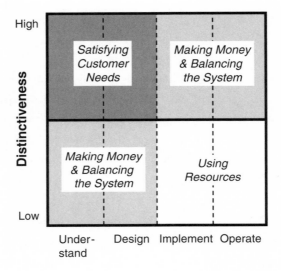

This explains where strategy comes from.

——— **MAKING IT REAL** ———

- Does the business you most admire in the world fit with this map?
- Does the way your business operates fit with this map?

Some examples of the world's most respected companies are listed below, together with the activities they are respected by other chief executives for being excellent at.[4] Opinions about which half of the map they operate in are the author's.

*General Electric:* Both halves. Most admired for its "management and leadership" (making money and balance). See also the "Running the Business/Changing the Business" box below.

*Microsoft:* Original Office programs (bottom half) had poorer functionality than its early rivals, but better distribution. Company is now respected for its vision and innovation (moving into top half).

*Sony:* Top half. Known for its vision and innovation.

---

[4]Source: Financial Times/PricewaterhouseCoopers report, "Companies Most Respected By Chief Executives."

*Coca-Cola:* Middle/bottom. Rated for its product portfolio (balance).

*IBM:* Both halves. Respected for its constant improvement and its marketing and advertising. Certainly this has been key in revitalizing the company and in moving it from the bottom half to the top.

*Toyota:* Both halves. CEOs rated the company for its focus on consumers. But what converts that focus into reality, cheaply, is the famous "Toyota Production System."

*PepsiCo:* Middle/bottom. Other food and beverage chief executives rated this company top for having "the best distribution system" (using resources, bottom right).

*Dow Chemical:* Bottom half. Respected by its peers for the way it "concentrates on its core business and outsources the rest" (balancing the system), and for its strength in chemical products and processes (using resources).

---

**IMPLICATIONS, PART 3: THE ORIGINS OF STRATEGY** Twenty years ago Michael Porter identified the three generic strategies available to businesses. They were:

- Differentiation:

  "... differentiating the product or service offering of the firm, creating something that is perceived *industrywide* as being unique." [his italics]

- Cost Leadership:

  "... to achieve overall cost leadership in an industry through a set of functional policies aimed at this basic objective."

- Focus:

  "... focusing on a particular buyer group, segment of the product line, or geographic market ... [so as to] serve its narrow strategic target more effectively or efficiently than competitors who are competing more broadly."

We can now understand that these are about being good at the first two core functions. Differentiation means being better than competitors at the activities to do with satisfying customer needs. Cost leadership means being better than competitors at using resources. And focus could be to do with either, but with a smaller number of customers.

And the map also explains why being what Porter called "stuck in the middle" can be successful.

Porter said that any firm that failed to "develop its strategy in at least one of the three directions" was "stuck in the middle . . . an extremely poor strategic situation." Yet businesses seem to be successful even while being "stuck in the middle," offering middle-ranking quality at middle-ranking prices.

The reason, as our map shows, is that there is a third way to be successful: to be good at the activities to do with balancing the business. Although this is less easily recognizable than the strategies to do with satisfying customer needs and using resources, it is no less valid as such—in fact it is probably the most important of them all, since it applies to most of the activities in the economy.

All businesses need to carry out the same fundamental activities. And as companies learn to get better at these activities over time, so they raise the bar for rivals and redefine the level of performance that is good enough in that part of the economy. After a few years, Darwin's principle of natural selection tells us to expect that the businesses that are better than their competitors at what is needed in their part of the economy will survive—"each slight variation, if useful, is preserved."

The businesses that provide more value to the customers who *want* more value will survive. The businesses that provide cost leadership to the customers who *want* cost leadership will survive, and so on.

The businesses that are less good at those things will fail. And the businesses that are good at doing the *wrong things* will fail also. The businesses that provide value to the customers who want cost leadership will fail. The businesses that provide cost leadership to the customers who want value will fail. (And the same, of course, goes for the relationships that the business has with its other stakeholder groups.)

If we then look (as Michael Porter did) for clues as to what makes a business successful, we will see some successful companies that are very customer-oriented, others that are low-cost, and others that focus on a small group of customers or services.

We might then easily make two mistakes. The first would be to assume that by copying them we will also make our own company successful. And the second would be to assume that the companies are successful *because* they have picked a particular strategy.

But strategy does not exist. Strategy by itself adds no value. Only actions add value. Only actions and activities exist. Like the emperor's new clothes, when we see strategy we are seeing something that is not there—we are confusing cause and effect, chicken and egg.

Reality is that each company has *become* successful because it was good at what its marketplace wanted: providing value where value was needed, or low cost where low cost was needed.

That meant it survived for long enough to become even better at the activities that mattered. Became good enough, in fact, for us to think there was a strategy.

Each company succeeded not because it picked a good strategy, but because it had a way of using resources to make money by satisfying customer needs that was a *good fit with its business environment,* a better fit than its competitors.

Success (as all those failed dotcom companies showed us) is not a question of choosing a brilliant strategy and then implementing it. Success is about listening to the marketplace that you are in, and then being good at the actions that will give it what it wants.[5]

This is the origin of strategy.

Every business is a system of activities that makes money by using resources to satisfy customer needs, now and in the future. Put a collection of those businesses together and you create an economy. The *natural* and *inevitable* result is then that these businesses will need to become good at different activities in different parts of this economy. And it will *seem* as if they need to follow different strategies.

---

[5]This implies that if you want to change the world, you need to change what you buy—the marketplace will then provide it. An alternative route to business success, as we saw in Chapter 6, is also to change to an environment that appreciates the things the business is good at.

But there is no such thing as strategy. There are only activities. And what drives success is how well they get carried out, in comparison with what customers (and other stakeholders) want, and in comparison with how well other businesses can do the same or similar things. A good strategy just means finding a way to do the activities in a way that brings them closer to the three dimensional "ideal quality" shape we have drawn.

This is like Isaac Newton realizing that two completely separate and unconnected things, an apple falling from a tree and the moon orbiting the earth, are both caused by exactly the same thing: gravity. Two completely separate and unconnected things, the strategic success of a business and the way an individual process gets carried out, are both caused by exactly the same thing: how well the activities within it match the three-dimensional economic landscape, the three-dimensional shape that defines what quality means in different parts of the economy.

*The same thing is driving both the small scale and the large scale.*

All the management fads, fashions, and fixes of the past twenty years are now clearly recognizable simply as techniques for improving *how* the business carries out one or more of its five fundamental processes:

- the three core functions (satisfying customer needs, using resources, and making money) and
- the two coordinating ones (balancing, aligning, and changing the business over time)

Benchmarking, focusing on core competencies, business process reengineering, activity-based costing, shareholder value accounting, balanced scorecards, sense-and-respond organizations, e-business, the Internet, customer relationship management (CRM), stealth marketing, viral marketing, SMS marketing—all of these are specific ways to improve *how* the fundamental activities get carried out. Each one raises the bar for competitors, but there will always be new techniques.

The key to determining whether each one will help or hinder a business is whether it will bring the cost-value balance of specific activities closer to the three-dimensional surface that represents quality, or whether it will take them further from it.

The underlying fundamentals of what a business needs to do to be successful will never change. Ultimately what matters is: what do customers (and other stakeholders) want, can you provide a service that *matches* a section of those needs better than competitors, can you *deliver* that service better than competitors, can you combine the two to *balance* your business and *make more money* than competitors, and/or can you *change* over time better than competitors?

Ultimately there are no panaceas: business is a never-ending race to improve a system that makes money by using resources to satisfy customer needs. Each part of that system offers the opportunity to do a better job than competitors—and so competitive advantage comes in layers like an onion, not as a single lump.

But once a business has learned to be good at its core activities, once it has learned to balance them and focus on the key activities that will make the most difference in its part of the economy, there is still another, final layer that can be added to the onion. It is a form of self-reinforcing competitive advantage that we will examine in the next chapter. There, we will learn how to add to our map the final part of our definition of a business: *changing over time.*

## RUNNING THE BUSINESS/CHANGING THE BUSINESS

If a business is represented on the map by a horizontal bar, doesn't that mean that every business needs to be good at *two* things—running the business and changing the business?

The answer is yes, and in a fast-changing environment it is the left-hand side that dominates; in a slow-changing environment the right-hand side.

But remember that a business is a system that makes money by using its resources and so on, and it is the *total system* performance that matters, the total system that competes. So the business needs to be good at more than just the two things shown. And it is competitors that define what level of performance is good enough in each area.

All athletes have to be physically fit to win—but runners need stronger legs, throwers need stronger arms, and pentathletes need a mix of both.

The map shows which part of the system is most important for businesses in each area. But although Ferrari, for example, needs to focus first on providing what customers think of as value, it would also benefit from discovering a way to deliver that same value for 50 percent less cost. And equally it would suffer if a competitor found a way to deliver 99 percent of the value for 50 percent of the cost.

Ultimately what matters is: what do customers (and other stakeholders) want, can you provide a service that *matches* a section of those needs better than competitors, can you *deliver* that service better than competitors, can you combine the two to *balance* your business and *make more money* than competitors, and/or can you *change* over time better than competitors?

Potentially any company can benefit by improving any one of these areas. The reason that General Electric has been so successful is because it has done *all of them:*

- exiting any business where it is not number one or two in the market (customer needs)
- introducing (for example) the six sigma quality improvement program (using resources)
- using tough financial performance measures (making money/balance), *and*
- pushing managers to reinvent their businesses before someone else does through the "DestroyYourBusiness.com" initiative (changing over time).

--------- MAKING IT REAL ---------

- In which of the five fundamental activities does your business most need to improve its performance?
- What key change projects is your business implementing today?

   What parts of the business will they improve the performance of?

   How will the improvements be measured: value, cost, or timing?

   Does this match with what the business needs?

   What key improvements are not being addressed?

## SUMMARY

The economy is made up of millions of businesses. We can draw a map of this economy by drawing the AUDIO process that represents each business and ranking them according to how distinctive they are.

We find that the balance between efficiency and effectiveness required for success is different in different parts of the economy. This means that in order to be successful in different areas of the economy, businesses will need to become good at different core functions.

What we think of as strategy is therefore nothing more than matching the core activities of the business to what the marketplace wants. There is no strategy: there are only actions that succeed (fit) and actions that do not.

A business does not succeed because it has a better strategy than a competitor—there is no such thing as strategy. A business succeeds (or fails) because it carries out its activities better (or worse) than competitors.

Ultimately what matters is: what do customers want, can you provide a service that *matches* a section of those needs better than competitors, can you *deliver* that service better than competitors, can you combine the two to *balance* your business and *make more money* than competitors, and/or can you *change* over time better than competitors? (And the same applies to the other stakeholders.)

The map we have drawn to identify the third layer of business advantage takes into account four of these five key things. The next chapter looks at the last of them: the ability to change over time.

LAYER 4

# THE EXECUTIVE PERSPECTIVE: CONNECTING THE SYSTEM

# CHAPTER 8

# Putting It All Together: The Escher Cycle

*"Curiouser and curiouser!" cried Alice.*

—LEWIS CARROLL, *ALICE'S ADVENTURES IN WONDERLAND*

THIS BOOK STARTED WITH a practical question: "What is the least a business needs to do to be successful?"

The answer, we found, is that a business is a simple system that makes money by using resources to satisfy customer needs. Balancing and aligning these three core functions improves the performance of the business as a whole, and this balance needs to be maintained and updated over time.

Each activity provides the opportunity for a business to deliver a better or worse performance than its rivals. So each activity provides the opportunity to create competitive advantage. And when large numbers of businesses come together to form an industry or economy, each business needs to become good at the activities that give it the best fit with its particular part of that environment. This explains what we call strategy.

All of this so far has provided a simpler explanation for things we knew already—about how businesses work and about the dynamics that naturally arise between them. It has shown that all successful businesses are based on just three things: satisfying customer needs, using resources, and making money. These things need to be done, they need to be balanced, they need to be updated over time, and they need to be fine-tuned to match the part of the economy where the business is operating.

This chapter introduces us to something new. It shows businesses how they can *connect* their improvements in those key activities to the natural flows of innovation and improvement that exist within the economy. By doing this, they will be able to accelerate their own evolution and create self-reinforcing business advantage.

The route we will take to understanding this is by thinking about the forces that act upon a successful business as it tries to expand into other parts of the economy.

We start by taking another look at the map we created in Chapter 7.

## UNDERSTANDING THE ALTERNATIVES

*WHEELS WITHIN WHEELS—THE "FRACTAL ECONOMY," REVISITED* If we want to understand what it takes for a business to expand and diversify, we need to understand what its alternatives are. To do that, we need to add a bit more detail to our map of the economy.

Copying the idea that a flock is made up of hundreds or thousands of individual birds, we created a map of the economy by charting individual businesses according to *what* they do (the outputs they produce) and *how* they do it (the four-stage AUDIO cycle).

On this map, any individual business is represented by a horizontal line or bar—the thicker the bar, the wider the range of services that the business provides. Ferrari, for example, would be represented by a thin line near the top of the diagram, while Ford would be a broader band lower down.

But no business works in isolation. Every business buys in services from outside. As we saw in Chapter 3, there are many things a business needs to do, and it does not matter whether they get done inside or outside the company, as long as they get done with the right balance of cost, value, and timing.

In Ford's and Ferrari's cases, one of the things that they probably both purchase is market research. Although they probably both need different information, and use different companies to get it, they both do the research for the same reason: to do a better job at the *understand* part of their business. And the reason they buy these services from outside rather than doing the job themselves is because that gives them a better mix of cost, value, and timing—it helps them to get closer to the target value-cost surface that we saw in Chapter 7.

The same applies to bought-in services across the whole of the AUDIO cycle.

Think of nuts and bolts. Ford and Ferrari probably do not manufacture their own nuts and bolts, although 100 years ago they may well have done so. The reason they now buy them from a specialist supplier is to do a better, cheaper job at the *operate* part of their business:

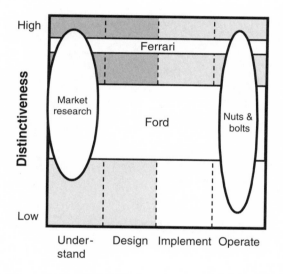

In the *design* phase they might buy software and services for computer-aided design. In the *implement* phase the companies might buy space at a motor show to help them launch new models. And so on and so forth. Every service that these businesses buy—from steering wheels to security, from paint to payroll, from airbags to executive recruitment—fits somewhere on the above diagram, according to the part of the AUDIO cycle that it supports. And because different suppliers sell different versions of the same service, ranging from high distinctiveness to low distinctiveness, companies selling a range of similar services will appear as a vertical "blob."

In every case, the service is bought because it helps the businesses that buy it to do what they need to, better—because buying the service gets them closer to their target mix of cost and value than carrying out the activity themselves. (For the sake of readability I will leave out the "and timing" part from this point on.)

From the suppliers' point of view, this means that the mix of price and value that they need to provide is whatever *fits* for the part of the customer's process they are being used to support:

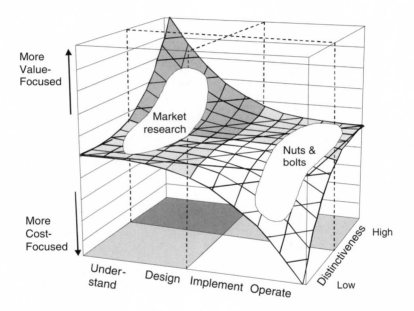

In other words, *the target mix of price and value that each supplier business needs to provide to be successful is the same value-cost mix that matches what the customer's business needs in that part of the economy.*

This means that we can look at our map of the economy in a new way, and use it not only as a map of the overall AUDIO process inside each business in an industry, but also as a map of the services that are sold into that industry.

Nuts and bolts companies now appear as vertical areas, supporting various customers in the *operate* part of the economy, market research companies appear as vertical areas, supporting clients in the *understand* part of the economy, and so on.

Whichever subset of businesses in the economy we look at—automotive manufacturers, market researchers, publishers, retailers, wholesalers, hotels, airlines, consultants, logistics and transportation companies, whatever—all will have a different set of suppliers. And they, in turn, will have a different set of suppliers, and so on.

We can think of the economy as made up of different layers. The earth-extraction industries, for example, supply the steel and petrochemical industries; these in turn supply the shipbuilding, automotive components, precision equipment, heavy equipment, paint, plastics, fabrics, and electricity-generating industries. These then supply their outputs to others.

Each of these industries is a subset of the total economy, all with the same structure as the map of the total economy. Each is a set of businesses with a four-stage AUDIO cycle, offering a range of services from highly distinctive to less distinctive. The more difference there is between high distinctiveness and low distinctiveness the more steeply the cost-value quality curve slopes. The less difference between high and low distinctiveness, the flatter the shape.

And because there is no precise definition of an industry (Chapter 7), the total economy can be sliced an infinite number of ways, all overlaid with a different set of suppliers, all with the same basic shape and structure, but no two slices exactly the same.

This "wheels within wheels" quality can be difficult to imagine, but is a property of the mathematical shape called a fractal. This may sound complex, but it is simply a sign that the apparent chaos is being created by an underlying simplicity.[1] In a mathematical fractal, the underlying simplicity is a mathematical formula. In our case it is the fact that all the different businesses share the same simple structure: making money by using resources to satisfy customer needs.

---

[1]For a superb free program which allows the user to zoom in and out of different fractal shapes in real time, visit: www.gnu.org.

But, quite simply, Ford and Ferrari are both part of a slice called the automotive industry, which is served by the nuts and bolts industry, which itself serves the *operate* phase of a slice called consumer needs.

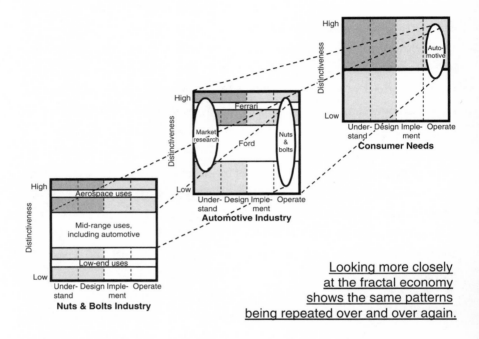

Looking more closely
at the fractal economy
shows the same patterns
being repeated over and over again.

In this way, the economy is a hologram of itself: every business *is a part of* the larger business processes it supplies, and so contains information about the larger process into which it fits. The specifications of different nuts and bolts depend on the uses to which they will be put. Every market research questionnaire is a summary of the particular information that matters most to the customer businesses. And so on.

Whether we can understand what a hologram or a fractal is does not matter.

What *does* matter is that this way of thinking is now going to show us how the structure of the economy helps businesses to expand once they have become successful.

As we look at the forces acting on a business trying to expand, we are going to need to think at two levels: first at the level of the AUDIO cycle within the business itself (as we saw in Chapter 7); and second in terms of the AUDIO cycle of the larger business processes that it supports. (This larger process might be another business, like Ford or Ferrari. Or it might a combination of businesses that cooperate, for example, to sell holidays/ vacations, fly planes, and manage hotels and car rentals.)

---

### THE IMPACT OF CHINA

The opening up of China to foreign trade and investment has given the world access to a source of manufactured goods that is significantly cheaper than existed before. For customers this is good news. But for existing manufacturers it represents a challenge.

At first sight there may seem to be only two options: create manufacturing bases in China that share the same cost structure, or quit. But the map of the fractal economy can help us to think about the problem differently and expand the range of available responses.

Simplifying hugely, we could say that the impact of China has been to lower the cost at which commodities can be manufactured. This changes the economic landscape in the bottom right-hand corner of any affected industry. And as the new manufacturers develop more premium services, the effect is spreading upwards:

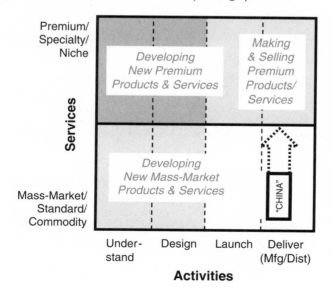

---

Any business that wants to survive in this industry needs to find a piece of territory that it can defend: a combination of activities and services at which it can do a better job than its new rivals.

Again, simplifying hugely, because the precise details will depend on the particular industry, we can see that *potential* options for an existing manufacturer could be to:

- set up operations in China, as before (bottom right quadrant)
- shift from manufacture into distribution (bottom right)
- move away from commodities into manufacturing premium services (top right)
- focus on developing new commodity services (bottom left) on the assumption that the new China-based rivals are good at copying but not yet at innovating
- get close to specific customers with distinctive needs, recognizing that skill at developing new specialty services is the activity that the new China-based rivals will find hardest to develop (top left)

Which of these alternatives is most appropriate will depend on the specific industry and business. But over the long term any sustainable solution will have to include either a low-cost manufacturing base (perhaps in one of the other BRIC countries of Brazil, Russia, and India, to which this analysis also applies), or to getting close to customers and taking the lead in developing new premium services.

This will position the business either in the bottom right or the top left quadrant of the industry. And these, as we shall see over the coming pages, are the two key sources of innovation and improvement in the economy.

## WHAT ABOUT CONSUMERS?

Some readers may be worried that not all customers are businesses: some are what we call consumers.

But everyone who works, whether employed or self-employed, fits our definition of what a business is. We all satisfy the needs of a customer or employer in one or more of the phases of the AUDIO cycle, depending on our job. We all make money (and borrow money) and use resources to do so. And we all improve our core functions through an AUDIO cycle that we usually call training, education, or experience.

Of course, "all work and no play makes Jack and Jill a dull couple," so we don't just spend time and money on work-related activities. The five Maslow levels show us there's more to life than that.

But if this applies to our smallest businesses, then maybe it should apply to our largest ones as well. Maybe all businesses should spend time and money on things to do with activities beyond their own existence, safety, and security. Maybe there's a business equivalent of belonging and esteem.

If it seems a little soulless to think of people as businesses, then the problem probably lies more in our definition of what we have come to expect a business to be than in seeing people as "making money by using their talents to fulfill a need, now and in the future."

If some of the businesses we have created lack humanity, then it is we who have made them so. Businesses were created to supply the needs of people, not the other way around.

AVAILABLE DIRECTIONS FOR DIVERSIFICATION This new diagram shows that every business activity is potentially a service that another company could provide. (Even Ford used to manufacture its own nuts and bolts.)

On this map, the "footprint" of each company shows the set of needs that it is competing with rivals to satisfy—anything outside the footprint is the so-called "white space" of needs that the business could expand to provide.

Let's think about how it might do so.

The simplest way to grow is by selling more of the existing services to new customers. For example, the market research company that worked for Ford could probably sell nearly identical services to General Motors, Procter and Gamble, or Nestlé. The nut and bolt manufacturer could probably sell to other car companies, or other countries. This would normally be counted as a diversification, but it does not change the footprint on the map and is shown as "0" in the diagram below. This makes the footprint deeper, strengthening the company's hold on its existing space, as we saw in Chapter 2.

The first way to diversify that changes the footprint is by creating more- or less-differentiated versions of its services. These might sell to the same customers or to different ones—it does not matter. These vertical diversifications are shown as "1" on the diagram below. For example, the market research company that worked for Ferrari could adapt a version of its services to be useful to Ford, or *vice-versa*. Similarly, the nut and bolt manufacturers could make higher-specification nuts and bolts for aviation or aerospace use, or weaker ones for gutters and shelving.

The second way is to extend horizontally. This is shown as "2" in the diagram. Market research and nuts and bolts each form a very small part of the total set of activities that the companies that buy them have to carry out in the *understand* and *operate* phases of their businesses. By understanding what customers do before and after the service they buy in, suppliers can find new services to provide. In this example, the market research company could expand from providing raw data to analysis, and then recommendations based on that analysis. The nut and bolt company could expand into providing whatever components and sub-assemblies the nuts and bolts are used to hold together. It could then extend its service to include fitting those sub-assemblies directly into the car on the production line. (This, in fact, already happens in several places around the world, where it is the component supplier, not the car manufacturer, who employs the workers on the production line.)

Horizontal diversification effectively works by taking over more of the internal process of the client business. Extend this far enough, and it becomes outsourcing, and can even take the company into completely different phases of the customer's AUDIO cycle, shown as "3" in the diagram below.

For example, the nut and bolt manufacturer might work more closely with its clients to understand their larger business process and perhaps design new fixings unique to the specific *design* process of each new car. The market research company could probably extend its services this way by forming a team to help implement its recommendations, or by developing research methods that are specific to other parts of the customers' process (specific to new launches, for example).

In any case, this way of thinking will help a business to broaden its perspective on what business it is in, help it to think outside the box:

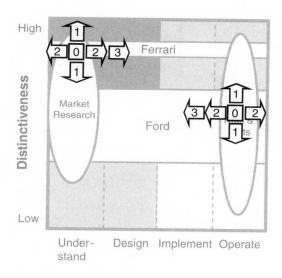

Let's look at some examples of how companies have significantly expanded like this in the past.

IBM started life as a computer manufacturer, providing value to customers only in the *operate* phase (bottom right-hand corner). Its turnaround in the 1990s depended heavily on expansion into consulting, design, and implementation services that helped customers to best apply those computers to improve their businesses. That shifted the business footprint upwards and to the left, and as a result, IBM now provides value (and earns revenue) in *all four stages* of its customers' AUDIO cycles.

Accenture operates in much of the same space, but came to it by a completely different route. Arthur Andersen was founded as an accounting firm, helping clients with the *understand* phase of their businesses (bottom left). It then expanded vertically into management consultancy by forming

Andersen Consulting (now Accenture), which in turn expanded horizontally from not only *understanding* the key drivers of the customer business but also *designing* and *implementing* computer systems that would improve its business performance in the light of those drivers. Accenture (the descendent of an accounting firm) now competes directly with IBM (the descendent of a manufacturing firm) in the top half of the diagram.

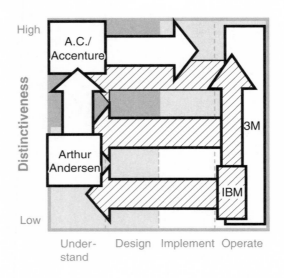

3M, on the other hand, is often considered to be one of the world's most innovative and diversified companies, with a range of products that includes Scotch™ Tape, Scotchgard™, Post-it® Notes, and the soles of the boots worn by the first man on the moon. These depend heavily on the company's ability to *understand* customer needs, *design* solutions, and successfully bring them to market (*implement*). But from this way of thinking, 3M doesn't seem diversified at all: almost all their services help customers only in the *operate* phase. Yet 3M contains a huge amount of knowledge about what it takes to *understand, design,* and *implement* new services—expertise that other companies would be willing to pay for, if 3M offered it *as a service in its own right.*

If successful businesses can expand in any direction, we might very well ask what's to stop one of them growing to take over the entire economy? The answer, as we know, is that different skills are needed in different parts of the economy. But this issue will be discussed on page 271 in the "What Gives Businesses an Edge" box.

For now, having identified the possible ways in which a successful business might diversify, the time has come to look closely at what would drive the success of moving in each direction.

But this issue will be discussed on page 271

───────── **MAKING IT REAL** ─────────

- What parts of the AUDIO cycle do your business's services support for its customers?

  How might it expand?

- What key suppliers does your business currently use, in which phases?

  How might their role be expanded to help your business?

## NOT A LEVEL PLAYING FIELD

In Chapters 2–7 we have seen how successful businesses all carry out the same fundamental activities and form industries that all have a similar shape and structure.

We know how individual businesses can diversify, and are now going to look at whether it is easier for them to expand in some directions than others.

In doing so we are going to have to think in terms of the sources of advantage, not only in the business's own industry, but also in the larger business processes that its services form a part of.

This will reveal the natural flows of innovation and improvement that exist within and between industries, which affect which directions are easier for businesses to expand in, and, more importantly, affect their ability to improve performance at the core functions or activities that provide strategic business advantage.

*VERTICAL DIVERSIFICATION, PART 1: SIZE MATTERS* Let's start by looking at companies in the right-hand half of an industry: businesses that support the implement and operate phases of the larger business processes they are part of.

We know that a successful company in the lower-right ("cost-cost") quadrant will be good at using resources, while a successful business in the upper-right quadrant will be good at balancing the core business functions and making money.

What happens when each develops a service that takes it into the other's space? Does one have an advantage? The answer is yes.

To become a low-cost provider in the bottom right-hand quadrant, a company has to become very good at just one thing: *using resources.* As we know from Chapter 3, this means it needs high volumes and to make use of the Experience Curve.

To become good at balancing the core functions (top right) a company only needs to be reasonably good at each one. The 80:20 rule, or the law of diminishing returns, means that this is easier than becoming very good at just one. The company that gains enough experience to be moderately good at using resources has also had enough experience to be moderately good at satisfying customer needs and at making money. To become very good at any one of these core functions requires experience, and that does not come easily or cheaply.

Putting it more bluntly, if a business is selling a standard bottom-right quadrant commodity such as pork bellies at 90 cents a pound, and the market price is 80 cents a pound, then customers will not give two hoots how balanced its business model is; they will simply go elsewhere.

This means that a business that decides to expand from the bottom right-hand quadrant of any particular industry into the top right-hand quadrant (by developing more differentiated services) has an advantage over any business that tries to do the opposite. Specifically, a business can leverage its low-cost delivery base to also provide more differentiated services.

*Being successful in the lower-right quadrant helps a business to do a better job in the top-right quadrant than operating in the top-right quadrant alone.*

This is indicated in the diagram below by the "Size Matters" arrow:

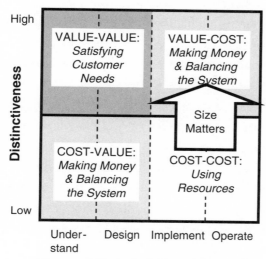

**Flows of Knowledge and Expertise**

In general, being successful in the bottom right-hand quadrant brings knowledge (experience) that helps a company to do a better job at the top right.

Putting this another way, the companies in the world today that are able to do mass customization are not small craft shops that grew larger, they are businesses that were good at mass production and made it more flexible.

And this transfer of knowledge happens whether the low-cost leader chooses to diversify or not: businesses in the top-right quadrant will always be on the look-out to hire the experience of people who know what it takes to be the low-cost leader, or to buy equipment that was developed to support those businesses.

It is easier for a supermarket to add a delicatessen counter than it is for a delicatessen to become a supermarket—the infrastructure needed to run the supermarket means the delicatessen can also be run more cheaply than a delicatessen on its own.

The experience gained from making large numbers of cars cheaply can be used to make luxury models cheaply, as well (see box on page 264).

Ten years ago, my local independent video store carried a large range of videos from art house and independent producers, as well as the Hollywood blockbusters. When the global chain came to town it lost the high-volume sales, and was forced to close because there was not sufficient local demand for an art-house-only store. The global chain could carry more independent movies than it does, but chooses not to.

Once a business, such as Direct Line, has put in place the resources needed to sell simple mass-market services like car insurance, it can easily branch out into more complex areas, such as house insurance.

The infrastructure needed to transport large numbers of low-value items around the country, or around the world, can be leveraged to transport small numbers of higher-value items more cheaply than a network dedicated to the high-value items alone. (This is true whether the items are foodstuffs, mail packages, or electronic data.)

If we talk again in terms of the terrain of the economy, we would say that there is a natural slope from the bottom right-hand corner of the economy to the top right. This counts as downhill and makes it easier for companies to expand in that direction than the other.

That does not stop businesses from successfully expanding in the other direction—after all, armies that attack uphill can still win—but the effect exists, and businesses can take advantage of it if they understand it (though the size of the effect will vary from industry to industry).

Next we will consider the left-hand side of the economy, and services that help their customers with understanding and design.

---

**CASE STUDY: THE AUTOMOTIVE INDUSTRY**

Consider as an example the automotive industry, the output of which helps customers in the *operate* phase, and where the number of independent makers has fallen as corporations increasingly own a full range of brands (luxury to economy) that compete directly against each other.

Ford and General Motors have both moved into the top-right quadrant by buying existing brands (including Jaguar and Saab) and then working to introduce their lower-cost manufacturing processes to those companies. Although this has been difficult, it has been relatively successful, compared with BMW and Mercedes, which have worked to expand in the opposite direction. BMW bought Rover in 1994, and then spent approximately $4bn trying to restructure the business before deciding to sell most of it to Ford in 2000. Daimler successfully produced the Mercedes-badged A-class (after some teething troubles), so did not need to buy a new brand to move down-market in the way that Ford and GM did in order to move up. But Daimler's merger with (or acquisition of) Chrysler continues to be difficult, and is said to have cost $2bn in the first year alone.

But the most successful expansion has come from Toyota. Although not the largest automotive manufacturer,[2] Toyota is the company that has been most successful at converting high sales volume into low-cost production through the famous Toyota Production System. Its luxury models, under the Lexus brand, are built using the same system, often at the same plant, and this approach has meant that it has not only avoided having to acquire another company, together with all the costs of integration that go with it, but also every Lexus model sold adds to the cumulative experience of the Toyota Production System, thus strengthening the cost advantage of Toyota models, as well!

Brand image can be bought, but it is worth nothing unless it is based on real technical ability, which in turn is the result of learning and experience. (Experience can be bought, in the shape of people or equipment—but if competitors can buy it, too, then it no longer provides advantage, only the ability to catch up.)

---

**VERTICAL DIVERSIFICATION, PART 2: THE TEFLON EFFECT** In the left half of the economy there are, again, two quadrants, and different skills are needed to be successful in each one. In the top-left ("value-value") quadrant, companies need to be good at satisfying customer needs, while in the bottom-left ("cost-value") quadrant they need to be good at balance.

Once again it is more difficult to be very good at the single function than it is to be moderately good at all of them. The explanation is the 80:20 rule, the law of diminishing returns. Putting it bluntly this time, if your

---

[2]In 2003 Toyota passed Ford to become (in sales unit terms) the world's second largest carmaker after GM.

customer is the government of the newly-reunified Germany, and has asked for designs to renovate the Reichstag parliament building in Berlin, they are not looking for a design that is quick, cheap, and easy to build. What they want is a design that is innovative, imaginative, and (preferably) astonishing. The firm of architects that understands satisfying customer needs well enough to win that kind of commission will find it easier to design a suburban house than the designer of suburban houses would find it to design the Reichstag. It is easier for a brain surgeon to remove tonsils than it is for a dentist to perform brain surgery.

On the left-hand side of the economy, then, downhill runs from top to bottom. Again the slope is to do with innovation, experience, and the flow of knowledge within the economy. But this time it is the experience and innovation to do with become leading-edge at satisfying customer needs, not using resources. This time the innovation is in terms of *what* the customer wants, rather than *how* to deliver it.

Necessity is the mother of invention, so the customer who pays for a new invention is usually the one who needs it most, who values it most (Chapter 2). Once the new service has been invented it can then be reproduced more cheaply for other customers and adapted to suit the needs of many more customers (Chapters 2 and 3).

The drive to put a man on the moon is a well-known example that led to the invention of many technologies that then found applications here on earth. Spin-offs from NASA include freeze-dried food, smoke detectors, trash compactors, virtual reality, quartz watches, customer service software, scratch-resistant lenses, and swim-faster swimsuits, to name but a few.[3]

Other examples of how services migrate from specialist to general use include surgical techniques developed in wartime, video recorders (used by television companies for around twenty-five years before they became common in homes), investment funds, and home photocopiers.

Again and again, what we see is that new services are developed in the top left-hand quadrant of the economy and then migrate downwards as

---

[3]See www.thespaceplace.com/nasa/spinoffs.html.

they are *understood* and *designed* into services and applications with wider appeal.

This means that businesses that occupy this "high ground" for new ideas have the opportunity to convert those into services with wider appeal, *if they choose to do so*—the mass-market Chanel or Gucci handbag, if you will.

If they don't, then companies in the lower half will always do it for them. It is easier to make a fake Rolex than to design a real one; easier to print a copy of John Constable's *Haywain* on a box of cookies than it is to paint the original picture; easier to take a cast of Michelangelo's *David* than to carve it from the original block of marble.

So, rather than controlling all of the process themselves, businesses can also license their intellectual property to other businesses, while remaining focused on what they do best.

And equally, businesses that want to be more successful in the bottom left-hand quadrant will benefit by looking to the top left for inspiration.

*Being successful in the top-left quadrant helps a business to do a better job in the bottom-left quadrant than operating in the bottom-left quadrant alone.*

Downhill in the understanding and designing of new services (often known as trickle down in marketing circles) runs from top to bottom, and this is shown below as the Teflon Effect. After all, the first use for Teflon[4] was not the humble frying pan, nor was it the last. (See diagram on next page.)

In fact there is a group of companies that are dedicated to enabling this Teflon Effect for their customers. These are the Information Technology (IT) service companies, such as Accenture and EDS. These businesses take the understanding of a computer technology that was invented by another business and apply it (under some form of licensing agreement) to improve a customer's business process. In 2002 this valuable role of enabling of the

---

[4]Teflon was initially so expensive that no cost-effective uses for it could be found. But then its unique anti-corrosive properties made it essential to the Manhattan Project and the first atomic bomb. Other military applications then included nose cones for proximity bombs and coatings for copper wires in radar systems.

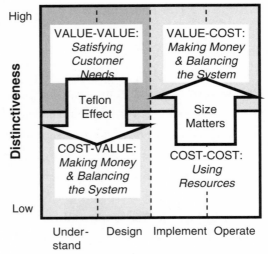

**Flows of Knowledge and Expertise**

Teflon Effect earned them worldwide revenues of more than $500 billion.[5] Sometimes they also implement and/or operate that process, so their service effectively becomes implemented strategic transformation. This is an example of the horizontal diversification that we shall look at in the next section.

---

**INFORMATION AND KNOWLEDGE**

Seeing each business as part of a larger business process, we realize that the whole economy is actually a vast processor of information and knowledge.

Each link in the chain, each business, is a specialist at taking data from one phase of the cycle, manipulating it, and transforming it into *information* that can be used in the next phase. How to carry out that transformation is the *knowledge* that gives the firm competitive advantage.

Nike understands what people want on their feet and transforms that into a set of instructions that a factory can use to make a shoe. The factories that know best how to make the shoes win the business. (Nike uses over 100 different contract factories in the US alone.) Information about orders and deliveries passes between the factories and

---

[5]Source: Gartner

retailers. The retailers who know how to sell the most shoes win more business, and provide information back to Nike about which shoes sell best. This information is key to understanding what customers want, which is why Nike owns almost 100 retail outlets worldwide, and employs 4,000 Nike retail associates in the US alone.

At the corporate level, Nike Inc. is competing with other footwear brands to be the best at *knowing* what teenagers want on their feet, *and* at *knowing* how to *manage the whole system,* cycle, or process to deliver it. (See also Chapter 7 for other horizontal flow examples.)

No wonder, then, that information technology has had such a huge effect on the world: it improves the efficiency and effectiveness with which every part can capture, manipulate, and pass on information.

This accelerates the natural flows of information and cycles of change within the economy, and also forces companies to focus on what they are really good at, what they truly have the *knowledge* to be able to do best. At the same time it expands the number of customers and suppliers that the business can work with, resulting in the so-called "winner takes all" economy, where the business with the best process/service for satisfying a certain set of needs is able to use that process to benefit any customer in the world.

These underlying currents or flows of information within the economy, and how a business can take advantage of them to change faster and become more successful, are really what this chapter is all about.

---

***HORIZONTAL DIVERSIFICATION: CHICKEN AND EGG*** Companies can also expand horizontally by delivering services that support more of the larger business process that they are part of.

The natural flow is from *understand* into *design,* then *implement* and *operate,* so the easiest way to expand might seem to be to move "downstream" into whatever phase or activity comes after the phase the business already supports. But the AUDIO cycle is a *cycle,* and knowledge flows in the opposite direction, too. Having a detailed knowledge of what it really takes to *operate* or *implement* will also help to build a better *design,* or a better *understanding* of what the situation really is. A plan (design) is more likely to succeed if it has been put together by people who have had experience of *doing* that kind of thing before. And if something goes wrong during implementation/operation then it may still be possible to be successful if the people *understand* the larger objectives that their actions were intended to achieve—this is, after all, one reason why companies spend time explaining mission statements and strategies to their people.

So, knowledge and information flow in both directions along the AUDIO cycle, and there is nothing that intrinsically makes it easier for a business to expand horizontally in one direction or the other.

In fact, as we saw in Chapter 6, managing that flow of information, deciding what information to pass from one phase to another, is a key part of managing the AUDIO cycle in any business: it is part of what determines whether Nike does a better job than Adidas, whether Ford does a better job than General Motors, and so on.

So for a business thinking of diversifying horizontally along the AUDIO cycle of its customer, the primary enabler/restrictor of horizontal expansion becomes the experience that can be gained in any *one* phase, rather than the benefits of integration *between* them. (See also the "What Gives Businesses an Edge?" box.) This means that the supplier business becomes limited/ defined by the resources it controls, and its market then becomes limited/defined by the different customers for which *its* resources/ processes can be used to deliver the best service for their need. New technologies and changing customer needs can alter that space, so survival becomes a question of maximizing the range of services that the business provides (in order to maximize experience curve effects, both for cost and value) and keeping a close eye on how the boundary (of which services add to the core experience of the firm and which do not) changes as needs and services and processes and resources all change over time.

The issue of passing information horizontally along the AUDIO cycle can then be left to the customer business (whose job it is anyway) and the business can maximize its own advantage by aligning itself with whichever customer it believes is best at managing that AUDIO cycle, one level up.

(In other words, working for a successful customer is better than working for a struggling customer.)

This can be done in a project-based way, as with the team of architects, consulting engineers, a sculptor, cost consultants, lighting consultants, a structural engineering firm, and a firm of construction advisors that won the competition to design the Millennium Bridge in London. Or it can be a more formal arrangement of a group of companies working together over the long term, as with the Japanese *keiretsu*, Korean *chaebol*, and western strategic partnerships.

Making money, as we know from Chapters 2 and 4, depends on the gap between demand for a service and its supply (from competitors). That gap can potentially be large in any part of the economy, anywhere along the AUDIO phases. But the *source* of any new gaps between what customers want and what competitors in general can provide is always some new innovation in either the top-left or the bottom-right quadrants of the economy. That is where new ideas for *what* to deliver and *how* to deliver it are created. And from there they then spread to the rest of the economy, through the Teflon Effect, because Size Matters, and now through the AUDIO cycle. The closer to those twin sources a business is, the more likely it is to be the first to spot a gap (and then be able to make money from it).

---

### WHAT GIVES BUSINESSES AN EDGE?

Consider two very different businesses: Nike and IBM Services. Each of them faces the same strategic challenge—how best to manage the AUDIO cycle—but each has found a different way of collaborating with other businesses to achieve that. Why?

Nike's business is about understanding what people want to wear on their feet[6] and satisfying that need better than competitors. For the types of shoes that Nike sells, innovative design is the key factor, so the company employs designers directly, inside the business. This keeps *control* of this key process, and also keeps inside the business the

---

[6]As well as other sportswear and equipment, but let's keep it simple.

*experience* that is necessary to remain a leading player. The next stage is manufacturing, and to an extent the designs are limited by what it is possible to manufacture, so there is a good case for Nike to own the factories as well. But manufacturing uses a completely different set of skills and resources, so by using contract manufacturers, Nike can simplify its business (focus on what it is good at) while enabling those manufacturers to also work for other customers (including Reebok and Adidas), which generates larger experience curves and lower costs for all of them.

After working with Nike for a while, these manufacturers will know what it takes to design and build a competing shoe, and might consider expanding their own businesses into some of the activities carried out by Nike—after all, the ability to manage the total AUDIO cycle can start from expertise in any one of the phases. But by using many manufacturers, Nike (as well as Reebok and Adidas) achieves two further benefits: they make it less likely that any single manufacturer will achieve a significant cost advantage over the others (which would be one way to start a rival chain), and they prevent any single manufacturer from gaining sufficient experience in the whole range of footwear to be able to compete with Nike in design first, and innovation second.

Finally, instead of relying on existing retailers, Nike has chosen to run some of its own retailing outlets. There are three good reasons for doing this. The first is that the innovative retailing experience can become an explicit part of what it is to buy a Nike shoe, extending the brand to satisfy more customer needs. Nike claims that their Nike-Town outlets "became the standard for interactive and immersive brand environments," so the second benefit is that it allows Nike to experiment with expanding into *their* larger business process, which is retailing. But the third, and probably most important reason, is that it brings Nike into direct contact with information about what it is that people want to put on their feet—what gets people excited about footwear, and what does not—and that can feed directly back into the design process, without filtering through any market research report.

In summary, Nike understands that its role is to *manage* the AUDIO cycle, not to carry out every activity itself. It also understands that the customer needs it satisfies are in the top half of the economy, so that its advantage comes from being best at understanding and designing those needs, while manufacturing is best done by third parties who provide a low-cost, but effective, part of the total chain.

Now consider IBM Services. They offer to understand a customer's business need, design a computer-based solution, install it, and then run or host the finished system: the full AUDIO cycle. Each of these stages could be run as a separate business—so why does it make sense for IBM to offer them all, rather than focusing on what it does best and using third parties to provide the rest more cheaply, in the same way that Nike does?

The answer is that this time the key resources used in all four stages are the same: people. The knowledge that a systems engineer gains from working in one phase of the cycle can be used to do a better job in another. So by offering services across all four phases, the company is able to gain more experience than it would by working in just one. And that experience can be converted into an integrated methodology that brings value to the customer in the form of lower costs, and lower risk for all parties.

The fact that the business shares the same name as the original computer manufacturer is almost irrelevant, apart from some recognition benefits. Because the resources used in the two parts of the business are different, the experience curves are "de-coupled." If not, it would not be possible for other IT services companies to survive, unless they also had links to a similar computer-manufacturing arm. But they do survive, and thrive, and like Nike they do so by using whichever manufacturer they choose.

In summary, the economy is a sea of different processes and activities. The footprint that defines a particular business is given by the space where *it* has the best solution for carrying out those activities. The knowledge that the business has gives it the potential to expand from there, either horizontally or vertically. What stops it from doing so, what prevents it from expanding to fill the entire economy, is a lack of experience, both in terms of *what* to do (value) and in *how* to do it (cost). Experience, in turn, is driven by the extent to which different parts of the economy use the same resources, the same technology. So a business is a process built around a technology, and the experience curve is what gives that business an edge.

So, the best way for a business to expand horizontally could be either upstream or downstream, and an effective two-way information flow within the AUDIO cycle is definitely important to the success of every business. If we look, now, at the level of the total economy we find that one direction of flow is more important than the other.

In the top half of the economy, where value matters more than cost, it is more important for a business to use experience from *implementation* and *operation* to improve its ability to *understand* and *design* than the other way around. This means that it is important for businesses in the top-left quadrant to use experience gained from the top-right quadrant (either by working there directly or by cooperating with businesses that do).

For example, when the Millennium Bridge in London was first opened it wobbled unexpectedly, and was forced to close for almost two years while corrective work was carried out. The vibrations did not prevent the consortium from winning the business in the first place—in the top left-hand quadrant the competition judges were bound to be more interested in the revolutionary new horizontal suspension technology and eye-catching "blade of light" design than in mundane considerations of whether the bridge could actually be built on time and on budget or not. But if another team had presented the same design *and* a better track record of being able to implement on time and on budget, then it would have had an advantage in winning the business.

This means that the arrow indicating downhill in the top half of the economy runs from right to left.

In the bottom half of the economy, for example when a government agency or council wants to build a standard concrete motorway or freeway bridge, the customer does not want cutting-edge technology—they want something that is functional, that matches their budget, looks reasonable, and is cheap to maintain. In the bottom, cost-focused, half of the economy it is more important for the *understand* and *design* phases to bring about the right result in *implement* and *operate* than the other way around.

Having an understanding of the bottom-*left* quadrant (again, by working there directly, or by cooperating with businesses that do so) can help a business do a better job in the bottom-*right* quadrant than working in the bottom-right quadrant alone.

So downhill in the bottom half of the economy runs from left to right.

There are many ways to achieve this horizontal integration and alignment, from the mission and vision statements already mentioned to simply having a collaborative approach to working with colleagues (either inside or outside the business). For architects and for fashion designers such as Issey Miyake, watching out for new materials and new ways of combining them represents an opportunity to achieve previously impossible designs. In the manufacturing industry, "design for manufacturability" is a well-known set of methodologies that help to integrate design with manufacture. In the top half of the economy this enables innovative designs to be manufactured more inexpensively. In the bottom half it recognizes that a 1 percent better design can pay for itself many times over in savings in production costs. Switching from considering only the purchase price to thinking about "whole-life costs" is another example of the same kind of thinking.

If we add these two new downhill arrows to our map of the economy, we find a clear picture of how information (or experience or knowledge) gained in one part of the economy can help a business to be more successful in a neighboring part. (That is to say, it helps the business to be more successful than if it operated in the second part alone.)

Not only does this advantage show a definite directionality (it *does* matter which direction a company expands in) but when taken together the arrows form a continuous cycle:

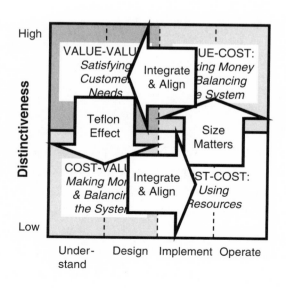

I call this the Escher Cycle because, like the famous picture by M.C. Escher, downhill in the economy goes on forever.

## A SELF-REINFORCING CYCLE

**THE ESCHER CYCLE—THE ULTIMATE SOURCE OF BUSINESS ADVANTAGE** Businesses are processes and are themselves made up of processes. And the whole economy is made up of businesses, so it must be a process also.

The picture shows us what that process looks like. It shows us how the thing that we call capitalism creates the effect that we call progress.

A business makes money by using its resources to satisfy a customer need. In order to do this better it chooses to improve something, either in what it does, or in how it does it. This alters the level of performance that is good enough for neighboring businesses, and a wave of change ripples through the economy.

This change can have a rapid and direct effect on the way other businesses work, as with close partners, competitors, customers, and suppliers. Or the ideas and knowledge that embody the change can take longer to transmit, moving through the economy as people change jobs from one firm to another or share it through books, conferences, and barbecue parties.

Eventually the innovation returns, in a different form, to the business where it started, and forces it to improve again: "What goes around, comes around." Or as it says in the Bible, "As ye sow, so shall ye reap." (See also "The Tao of Economics" below.)

The Escher Cycle is a flow of innovation and improvement that flows like a never-ending current through the economy. Understanding this can help businesses (and economies) function better.

In 1776 the economist Adam Smith[7] famously wrote about the "invisible hand" of the marketplace. Specifically, he said that:

> "Every individual necessarily labours to render the annual revenue of the society as great as he can. He generally, indeed, neither intends to promote the publick interest, nor knows how much he is promoting it. . . . He intends only his own gain, and he is in this, as in many other cases, led by an invisible hand to promote an end which was no part of his intention."

What the Escher Cycle shows us is the mechanisms by which this invisible hand operates.

It shows that what "leads" us all is not so much an invisible hand as an invisible *process*.

---

[7] *An Inquiry into the Nature and Causes of the Wealth of Nations,* bk. IV, ch. II (1776)

The reason that the set of policies we call the free market works is because it enables the Escher Cycle to work faster. Both the US and the USSR developed the technologies needed to put a man on the moon. Indeed, during the early stages of that race the Soviet Union was ahead. But the free market approach of the US then took those technologies and converted them into other inventions with more mass-market appeal (the Teflon Effect), which then helped to pay for the development of more innovations (Size Matters). The USSR could have done exactly the same thing. But the centralized, directive approach to organization that worked so well for achieving a single, concrete goal was completely unsuited to the task of coordinating an entire market. Repeating this example on a larger scale, we see that without the unplanned Escher Cycles of the West to compete with, the Soviet Union might have evolved forever at its own gentle pace, and the Iron Curtain might never have come down.

Governments *can* stimulate their economies (whether deliberately or accidentally) through policies and mechanisms that encourage the processes of the Escher Cycle to work faster. But the way they go about this has to be facilitative (bringing ideas and information to the parts of the economy where they are *likely* to have the most benefit) rather than directive (forcing businesses to do things in a certain way).

And businesses that deliberately set out to copy the Escher Cycle can build themselves an additional layer of competitive advantage, too. A business that understands the flows of the Escher Cycle is like a yacht that understands the currents and the winds: by working *with* them it can travel farther faster than one that tries to sail against the weather. By taking improvements that would have happened eventually, and consciously making them happen sooner, it can create directed evolution.

To do this, a business needs to do three things.

The first is to make the Teflon Effect happen. Identify and get close to the most distinctive customers (often also the most difficult and demanding customers!), find new ways to bring them value, and improve the return on that investment by reusing those innovations in services for less-differentiated customers.

The second action is to realize that Size Matters. Use the Experience Curve to deliver high-volume services at a low cost, and then to use those resources to deliver more differentiated services, also at a low cost.

The third thing is to integrate and align the business along the AUDIO cycle. This means sharing information and knowledge (to learn from and teach others) on *three* levels:

- inside the business, with the resources and activities it controls directly

- outside the business, downwards, by getting suppliers to align themselves more directly with what the business needs (perhaps through new contracting arrangements)

- outside the business, upwards, by connecting into the larger AUDIO cycle of the business process it supports. This brings information about what the customer wants, and the whole cycle begins again.

The first of these actions is about doing what was discussed in Chapter 2, satisfying customer needs. The second action is about using resources, Chapter 3. And the third is about balancing and aligning, a combination of Chapters 4, 5, and 6.

In other words, what a business needs to do in order to create an Escher Cycle, to create the ultimate competitive advantage in the economy, is to become a system that makes money by using its resources to satisfy a customer need, now and in the future, and we have returned to where we started.

---

**THE ESCHER CYCLE—AN EXAMPLE**

In case this all seems to be getting a bit abstract and theoretical, I want to give just one more example to show how very practical and simple the Escher Cycle is, as well as the enormous power and impact it can have.

The example I want to use is Bloomberg L.P., a global company providing news, information, and analysis to people who work in the financial markets. When it was founded in 1981, it faced two huge and well-established competitors, both more than 100 years old, and both with impeccable credentials. These were Dow Jones & Co. in the

United States, and Reuters in Europe. But within ten years Bloomberg's services were challenging and beating them both. And the company is now widely recognized as a leader, if not *the* leader, in this marketplace. How did this happen?

In his 1997 book *Bloomberg on Bloomberg* the company's founder, Mike Bloomberg, explained what he did. I have extracted some of his key insights below:

1. *Knowledge is what matters—knowing how to use resources to satisfy customer needs:*

    "There were better traders and salespeople, . . . managers and computer experts [than me]. But nobody had more knowledge of the securities and investment industries *and* of how technology could help them."

2. *Focus on what customers want—understand the difference between services with high and low distinctiveness:*

    "Bloomberg is in the business of giving its customers the information they need . . . where and when they need it, in whatever form is most appropriate."

    "Bloomberg offers two kinds of media: *broad*cast communications, where many consumers get the same information simultaneously; and *narrow*cast communications, for small groups."

3. *Size Matters—use the resources that support the mass market to cheaply deliver more differentiated services:*

    "In the Bloomberg terminal, we had a distribution device par excellence [and] revenue from terminal rentals, which meant we didn't have to worry about [a new] service paying for itself as a stand-alone product—one heck of an advantage."

4. *Leverage the Teflon Effect:*

    "We have the necessary information . . . so broadcasting's an easy extension of what we do elsewhere. . . . Radio and television simply became other delivery mechanisms for the same content."

    "The economics of this multiple utility let Bloomberg do things for thousands of dollars per piece when the competition's spending millions."

    "[When developing new services we] worked step by manageable step, each one valuable in its own right, each instantly upon completion providing a service to our customers and producing revenue to fund the continuing [service development] process."

"Radio stations . . . around the world could insert discrete Bloomberg-supplied stories into their lineups, or take our programming in a different order from the one we broadcast in New York. They just told the computer which story they wanted, where and when—and out it came. . . . Bloomberg was breaking and remaking all the rules."

5. *Integrate and align the business across the AUDIO cycle:*

"Our reporters periodically go before our salesforce and justify their journalistic coverage to the people getting the feedback from the news story readers. . . . In turn, the reporters get the opportunity to press the salespeople to provide more access, get news stories better distribution and credibility, bring in more business-people, politicians, sports figures, and entertainers to be interviewed."

"Understanding and reinventing how news should be produced and delivered, as opposed to doing it 'the way it's done,' lets us beat the competition. Such new strategies are more efficient for ourselves, and they give better allocation of resources to fulfill our customers' needs."

6. *Realize that your business system does not stop at the edge of the company:*

"The alliance of Bloomberg and Merrill Lynch was mutually beneficial. Merrill . . . got a customer service edge by putting its information on the Bloomberg system. Bloomberg needed [and got] real-time prices to provide timely analysis."

"We provide what so many newspapers have in short supply. . . . The newspapers, in turn, provide what we need."

In other words, although he probably did not realize it at the time, Mike Bloomberg built himself an Escher Cycle. And then the business built itself.

Let me be clear about exactly what I mean by this.

By focusing on the principles and processes for developing and delivering new services (and new delivery mechanisms) Mike Bloomberg enabled the business to build whatever levels of performance were *appropriate to the market at that time:* services that were appropriate to the needs of customers; ways of using resources that were appropriate to employees and suppliers (and the available technologies); and financial returns that were appropriate to lenders and investors. Whenever new ideas turned out not to fit with all three, Bloomberg "pulled the plug."

As the market changed, so the services (news, analysis, company information, . . .) and the delivery mechanisms (radio, TV, Internet, . . .) adapted automatically.

Rather than focusing on achieving a specific level of performance in a service or delivery technology, Bloomberg focused on putting the processes or procedures in place, and letting them listen to the market and give it whatever it wanted (and would pay for). That, essentially, is what the Escher Cycle is all about.

As we have seen, the processes for doing this did not need to be very complicated. But so long as the competition had no similar processes (so long as they focused on what the market *should* want, rather than what the market *could* want) simple processes were all that was needed.

It is advantage in the individual processes that make up the Escher Cycle that creates competitive advantage: in satisfying customer needs, in using resources, and so on. Linked *together,* they create self-reinforcing business advantage.

<hr>

**———— MAKING IT REAL ————**

Teflon Effect:

- Who are your most demanding/leading-edge customers?
- How could you turn (some of) the new things you do specially for them into services with wider appeal? Who would buy them? How?

Size Matters:

- What parts of your business do you have advantages of scale/experience in?
- How could you leverage and increase those advantages
  - for more distinctive services of your own?
  - for other businesses?

AUDIO Cycle:

- How can you increase the understanding that people in your business have about each other's areas? (What recent problems would that have solved?)
- Which key suppliers could significantly improve your performance by taking on more risk? Is the barrier one of understanding or contractual arrangement, or both?
- How could you improve your contribution to your customers? Is the barrier one of understanding of their aims or ability to understand/ implement improvements?

## YIN AND YANG: THE TAO OF ECONOMICS

There are two engines of change within the economy.

One is in the top-left quadrant, and has to do with improving *what* the business does.

The other is in the bottom-right quadrant and focuses on *how* to do it.

More simply, one is a source of *creativity* and the other is a source of *efficiency*.

Each set of changes flows through the economy via the Escher Cycle in the ways that we have described, and in doing so each contains the knowledge that begins the other.

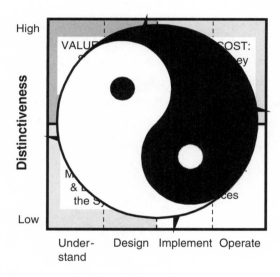

All of this is a direct echo of the Yin and Yang of Eastern philosophy, where Yin and Yang each represent complementary aspects of a complete whole, such as 'female and male,' 'dark and light,' and so on.

Given that our map shows processes, and everything is a process, it seems clear that the fractal economy extends much further than we realized.

## SUMMARY

Our map of the economy is also a map of the total set of needs that exist within the economy. The needs that any business satisfies can be drawn as a footprint on that map.

By looking at what happens when businesses seek to diversify, we find that there is a continuous flow of knowledge and innovation within the economy, the Escher Cycle. Mimicking this would accelerate the natural process of progress within the economy, and so create competitive advantage.

To achieve this, a business must use the Teflon Effect and Size Matters to harness the twin economic forces of the Demand Curve (*creativity*) and the Experience Curve (*efficiency*). It must also integrate and align its resources on three levels: internally, with suppliers, and with partners and customers.

By doing so it creates a self-reinforcing cycle of competitive advantage that is difficult for competitors to catch.

This is the *same* as saying that a business is a system that makes money by using its resources to satisfy customer needs, now and in the future, and so we have returned to where we started:

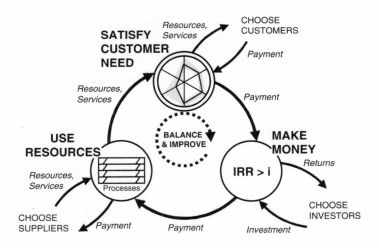

What the Escher Cycle shows us is the ultimate methodology for *how* to achieve that.

284

CHAPTER 9

# Conclusions

*You must remember this,*

*A kiss is still a kiss,*

*A sigh is just a sigh.*

*The fundamental things apply*

*As time goes by.*

<small>—"As Time Goes By" by Herman Hupfeld,

© 1931 Warner Bros. from the film *Casablanca*</small>

THIS BOOK HAS UNCOVERED the standard activities that go to make any business successful. It has shown us how to carry them out and how to balance them against each other. And it has shown us how to create a successful strategy, by fine-tuning these activities to match the part(s) of the economy where the business is operating. In doing all of this, the book has helped our businesses become more successful, by revealing the key minimum activities they need to focus on at each level.

In revealing to us how strategy and action are connected, the book has also shown that what we think of as the big picture is just the little picture repeated many times. There is no such thing as an industry or economy—only businesses and business activities. And flowing between and among them all is a continuous current or stream of information, driving progress. This is the Escher Cycle. And understanding how it works and how to copy it can make a business even more successful, by creating strategic advantage that not only lasts in the face of competition, but actually *grows* the more of it a business has. That advantage is already creating the successful businesses of tomorrow.

This chapter marks the conclusion of this book, but it is not the end of the story. This chapter summarizes the book and looks at implications for the future.

## SUMMARY OF THE BOOK

*BEHIND COMPLEXITY THERE IS ALWAYS SIMPLICITY* The film *Casablanca* is set against the chaotic background of wartime French North Africa. The resulting situation is a complex mixture of conflict and danger, agents and spies, mistrust, deceit, integrity, and corruption. But to the audience, out of all these competing themes there is only one story that really matters: will Ilsa stay with Rick, or will she fly to freedom with her husband?

Although the world can seem a complex place, when we strip away the detail we find that what matters is very simple.

In the world of movies, it is said that all great drama consists of just nine basic plots retold in different ways. These can be found all the way back to ancient myths and fairy tales. The major theme in *Casablanca*, for example, is the same as the one in *Romeo and Juliet*: "boy meets girl, with obstacles."

Switching to the physical world, the same applies. But here the fundamental building blocks are not situations but atoms. A diamond and a piece of charcoal may *look* very different, but both are made of identical carbon atoms. The reason that they appear different, have different properties, and are worth such different sums of money, is because the identical atoms inside them are *arranged* in different ways. In the diamond they are stacked at the points of millions of interlocking three-sided pyramids. In charcoal the arrangement is not geometric, but organic.

The whole of the physical world around us, the nearly infinite variety of rocks and minerals, plants and animals, buildings, streets, and stars, is made up of just ninety different kinds of atoms, arranged in different ways.

Complexity is just simplicity repeated many times.

286

CONCLUSIONS

If we can understand the fundamental simple structures of stories, then it can help us to write better scripts, like the one for *Casablanca*.[1] If we can understand the fundamental simple structures of matter, then it can help us to build better bridges and buildings, cameras, cars, computers, and CD players. And if we can understand the fundamental simple structures of businesses, then it can help us to achieve more of whatever results we want our businesses to create.

This book has set out to unravel the complexity of capitalism to show the simplicity that lies behind it.

*FUNDAMENTAL BUILDING BLOCKS OF BUSINESS* In the same way that atoms are the fundamental units of matter, so businesses are the fundamental units of capitalism. And, like atoms, businesses are also made of smaller units.

All the different atoms in the universe are made out of just three standard particles: protons, neutrons, and electrons. Businesses, as this book has shown, are processes, and so what they are made up of is smaller processes or activities.[2]

All the busy-ness of the commercial world around us can be boiled down to just *three* core processes or activities: satisfying customer needs, using resources, and making money.

*Doing* these activities well forms the first layer of strategic business advantage. *Balancing* them against each other and maintaining that balance over time forms the second layer. *Fine-tuning* the activities to match the particular part of the economy where the business is operating forms the third layer. And *connecting* the activities together within the business and with customers and suppliers forms the fourth and final layer of business advantage.

---

[1] Part of what makes *Casablanca* so special is that it contains interwoven elements of all nine key themes: the wandering loner, the love triangle, the fatal flaw, and so on—the ultimate in "something for everyone."

[2] Capitalism, in its turn, is made up of businesses, so capitalism is also a process. This is what the Escher Cycle shows us: *the process of capitalism.*

*How* these various activities or functions get done is different for every business, which is why they all seem different. How they get done also changes continually over time, as changing customer needs redefine what is *desirable*, new technologies redefine what is *possible*, and new competitor behaviors redefine what level of performance is *acceptable*.

But no matter *how* they get done, they always define *what* any business needs to do to be successful. They are fundamental, and will continue to apply "as time goes by."

*LAYER 1: THE THREE CORE PROCESSES* In order to satisfy customer needs, a business has to understand what those needs are, pick the set of needs (and customers) that it wants to satisfy, and then bring those chosen customers and the service together. The heart of this activity is about getting close to customers: understanding them and having them understand the value that the business can bring. The second part, choosing which customers' needs to support, determines the intrinsic basic mix of risk and reward that the business faces from its marketplace.

The second core process, being good at using resources, is about putting in place a business model to deliver the chosen service. This has three parts. The first is to identify the key resources that the business will use, and the second is to organize them together into a business model that will provide the mix of efficiency (cost), effectiveness (value), and adaptability (rate of innovation) that the chosen customers want. The third part is to make this real, by assigning the activities of the business model to suppliers and employees either "inside" or "outside" the firm. The choices made will be a balance between two factors. One, the heart of this core process, is the Experience Curve, which determines how firms are able to drive down the unit costs of delivering the service. The other is the degree of flexibility and control the firm has over activities carried out either inside or outside the firm. The chosen balance determines the intrinsic mix of *operational* risk and reward that the firm faces.

In order to be good at the third core activity, making money, a business needs to do just four things: optimize the size of future cash flows, optimize the timings of future cash flows, reduce (or optimize) the amount of money invested in the business, and minimize the effective interest rate that is paid to lenders and investors. By doing this, the *operational* risk/reward of using resources and the *market* risk/reward of the chosen customers' needs are converted into the *financial* risk/reward that faces lenders and investors. In this way all three functions are interlinked, which leads naturally to the need for the two coordinating activities.

*LAYER 2: BALANCING AND ALIGNING OVER TIME* Each of the three core processes is closely linked to the other two. Altering the service offered to customers automatically changes the way resources are used, which alters costs and changes how much money the business then makes. Paying more money as dividends to investors leaves less money to spend on developing new services for customers, and so on.

Every business is essentially a negotiating intermediary between three groups of people:

- customers
- employees and suppliers
- lenders and investors

Every transaction that it carries out involves the redistribution of risk and reward (money or value) between the business and one of these three groups. From a negotiation analysis perspective this is what all business is about, and it explains why *three* core functions are needed: one to interface with each external group.

In order to succeed, a business needs to negotiate effectively with all three groups. That means achieving "win-win" in each case. And for that to happen, all three groups have to want compatible things. Specifically, all three have to want compatible mixes of risk and reward.[3] In the wider

---

[3]Coincidentally, a study has found that the major driver of success and failure in international mergers and acquisitions is how well the attitudes to risk of the two businesses match. [Schoenberg, R. (2003) "Management Style Compatibility and Cross-Border Acquisition Outcome," Imperial College Business School Working Paper No. SWP03/01/BSM, 2003.]

scheme of things, this means that the role of the business is to bring together, match, balance, and align three groups of people.

*How* it does so is by bringing together, matching, balancing, and aligning the three core functions, together with their three associated sets of risk and reward (market, operational, and financial).

Doing this is the first coordinating process, function, or activity. It is achieved through three sub-processes:

- Managing the mix of services that the business provides
- Putting an organization structure in place that helps people to do what the business needs to do, and change what the business needs to change
- Using a measurement and reward system that keeps the business focused on the results that matter most today (while leaving it the flexibility it needs to adapt and grow into the future)

All three activities involve trade-offs between the three core processes and the three external groups—there is no single perfect mathematical solution. The narrower the band of options that represent win-win, the less room for maneuver the business has to achieve success. And without win-win in all three areas, the business is not sustainable.

All three of these sub-processes also need to trade-off and balance with the second coordinating activity, which is to adapt and change the business over time.

Changing over time is (of course) a never-ending cycle. It has four stages. The first is to convert a general Awareness of how the outside world is changing into an Understanding of what really matters to the business. The second is to convert that understanding into a Design for a better way of doing things. And the third and fourth stages are then to Implement and Operate that new design. Together, these become the AUDIO cycle, and success in business requires competitive success at *all four* stages. Changing the business is now as important as operating the business, as the amount of money spent on change consultants shows.

In these ways, the core and coordinating processes can be broken down into various sub-processes or activities. Together these define the least a business needs to do to be successful.

But how *well* does it need to carry out each activity?

*LAYER 3: FINE-TUNING THE SYSTEM* In order to be successful a business needs to carry out all these fundamental processes and activities. But how well it needs to do so will vary from business to business.

What level of performance counts as good enough depends on the performance of other businesses that are competing to fulfill the same or similar customers' needs. Over time, businesses will become better at the core activities that matter most in *each particular part* of the economy. (Those that become good at other things will simply fail.) So what we think of as picking the right strategy is actually about listening to the marketplace and matching the core activities of the business to provide what that marketplace wants. And the marketplace, of course, is made up of customers, suppliers and employees, and lenders and investors. And it is the relative importance or negotiating power of these three external groups that varies in different parts of the economy.

A business does not succeed or fail because it has a better or worse strategy than a competitor. It succeeds (or fails) because its activities are better (or worse) than competitors at delivering the mix of value and cost, risk and reward that customers, employees and suppliers, and lenders and investors want *in that particular part of the economy.*

This means that businesses can use the list of fundamental processes and activities as a *checklist for creating competitive advantage.*

---

**A CHECKLIST FOR CREATING BUSINESS ADVANTAGE**

For new startups the approach is simple. A complete business plan can be created simply by defining *how* the startup intends to carry out each of the fundamental activities.

For example, it might say:

- This is the general set of customers and needs we will be working in
- These are the specific needs we shall focus on, and here's why that is the best combination of value to customers, value to the business, and competitive advantage
- This is our customer chain: the actions we will take to shift customers from being unaware of our existence to becoming loyal
- These are our key resources (and how we can control/protect each one)
- This is how they combine to form a business model
- These are the key processes we will carry out in house, and these we will outsource
- This is how the business will optimize the size of its revenues and costs
- This is how it will manage the timings of those revenues and costs
- This is how the capital employed will be kept to a minimum
- These are the payouts to lenders and investors
- This is our portfolio of services, and how it will be managed
- This is our organization structure
- This is the measurement and reward system
- This is how we will monitor performance compared to competitors
- This is how we will carry out the four parts of the Escher Cycle

The business does not have to achieve world-class performance at every activity on day one. But it will not be sustainable until every process is being carried out *in some form*. Until then it is just a collection of loosely related activities, not a true business.

Starting from Layer 1 and building layer by layer, the more activities it carries out and the better it becomes at carrying out each one, the stronger its business advantage will become.

For existing businesses, a similar approach can be used. Starting from the list of fundamental processes and activities, the first step is to identify the (main) ways in which each activity gets carried out today. Comparing the level of performance for each activity today with the performance that will be needed in the future shows where the biggest change is needed. And the business plan is then the plan to build the levels of skill and competence that will be needed for each activity in the future (as we saw with Future Blueprinting in Chapter 6).

The focus switches from fixing problems in isolation (which only moves the problem to some other part of the business) to building a successful *total business*.

Understanding the same picture for competitors' businesses can teach us how to achieve their level of performance, as well as help to identify the areas that need improvement. It can also (perhaps more importantly) identify the *specific activities* at which the business is better than competitors—for this is where the business actually makes money.

In this way, the basic activities and sub-processes form a hierarchy of business advantage, similar to Maslow's hierarchy of human needs.

## The Hierarchy of Business Advantage

**Layer 4:**
Escher Cycle

**Layer 3: Strategy**
Fine Tune to Fit Environment

**Layer 2: Leadership**
Balance/Align, Lead Over Time

**Layer 1: Operations**
Satisfy Customer Needs, Use Resources, Make Money

Each level, and the individual processes on that level, offers the opportunity for a business to do a better job than its competitors. If two businesses have achieved similar performance at the first layer of activities, then advantage comes from being better at the next level up, and so on.

But remember that it is the total picture that matters, and woe to the business that focuses only on the higher source of advantage and forgets to maintain at least competitive parity on the more basic, lower-level activities.

*LAYER 4: THE ESCHER CYCLE* Because different activities matter more in different parts of the economy, different businesses are better at carrying out some of the standard processes and activities than others. And because it is always easier to copy someone else than it is to reinvent the wheel yourself, there is a flow of ideas and knowledge through the economy about how to carry out each process well: a flow from businesses for which high performance at an activity is very important, to businesses for which it is less important.

There are two sources to this flow, two springs of innovation—the twin engines of the economy. One focuses on maximizing the value that the business brings to its customers—this source is creativity. The other focuses on finding cheaper ways to deliver the value that has been identified—this is efficiency. (And the balance between them is what defines quality, or value for money.)

The innovations from these two sources then flow out into the rest of economy, through the Teflon Effect and because Size Matters. These in turn are linked by the coordinating processes involved in changing and improving businesses, to form a never-ending current of know-how running through the economy. This is the Escher Cycle, and it is the mechanism that drives the thing we call progress—the invisible hand of the marketplace. It is both the process and the consequence of the system we call capitalism.[4]

A business that understands how this cycle works can copy it. In doing so it creates directed evolution: it mimics the natural processes that brought us from the Stone Age to the Space Age, and so accelerates its own natural processes of improvement and development.

A government that understands how this cycle works can accelerate the evolution of its economy by putting in place policies, forums, and processes that encourage the four parts of the cycle to happen.

By taking the services created for the most demanding customers and adapting them for a wider market; by leveraging the scale of the resources needed to deliver to that wider market, to deliver cheaply to all; and by integrating the business into an organism of continuous seamless change, the

---

[4]And perhaps of evolution as a whole—see the Epilogue.

Escher Cycle creates a self-reinforcing loop of learning and competitive capability that represents the ultimate competitive advantage for any business.

It is the ultimate competitive advantage for two reasons. First, because it is always at the top of the hierarchy of competitive advantage. No matter what the relative competence and skill of rivals and competitors at activities on lower levels of the hierarchy, the Escher Cycle is always at the top because it represents the ability of a business to combine all the fundamental activities —to coordinate them in a synergistic way that enhances them all. It is the *virtuoso* level of skill in managing a business.

And the second reason why it is the ultimate competitive advantage is because once it is switched on it becomes much more difficult for competitors to catch up—it creates a chain reaction of accelerating competitive advantage, a bit like the first time the sun "switched on" four and a half billion years ago. Up until that time the sun was just a huge ball of ionized hydrogen gas—protons and electrons—more than a million times the size of the earth. But then a very rare event happened: four protons at its center were squeezed together so hard by the intense temperature and pressure that they fused together to form the nucleus of a helium atom. As they did so they released energy and light. That increased the temperature around them, which encouraged four more protons nearby to fuse—and then four more, and four more until the whole central core lit up.[5]

In the same way, the Escher Cycle gets the separate "protons" of business, the fundamental processes, to fuse together. When this happens, skill at one process enhances performance at another, which then improves another and another and another, until the original process itself is improved *and the whole cycle repeats.* By focusing on *improvement* as the key thing to be good at, rather than *performance* at any one activity, the business frees itself to go wherever the market wants to take it, and to be successful wherever that turns out to be.

---

[5]This is nuclear fusion, and temperatures and pressures are only high enough for it to occur at the core of the sun. The light produced takes about a million years to reach the sun's surface, and then about eight minutes to reach us.

As this happens, something else happens, too. In the same way that the four separate protons combined to create a helium nucleus, so the five fundamental processes now combine to create a synergistic true business. They become a truly integrated whole, instead of simply a collection of related activities.

What makes this difference? What enables skill at one process to be converted into improved performance at another? What enables the Escher Cycle? The answer is: information.

Information by itself is just data. Information gathered, applied, and directed to improve one of the fundamental five processes is knowledge. And knowledge applied to running an Escher Cycle is wisdom, power, and money.

That is why the potential of information technology and knowledge management is so huge. And the reason they have so often failed to deliver on that potential is because they have been applied to projects that did nothing to improve the five basic processes. Technology by itself adds no value—technology adds value only *when it improves one of the fundamental business processes.*

And that is why the so-called Information Age, despite all its hype, is bringing the biggest changes to our lives since the Industrial Revolution: not because of any snazzy technology or sexy buzzwords *in themselves,* but purely and simply because taking knowledge from one part of an Escher Cycle, and applying it to another, can help things to get done better, faster, and/or cheaper.

That is why the Information Age is exciting: because it is about to make the Escher Cycle happen.

What will the world be like then?

## IMPLICATIONS—WHAT NEXT?

With the fall of the Berlin Wall, and the so-called triumph of capitalism over communism, there was some discussion about the different flavors of capitalism that exist around the world, and which of them might be best. Comparisons were made between American capitalism, which supposedly sees the purpose of business as purely to enrich the shareholder, and

European capitalism, which (supposedly) places more emphasis on the benefit of the employees. Chinese capitalism ("for the good of the family") was compared with Korean capitalism ("for the good of the nation") and Japanese capitalism (which supposedly sees the prosperity of the *keiretsu* as its highest aim), and so on.

What the Escher Cycle tells us is that different strengths will always be important in different parts of the economy, and that the type of capitalism that ultimately succeeds will be one that can combine and coordinate all these different viewpoints in different areas, creating win-win agreements between all three of the groups of people that it interacts with.

Predicting the future is always a tricky business, so before reviewing the implications of the Escher Cycle it is probably worth looking back at the implications we have already been able to draw about how the small-scale characteristics of individual businesses affect the nature of the large-scale world around us. Some of these are given in the "Understanding the Implications" box.

---

**UNDERSTANDING THE IMPLICATIONS: LINKING SMALL-SCALE CAUSES TO LARGE-SCALE EFFECTS**

This book has looked at the implications of assuming that all business can be reduced to just three things: making money, using resources, and satisfying customer needs.

It has found that many of the effects we see operating at the large-scale level of the total economy can be deduced from specific characteristics of individual businesses on the small scale. Some of these are listed below.

Because customers buy from businesses that most closely match their needs, businesses that deliver standard needs shared by large numbers of people will be large, and businesses delivering more specific, differentiated needs will be smaller.

Because the Experience Curve enables businesses to deliver a cheaper service by doing the same thing over and over again, businesses will survive as useful social organizations (because they make things more cheaply than people can make them for themselves), and outsourcing of processes to other businesses may give a better mix of cost and value.

When technologies change we can expect new businesses to appear and others to die, as the new technology dramatically alters the landscape of cost and value and so changes the boundaries that constitute a survivable business.

Businesses negotiate between three external groups of people, so there will be conflict between businesses and their customers, employees/suppliers, and lenders/investors, as each group pushes (negotiates) for a bigger slice of the value that the business creates.

Businesses themselves have no ethics or values. To a business, the only value any person or thing has is the present value of the future cash flows it can be used to create. This means that we can expect to see business in conflict with people (who do have values), over items that have emotional significance for them, such as animals, the environment, and their children's health. But their conflict is not actually with the business itself (which has no values), but rather with the values of the people who get benefit from the business—namely its customers, employees and suppliers, and its lenders and investors.

A business consists of operating and changing three basic sets of processes, so a business that measures and manages the performance of all these parts will perform better than a business that concentrates only on a single set of (financial) measures.

Different organization structures enable businesses to optimize different parts of their operations and activities, so we expect businesses operating in different parts of the economy to have different internal organization structures.

Finally, we saw that bringing many businesses together leads to a flow of ideas and improvements that naturally result in the thing we call progress.

All of the above come logically from our simple definition of a business. And all are readily observable in the business world around us.

And in the same way, though we may not be able to predict exactly *which* companies will mimic the Escher Cycle first, we can say that *all* the successful companies in 100 years (or maybe ten?) will be operating it *in some form*. And we can make predictions about what the world will then be like.

In the same way that we have been able to draw conclusions from the properties of individual parts of a business for businesses as a whole, so we can also make predictions about the effects that the Escher Cycle will have.

We may not be able to predict which companies will be the first or best at implementing it, but we *can* say that the advantage they will gain means that in 100 years (or maybe just ten years?) all the most successful companies will be operating an Escher Cycle, in some form, continuously improving it as they go.

It means, for example, that there will be increasing emphasis placed on the intuitive side of management. Managing and coordinating the different parts of an Escher Cycle is a lot like playing chess, so top CEOs will need to be like chess grandmasters, combining different pieces to form an effective whole.

What enables grandmasters to play exhibition matches of 100 or more games at once is the ability to sense intuitively the whole arrangement of pieces on the board without having to think through every possible move and counter move. In the same way, CEOs will increasingly need their intuitive skills and "gut feel" *in combination* with the traditional, "hard" emphasis on results, deadlines, and control. Those who demonstrate the ability to combine both approaches, both halves of the brain, will command even higher salaries, in line with the greater benefits they are able to bring.

At the same time, because gut feel can be difficult to prove to others, we can also expect to see a rise in the alternative approach, which is the one that eventually enabled the Deep Blue computer to beat Gary Kasparov. We can expect to see a rise in the use of computer simulation and modeling to aid business decision-making.

Many of the pieces that CEOs will need to coordinate will be outside their own businesses. These may provide vital sources of information, or the ability to act on that information. Alternatively, a business may find itself playing a key role in somebody else's Escher Cycle. Whatever the situation, strategic alliances will become even more important than they have been over the past decade.

In fact, it is important to realize that an Escher Cycle does not have to be formed out of a single business. (That has never been the case in the past, and it does not have to start now.)

We know that businesses operating in different parts of the economy need to focus on optimizing different things—this is why they can be useful to each other. It also means, as we saw in Chapter 5, that they need different organization structures and cultures in order to be most effective.

So, a single, *uniform* company culture will *never* be able to create a successful Escher Cycle. Just as a single corporation needs different cultures in its different parts, so a successful Escher Cycle does too, but on an even larger scale. This means that companies which cooperate together may be able to create Escher Cycles that are as strong or stronger than cycles made within a single corporation. For multiple businesses working together, the issues will be ones of trust, sharing of information, and sharing of rewards. (This will create work for consultancies and IT companies.) For single-business Escher Cycles, the issues will be to do with power, control, and the ability of leadership to create a common shared vision that transcends the viewpoint of each part. (This will probably *also* create work for consultancies and IT service companies!)

Both approaches—single- and multi-company Escher Cycles—have their advantages, and both have their disadvantages.

But in general, we can say that "flatter" industries (see Chapter 7), such as electricity and gas, where there is little difference between a highly differentiated service and a standard one, will tend to favor Escher Cycles made up of a single, large business. And in more highly-sloping industries, such as garment manufacturing, consultancy, and cars, where the standard service is very different from the customized one, the Escher Cycles will probably need to be formed from more than one business.

In either case, ownership is not the issue: collaboration, cooperation, and the sharing of information from one part to improve the performance of another *is*.

The recent merger between AOL and Time-Warner makes a good case in point. This can clearly be seen as a very sensible attempt to create an Escher Cycle in the "infotainment" industry by combining the efficiency and delivery of AOL with the content and creativity of Time-Warner. But rapid legal and financial integration of the two businesses has led not to improved results, but rather to huge write-downs in the companies' combined market value, and large amounts of wasted time and effort as the two sets of management start to learn *all* about each other's innermost secrets, working to develop a single new corporate direction, branding policy, and so on.

This represents a huge waste, an unnecessary effort, changing and standardizing things that do not need to be changed or standardized—at least not yet.

If the two companies had, instead, realized that the aim of their merging was to create an Escher Cycle, then they would have been able to define their goals more precisely, and so could have focused specifically on projects where each could bring most value to the other. This would have brought immediate benefits (instead of immediate cost), and the two companies could then have moved closer together over time, learning more about each other as and when it became clear that there was business value in doing so.

Instead there was the equivalent of a rushed wedding between two corporations that met and got drunk at a party.

The issue in the short term appears to be one of ownership and control. But the issue in the long term is one of cooperation and sharing of information in order to be able to create results better, faster, and cheaper.

Cooperation can be more difficult than control, so many businesses will resist the risks that the Escher Cycle represents. Indeed, many businesses will not be *able* to implement the Escher Cycle, if they have not already achieved substantial competence at the first three layers of business advantage.

But with a lot of hungry businesses in the world looking for new ways to make money, and a lot of smart and clever people in them, somebody someday is going to find a way to make it work for their business.

And when they do, when they find a better, faster, cheaper way to do what customers want, the customers will go to them. When that happens the only survivable competence will be to be better, faster, and/or cheaper at giving customers what they want next. And the best way to do that is to create an Escher Cycle. If you are not part of the first one created in your industry, you had better be the fastest (to catch up).

The IBM example, in Chapter 5, showed that it *is* possible to get different business units to cooperate together for the greater good. The key for

Lou Gerstner was the measurement and reward system, and the same will apply in the larger economy—we just don't know how to make it work, yet.

But many of the building blocks are already there. And the companies that have the most to gain will find a way to make it work. And after they have paid for a few consultant-years of studies, we can expect to see more "constellations" of businesses being formed, tightly linked (like Japanese *Keiretsu*) to form a mutual Escher Cycle. The value of the information that they share will be included as an explicit part of the value traded in the contracts and agreements formed between them.

Success for an individual business in such a world will come from its ability to see itself as part of a much larger process, a flow of information—a flow that (both implicitly and explicitly) will come to form the basis of a whole new trading system across the world. And most valuable of all this will be the information that helps businesses to do a better job at the four parts of Escher Cycle. So, information brokerage—knowing what information to look for, where to find it, and how to apply it—will be a new key business. Who knows, perhaps this will be the source of the next Google.

*IN CLOSING* All of this may seem to imply that the future is inevitable. And, in a way it is, but in a way it is not.

We discovered the Escher Cycle because we found that the different parts of the economy go downhill forever. So, in the same way that we know that a ball dropped at the top of a hill will definitely roll downhill, we can be sure that the Escher Cycle will come. (It's already brought us from the Iron Age to the Information Age, the Stone Age to the Space Age; we just haven't learned to manage it yet.)

But in the same way that we do not necessarily know which side of the hill the ball will roll down, or what rocks and trees it might bounce off on the way, so we also do not know which specific businesses will be fastest to adopt the Escher Cycle, or how the value they create will be divided amongst the three external groups that each business negotiates with.

How this happens will have a lot to do with the laws and cultures of the different people around the world—the equivalent of the rocks and trees—and these are outside the scope of this book.

But we do know that whichever businesses manage it first will create an accelerating competitive advantage that will shift the competitive edge of businesses away from individual activities to the ability to coordinate the whole.

At that stage, as we saw briefly in Chapter 2, differences in corporate values (a combination of corporate identity and brand values) will become important. Competition between Escher Cycles will become competition between sets of values that are shared between the companies and businesses that make up each Escher Cycle. And then competitive differentiation will shift to the overlap *between* industries. But that's another level of detail, and another story.

All architects must obey the law of gravity, and are limited by the strength of the materials they use. What they build is up to them.

All sailors are subject to the winds and the tides, but where they sail to, how far and how fast, is up to them.

All business is subject to the laws described in this book. Understanding them can help you build and navigate your business better, faster, and cheaper. But what you build, and what results you choose to create, is up to you.

# The Escher Cycle and Evolution

PEOPLE WHO "GET" THE ESCHER CYCLE will implement it. Those who do not will not.

If the Escher Cycle matches reality—if a successful business really *is* a system that makes money by using its resources to satisfy customers' needs, now and in the future—then the people who successfully implement Escher Cycles will create better results than those who do not. And so they will gain more control over the world's resources and the way that they are used.

In this way, an idea will help to change the way that human history evolves—just as Deming's work in quality management helped to rebuild postwar Japan.

In his book *The Selfish Gene*, Richard Dawkins described how genes reproduce themselves through plants and animals, rather than the other way around. And he also introduced the idea of "memes"—ideas that reproduce themselves, just as genes do. The most useful memes survive, the least useful fall into disuse.

As we saw with the "Nine S" model in Chapter 3, businesses are the perfect mechanism for transmitting these ideas. Memes that help to create a successful business get reinforced within that business—and then spread to other parts of the economy, as people change jobs, as articles get written about the company's success, and so on.

But the links with evolution go further than this.

*A BRIEF HISTORY OF HISTORY* Ten thousand years ago, the glaciers of the last ice age retreated, and farming and civilization began.

Up until that point we could say that the key drivers of evolution for humans were the same as they were for animals: success at hunting and gathering. What determined success at those activities were genes.

There is no abrupt transition date, but after the Ice Age ended we can broadly say that the success of individual groups of people became less about competition between the people and their environment, nature, and more about competition between them and other groups of people. What determined success at *those* activities were memes.

If a generation lasts around twenty to thirty years, then there are only around 300 to 500 generations separating us from our ice-age ancestors. Not a long time for genes to evolve, but plenty of time for memes to do so.

At around that point, 10,000 years ago, farming effectively became the first business, in the sense that the word is used in this book. Farming created a surplus by using resources to satisfy the farmer's family's need for food. If the processes the farmer used were not efficient, effective, and adaptable enough to create a surplus to get the farmer's family through the winter and provide enough seed for next year's crop, then that way of doing farming, that business, would not survive. The more successful the farm was, the more the farmer's family (and its successful memes) could expand.

As farming methods improved, the surplus food could be used to "pay" for people to spend time doing other things than growing food: making pottery and cloth, building weapons and children's toys.

Competitive advantage for the different groups of people now shifted away from being the best at farming to being good at other things. It shifted to being able to make the best glassware that others would pay large sums for. It shifted to the skills needed to be able to organize expeditions to trade with other groups in far-off lands. It shifted to having the best processes for attacking other groups, or defending your own.

Competitive advantage between groups also shifted to the different forms of government they chose, because this affected their ability to organize large numbers of people to carry out different specialized tasks, all built around a shared culture, a common set of memes.

Different groups placed different priorities on the different activities—they chose different areas to be their identity and primary processes—and they all moved forward through time, with different results.

That was how history evolved, and how the complex system we now call the global economy came into being. And from the very beginning it was driven by the Escher Cycle. That is what brought us from the Iron Age to the Information Age.

We have now reached a stage where competitive advantage for a group of people comes (broadly) from their economic strength—their ability to create a surplus that will pay for *whatever* is needed . . . and which they obtain by providing whatever the market asks them for.

In other words, competition between businesses is not *like* evolution, it is *part of* evolution: part of the evolution of people, and hence part of the evolution of nature.

And it goes further.

NATURE IS A PROCESS This has been a book about business, but its underlying logic is really about processes.

The book has looked at what happens when there is a process (called a business) that creates a surplus (makes money) by using inputs to provide value for other processes (other businesses), and adapts or evolves over time. It has looked at what happens when many of these processes come together in an economy, and it has found the Escher Cycle.

But life is a process too. And just as customers/people can be thought of as businesses (Chapter 8), so living creatures of all kinds *take in inputs* (food, water, air, and sunlight) and *provide value* to other species (as food or habitat). Every species must also *create a surplus,* because (as Darwin pointed out) if there are fewer offspring than parents, then that species will inevitably die out. And every species, as we know, also evolves.

So, if this book is really about what happens when a collection of *processes* come together, then its conclusions must apply to any set of processes that share those same properties and characteristics, whether we call them businesses or living creatures.

This implies that there is an Escher Cycle for life, too.

In that case, what we have thought of in this book as an industry would now become a species. Instead of an industry made up of individual businesses we would see a species made up of individual plants, people, or animals, each of them slightly different.

Each individual would go through one or more AUDIO cycles and (remembering Richard Dawkins's argument that it is the *genes* that reproduce) their genes would then be passed on to the next generation. Like "Windows 2000," I am "Jackson 1962," if you like, and my children will be the next generation of a similar but not identical set of genes and memes. Just as there are multiple different versions of Windows (and other services) in use around the world, so multiple generations of the same family can live side by side.

And finally, just as industries come together to form an economy, so species would come together to form an ecology. Some of those ecologies would be very "flat," like deserts. Others would contain a great variety of life, like the rainforests.

This may seem a million miles from where we started in Chapters 2 and 3. But it is really no more remarkable than saying that an airline business, a hotdog vendor, and a convenience store all do the same things.

IMPLICATIONS On a metaphysical level this implies that the fractal economy extends much, much further than we thought. And it means that biology may have as much to learn from business as business has been able to learn from biology.

But this is a book about the least a business needs to do to be successful, and about creating sustainable business advantage. What are the practical implications for these two things?

Well, there are two. The first is a warning, and the second a possible solution.

Darwin taught us that species evolve. But Bateson[1] showed us that a single species cannot survive or evolve on its own. The species evolves in

---

[1]"Steps to an Ecology of Mind," Gregory Bateson

response to changes in its environment, and the environment (an ecology made up of other species) evolves in response to changes in each species. Simplifying: taller giraffes create taller trees, faster leopards create faster antelope, and so on.

So, the unit of successful evolution is the species *and its environment.* Only a species-and-its-environment can survive. And so we need to stop thinking of business and nature as separate things. They are not even two separate processes. They are different parts of the same, much larger system, and destroying one will destroy them both.

As Chapter 3 showed us, there is no inside or outside to the business.

The second point is that the "species-and-its-environment," which is the unit of successful evolution, sounds a lot like an Escher Cycle (made up of multiple businesses). As we saw in Chapter 9, the future of business looks set to be based around competition between groups of firms organized into Escher Cycles, built around common sets of shared values.

"A group of firms, organized into an Escher Cycle, built around a common set of values" sounds like a pretty good description of how an old-fashioned national economy used to work. But in the future, the boundaries that define the different trading groups will become ethical/cultural, rather than geographic.

Among these different groups, those that work *with* natural processes rather than against them will find that they automatically have *fewer activities* they need to do to be successful. That gives them a built-in advantage in the short term, which also makes them more sustainable in the long term. What determines whether this advantage is realized is the manmade policies that define the legal framework within which all businesses operate. They determine which businesses succeed, which then determines which ecologies succeed/survive.

This book has been about how the large scale is connected with the small scale. Hopefully it will help to create not only more efficient, effective, and adaptable businesses, but also policies that help to make sure the future economic landscape less like a desert, more like a rainforest.

# A Personal Example of the Escher Cycle "Try Thinking in Circles"

A FRIEND OF MINE IS A HOUSE and garden designer. Her particular focus lies in designing spaces that not only look great, but also create a sense of well-being for the people who use them.

She came to me excited one day about her plans to grow her business. She told me how she was going to research top hotels around the world and find out how they manage to make clients feel instantly at home. She would then turn her findings into a book, which would lead to magazine articles, television appearances, new design projects, and so on. She had it all mapped out over a three-year time plan, and wanted my advice.

"Gayle," I said, "your plan looks good, but I know nothing about house and garden design, or what that sort of publisher is looking for, or whether you provide it. So, I really don't have the expertise to be able to comment on how feasible, practical, or achievable your plan is. But instead of thinking in straight lines, why don't you try thinking in circles?"

These next three years do not exist in isolation: they are part of a cycle.

You have been doing house and garden design for many years now. This book will be just another cycle of what you have been doing all your life.

You understand what house and garden design is, and you know how to do it well. You also know that the most important result for you is to create a sense of well-being for the people who will use the spaces you create. All this puts you in the awareness stage (the "A" of AUDIO) of the cycle.

What you want to do next is to study these hotels and understand ("U") even better how to do what you do. That will enable you to design ("D") better spaces for clients. Those spaces will then be implemented ("I") by contractors, and used (or operated, "O") by your clients. That is your AUDIO cycle. It started a long time ago, and it will continue long after these three years are up.

In other words, this plan:

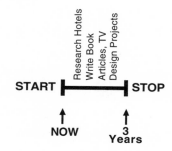

is better thought of as a repeating part of a larger plan:

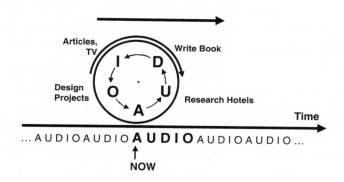

Understanding this, we realize that it makes sense to spend less time planning out specific individual activities (articles, TV appearances, or whatever) in great detail, creating a plan that will *never* match the way reality actually turns out, and more time making sure that there is at least one activity in each part of the A-U-D-I-O sequence: pick the best two or three activities for each section, and then go make them happen. The cycle will take care of the rest.

In other words, realizing this encourages us to spend less time planning out in detail how we think the world might work, or *ought* to work, and more time finding out how it actually *does*.

(By realizing that our plan for the next three years is just one more turn of the AUDIO wheel, and will be followed by another and another, we can also realize that we are living our lives *now,* and improving every day— rather than endlessly setting goals and making plans to become happy when we achieve them at some point in the future. So long as we do some kind of activity in each of the AUDIO phases, either one after the other or all at the same time, we will grow as individuals.)

Business and life are both processes, with inputs, outputs, and transformations. But while the quality of a *business* depends on the results or outputs that it creates for its customers and shareholders (and employees/ suppliers), the quality of a *life* depends on the quality of its processes: the relationships and transformations, as they occur.

My friend can turn her life into a business by using each part of the AUDIO cycle to provide valuable deliverables for others. She might make money during the understand phase by providing feedback to each hotel on how it compares with others. She can make money from the design phase by capturing her design principles in a book. Articles and other appearances in the media also summarize her design principles, and may even make some money, but mostly they help with the implement phase, by getting her name known. Finally, the bulk of her activity will be in the operate phase, designing spaces that look great and create a sense of well-being for new clients. And having done all that for three years, she will then reach a new level of awareness, which will enable the person that she has then become to choose what to do next.

In these ways (and more) my friend would build herself an Escher Cycle. (See diagram on next page.)

Study the best hotels to gain understanding. Convert that knowledge into design principles, in the form of a book (for example) that makes it useful to a wider audience. The book alone spreads her name, but media exposure also helps generate client work. If some of those clients are the

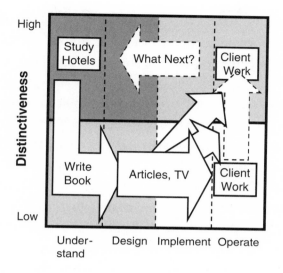

leading hotels then this will automatically create the knowledge and experience needed to kick-start the next cycle. If not, then another source will be needed.

Once this business is established, it could go anywhere.

Where it actually *does* go will depend on:

- how many people have a use for this particular knowledge ("designing for well-being")
- how easy it is to adapt these ideas to other services, and
- what economies of scale (or Experience Curve effects) exist within the technologies used to deliver the different services

(As well as finding the financial backing, of course.)

If it turns out, for example, that the only customers interested in paying for this kind of design are 100 hotels around the world, then my friend might form a consulting business focused around them, flying to wherever the clients are.

If there are 10,000 high-net worth individuals worldwide who would benefit from her ideas, then the best solution might be to form a different kind of business: hiring other people to carry out different parts of the AUDIO cycle to her specifications, and possibly (for example) forming close links with particular architects who are building new houses for these individuals. If her ideas turn out to be especially useful and valuable in building projects, my friend *might* then find her business being bought out by a firm of architects (or vice-versa).

If there turn out to be ten or 100 million people in the world who find this kind of house and garden design service useful, then an entirely different business model will become appropriate, perhaps using franchising or an Internet-based approach.

And, finally, if her design approach turns out to be valuable to car designers, hospital waiting rooms, and refrigerator manufacturers (unlikely but possible!), then she might find herself shifting to offer a much wider "Designed for Well-Being" service, rather than one tied explicitly to houses and gardens. In this case her role would shift to being best at providing just one piece of other people's Escher Cycles.

Following the AUDIO cycle and the Escher Cycle in this way allows the business to adapt to become whatever the world most wants it to be.

And the same possibilities, in essence, apply to any business.

# *Index*

# C

ABOUT THE TYPE

The text of this book was set in Adobe Minion, a typeface
designed by Robert Slimbach and issued as a digital original by the
Adobe Corporation in 1989. It is a typeface of neohumanist design,
inspired by the classical, old-style types of the late Renaissance.

*Printed and bound by Edwards Brothers, Inc.,*
*Ann Arbor, Michigan*

*Designed by Kevin Hanek*